The Art of Career Advancement for Law Enforcement and Public Safety Leaders

This book offers a comprehensive guide to the complex landscape of professional growth within law enforcement and public safety. Blending empirical research with the real-world experiences of seasoned professionals, each chapter delivers practical insights and proven strategies, carefully designed to address the challenges faced in career advancement. With a focus on the importance of self-assessment, leadership development, and strategic career planning, this book equips readers with the tools to navigate their professional trajectory with resilience, adaptability, and purpose. "Concept Bootcamp" boxes offer digestible summaries of key concepts surrounding leadership theory, contemporary issues, technology, community relations, policing models, and other foundational concepts that can and should be leveraged for success in the promotional process. Unique "Voices from the Field" boxes share insights from hundreds of diverse law enforcement professionals on the promotional process and professional development.

From the seasoned officer eyeing promotion to the newly minted recruit envisioning career progression, this book serves as a guide offering clear, actionable strategies for success in the evolving world of law enforcement leadership. For law enforcement and public safety leaders, educators, trainers, and human resources professionals dedicated to cultivating leadership excellence, this book provides a comprehensive framework for fostering talent, driving organizational transformation, and developing a culture of continuous improvement. By combining evidence-based approaches with hands-on, practical guidance, the authors empower readers to elevate their careers and create lasting, positive change within their organizations and avoid passive dependence on whatever mentoring and succession planning their agency may or may not offer. Whether you are a frontline officer looking to rise through the ranks, or a seasoned leader seeking to refine your leadership approach, this book is the essential resource for mastering career development, enhancing leadership effectiveness, and achieving lasting success in the dynamic field of law enforcement and public safety leadership.

Jonni Redick is a retired Assistant Chief of the California Highway Patrol, where she served twenty-nine years and advanced through the ranks from entry-level to executive leadership. Her work reflects a comprehensive command of organizational leadership, workforce development, public safety strategy, and culture transformation, grounded in her practitioner experience. Redick is a published author, contributor to national policing publications, national speaker, and consultant specializing in leadership development, career advancement, and building resilient, people-centered organizations. She serves as an adjunct faculty member at the University of San Diego, contributing to the development of current and emerging public safety leaders. She holds a M.S. in Law Enforcement and Public Safety Leadership from the University of San Diego and a Doctor of Education in Organizational Change and Administration from California Baptist University.

Erik Fritsvold serves as the Academic Director for the Master of Science in Law Enforcement and Public Safety Leadership program at the University of San Diego. He was the founding faculty member for the program and part of the team that shepherded it from concept through launch—a process that included three years of research and collaboration with law enforcement. Fritsvold directs all aspects of program academics, including curriculum, faculty, admissions, accreditation, and any issues related to students. Fritsvold's primary expertise is applying core tenets of academic criminology and criminal justice to dynamic, modern-day law enforcement. Fristvold earned his B.A. in Sociology from the University of San Diego in 2000, and his M.A. and Ph.D. from the Criminology, Law & Society Department at the University of California at Irvine in 2003 and 2006, respectively.

Routledge Series on Practical and Evidence-Based Policing

Books in the Routledge Series on Practical and Evidence-Based Policing disseminate knowledge and provide practical tools for law enforcement leaders and personnel to protect and serve the public and reduce crime. With an aim to bridge the "translation gap" between frontline policing and academic research, books in this series apply sound scientific methods as well as practical experience to make everyday police work safer and smarter. These books are an invaluable resource for police practitioners, academic researchers, public policymakers, and students in law enforcement and criminology programs to guide best practices in all aspects of policing.

Human Rights Policing
Reimagining Law Enforcement in the 21st Century
Peter Marina & Pedro Marina

Interviewing Vulnerable Suspects
Safeguarding the Process
Edited by Dr Jane Tudor-Owen, Dr Celine van Golde, Dr Ray Bull & David Gee MBE

Reframing Police Education and Freedom in America
Martin Alan Greenberg & Beth Allen Easterling

Gold Medal Policing
Operational Readiness and Performance Excellence, 2nd Edition
Judy M. McDonald

Understanding Police Operational Performance
James E. McCabe, Paul E. O'Connell, Demosthenes Long, and Carol Rasor-Cordero

Cutting Crime Using the Rule of the Few
Shannon Linning, Daniel W. Gerard and John E. Eck

Future Policing
Technology and Transformation
Laura Huey, Lorna Ferguson and Ian T. Adams

The Art of Career Advancement for Law Enforcement and Public Safety Leaders
Mastering the Seven Pillars of Professional Readiness
Jonni Redick and Erik Fritsvold

"The *Art of Career Advancement* is the resource our profession has been missing. Jonni and Erik deliver a transparent roadmap ensuring quality people reach leadership, not just the well-connected. A must read if you want to successfully climb the ladder."

Jason P. Armstrong
Chief (ret.), Ferguson Police Department
National Law Enforcement Officer Hall of Fame

"This book captures the art of the oral interview by translating key leadership and policing concepts into practical guidance, preparing candidates to stand out, perform with confidence, and secure their place at the table."

Julie Rodriguez
Captain, Los Angeles Police Department
President, National Association of Women Law Enforcement Executives (NAWLEE)

"What stands out in *Art of Career Advancement" is how* personally Redick and Fritsvold address the challenges of promotion and growth. They bring clarity to complex promotional systems while encouraging intentional career advancement, helping readers feel understood and prepared to move forward."

Dr. Tarrick McGuire
Chief, Alexandria Police Department

The Art of Career Advancement for Law Enforcement and Public Safety Leaders

Mastering the Seven Pillars of Professional Readiness

Jonni Redick and
Erik Fritsvold

Routledge
Taylor & Francis Group
NEW YORK AND LONDON

Designed cover image: Getty Images

First published 2027
by Routledge
605 Third Avenue, New York, NY 10158

and by Routledge
4 Park Square, Milton Park, Abingdon, Oxon, OX14 4RN

Routledge is an imprint of the Taylor & Francis Group, an informa business

Library of Congress Cataloging-in-Publication Data
Names: Redick, Jonni author | Fritsvold, Erik D. author
Title: The art of career advancement for law enforcement and public safety leaders : mastering the seven pillars of professional readiness / Jonni Redick and Erik Fritsvold.
Description: New York, NY: Routledge, 2027. | Series: Routledge series on practical and evidence-based policing | Includes bibliographical references and index.
Identifiers: LCCN 2026022563 (print) | LCCN 2026022564 (ebook) |
ISBN 9781041217497 paperback | ISBN 9781041217510 hardback |
ISBN 9781003728849 ebook
Subjects: LCSH: Law enforcement–Vocational guidance | Career development |
Public safety–Vocational guidance
Classification: LCC HV8142 .R43 2027 (print) | LCC HV8142 (ebook)
LC record available at https://lccn.loc.gov/2026022563
LC ebook record available at https://lccn.loc.gov/2026022564

ISBN: 978-1-041-21751-0 (hbk)
ISBN: 978-1-041-21749-7 (pbk)
ISBN: 978-1-003-72884-9 (ebk)

DOI: 10.4324/9781003728849

Typeset in Helvetica Neue and Optima
by Newgen Publishing UK

Contents

Introduction

A Culture of Leadership

Leadership may be the most important element of a successful law enforcement organization. Society is asking more and more of this noble profession—from addressing a broader variety of social problems,[1] to combatting rising violent crime,[2] to co-creating public safety in meaningful collaboration with the community.[3] Executing the widening and complex mission of a contemporary law enforcement organization mandates that leadership is systematic and intentional in creating a *culture of leadership*. Thus, the process of identifying, mentoring, and developing emerging leaders is one of—if not the—single most important task for any law enforcement agency.

Despite the centrality of leadership in law enforcement, there is widespread dissatisfaction with leadership quality and effectiveness in the profession. 2023 constituted the third iteration of Police One's annual "What Cops Want" report. The heart of this report is survey results from over 4,000 law enforcement professionals from a diversity of agencies across the United States. Arguably, the most glaring finding was the strikingly consistent criticisms of leadership efficacy in the profession. According to contributing author Bob Harrison: "One trend that carried over from the 2022 survey was perspectives regarding agency leadership. Throughout that survey, when asked about the effectiveness of their agency's leadership, sentiments were far more critical than positive."[4] Several quotes from respondents vividly support this claim:

> The overall quality of LE administrations is abysmal. Degrees, demographics and politics rather than proven ability and record determine who runs PDs.[5]

DOI: 10.4324/9781003728849-1

> Leadership tends to be the same: blind and ignorant. Decisions aren't made about staff anymore.[6]
>
> I do not want to see people invest that much effort to be disappointed and get railroaded. This area has many common problems in various PDs. Poor leadership breeds poor officers and poor morale.[7]

In the quest for effective and human-centric leadership, *process* is of critical importance. In any type of organization—military, pseudo-military, corporate, or academic—transparent, equitable, and process-centric leadership selection and development are cornerstones of organizational success. However, consistent processes are particularly challenging given the fragmented nature of modern law enforcement. According to the Department of Justice and FBI data:

> [t]here are more than 18,000 local police departments in the United States. These departments are subject to different state, county, and city laws and codes, and they have different policies, practices, and officer training programs. There is no universal standard for the structure, size, or governance of police departments in the United States.[8]

Of those roughly 18,000 agencies, most are comparatively small. Approximately 90 percent of agencies have fewer than fifty sworn personnel, and nearly 50 percent employ ten sworn officers or fewer.[9] Despite their prominence in public discourse and the media, the structure and size of agencies like the NYPD, LAPD, and California Highway Patrol are the exception.

Considering the balance between standardization and local control, the supremacy of local control of policing is laudable and largely appropriate. Policing being primarily a local endeavor allows law enforcement to be more engrained with, and responsive to, the particular needs of the particular community they serve.

However, one of the challenges of this fragmented policing landscape is the extreme variation in leadership development and promotion. The evidence suggests that promotional processes vary from transparent and procedurally just processes, to informal and uncodified "ole boy network" whimsical decisions based on personal preference and individual relationships. This book seeks to remedy that problem by providing a sequential and transparent playbook for ascending the law enforcement ladder, regardless of agency.

ASCENDING THE LAW ENFORCEMENT LADDER: THE EQUITY AND EMPOWERMENT MISSION

The mission of this book is to provide equitable access to the tools, strategies, and best practices that have proven to lead to promotional success.

Readers no longer have to rely on their organization's training budget, formal or informal mentoring system, or existing pipeline to promotion. Collectively, we can end-run the common pitfalls, possible "good ole boy/girl" nepotism,[10] and other organizational dynamics that historically, in some agencies, have poisoned the meritocracy that should underlie the promotional process.

We accomplish the mission of the book by employing a unique and utility-centric structure. This is three-pronged approach:

1. *The Promotional Process*: The foundation of the book is tangible and actionable information about the promotional process itself. Readers will know what to expect at each level as they ascend the law enforcement promotional ladder. This information is coupled with concrete and proven strategies, timelines, and techniques to prepare and successfully execute the complexities of this task. This book builds on a legacy of high-utility and high-impact books in this area from the authors,[11,12] by updating its focus and substance to be in line with the contemporary and fast-moving field of public safety.
2. *Concept Bootcamp*: *The Art of Career Advancement* offers a valuable and unique resource by providing a comprehensive guide to the key issues, themes, and concepts that every public safety professional should understand. These concept bootcamp sections are designed to be efficient and digestible summaries of these key concepts, always with the promotion-centric mission of the book in the forefront. These concept bootcamp sections will include leadership theory, contemporary issues in the law enforcement and public safety field, technology, community relations, policing models, and other foundational concepts that can and should be leveraged for success in the promotional process.
3. *Voices from the Field*: This book is also unique because it leverages the collective wisdom of approximately 1,500 public safety professionals from across the United States and beyond. From chiefs of police, sheriffs, and U.S. marine colonels to second-year correctional deputies and newly hired crime analysts, the authors surveyed a wide range of law enforcement professionals. This diverse group represents nearly every rank, role, state, and organization within the broad public safety field. They were kind enough to share their experiences, advice, successes, failures, and pitfalls to add layers and depth to this book that is simply unavailable elsewhere.

Leadership is the most important, most coveted, and most valuable asset in any organization. The authors are honored to serve the law enforcement and public safety community by creating this unique and practical strategy guide and conceptual toolkit to ascend the law enforcement ladder.

NOTES

1 Center for Evidence-Based Policing (n.d.) Homelessness and Mentally Ill Working Group. California Police Chiefs Association. Accessed on January 27, 2024 from: https://cebcp.org/wp-content/halloffame/Homeless-Working-Group-Report.pdf

2 University of Pennsylvania: Department of Criminology (n.d.) Is Violent Crime Increasing? Accessed on January 27, 2024 from: https://crim.sas.upenn.edu/fact-check/violent-crime-increasing#:~:text=Violent%20crime%20recently%20has%20been,increases%20have%20continued%20into%202022.

3 International Association of Chiefs of Police (n.d.) Community-Police Engagement. Accessed January 27, 2024 from https://www.theiacp.org/topics/community-police-engagement

4 Harrison, Bob (2024:7) What Cops Want in 2023, Police One.

5 Harrison, Bob (2024:7) What Cops Want in 2023, Police One.

6 Harrison, Bob (2024:7) What Cops Want in 2023, Police One.

7 Harrison, Bob (2024:7) What Cops Want in 2023, Police One.

8 Department of Justice (n.d.) Policing 101. Community Relations Services Toolkit for Policing. Accessed January 27th, 2024 from https://www.justice.gov/d9/policing_101_content.pdf

9 Berman, Mark (2021) Most police departments in America are small. That's partly why changing policing is difficult, experts say. Washington Post. Accessed January 27th 2024 from https://www.washingtonpost.com/nation/2021/05/08/most-police-departments-america-are-small-thats-partly-why-changing-policing-is-difficult-experts-say/

10 Morgan, C. (2014) *How the 'good ol' boys club' mentality hurts us.* Corrections1. Accessed from https://www.corrections1.com/2014-year-in-review/articles/how-the-good-ol-boys-club-mentality-hurts-us-nlcSK8ABGJlrFXmx/

11 Redick, J. (2022). *Survival Guide to Law Enforcement Promotional Preparation.* Curry Brothers Publishing

12 Redick, J. (2022). *Black, White, and Blue: Surviving the Sifting.* Curry Brothers Publishing

REFERENCES

Berman, M. (2021, May 8). Most police departments in America are small. That's partly why changing policing is difficult, experts say. *The Washington Post.* https://www.washingtonpost.com/nation/2021/05/08/most-police-departments-america-are-small-thats-partly-why-changing-policing-is-difficult-experts-say/

Center for Evidence-Based Policing. (n.d.). Homelessness and Mentally Ill Working Group report. California Police Chiefs Association. https://cebcp.org/wp-content/halloffame/Homeless-Working-Group-Report.pdf

Department of Justice. (n.d.). Policing 101: Community relations services toolkit for policing. https://www.justice.gov/d9/policing_101_content.pdf

Harrison, B. (2024). What cops want in 2023. Police1.

International Association of Chiefs of Police. (n.d.). Community-police engagement. https://www.theiacp.org/topics/community-police-engagement

Morgan, C. (2014, December 31). How the 'good ol' boys club' mentality hurts us. Corrections1. https://www.corrections1.com/2014-year-in-review/articles/how-the-good-ol-boys-club-mentality-hurts-us-nlcSK8ABGJlrFXmx/

Redick, J. (2022). *Black, white, and blue: Surviving the sifting.* Curry Brothers Publishing.

Redick, J. (2022). *Survival guide to law enforcement promotional preparation.* Curry Brothers Publishing.

University of Pennsylvania Department of Criminology. (n.d.). Is violent crime increasing? https://crim.sas.upenn.edu/fact-check/violent-crime-increasing

PART I

The Inner Architecture of Readiness

CHAPTER ONE

Laying the Foundation

Leadership Before the Title

Leadership in public safety does not start the day you put on a badge, walk into a courtroom, or lead a team. It starts long before that, even as a student, a criminal justice major, or a new Academy recruit. Whether you are just beginning in law enforcement, corrections, probation, dispatch, or emergency management, leadership is personal before it is professional. It is not about your job title or your rank. It is about how you show up, the values you stand for, and the choices you make when nobody's around to notice.

While there are innate elements to all human characteristics, leadership is not primarily innate. It is a perishable skill, like physical fitness or professional readiness, that must be continually practiced, sharpened, and renewed. As Simon Sinek emphasized: "You must be a student of leadership. If you desire to lead, you must study."[1] This truth brings us back to something simple but important: leadership starts long before the title ever does. If leadership is a skill, then it is not something you wait to be given; it is something you begin practicing from day one, in the small, everyday choices you make throughout your career.

In the early days, there are three building blocks to consider that can make a significant difference in your leadership growth. First up: *personal discipline.* Truly, at its core, it is about consistency, structure, and self-governance—the ability for you consistently to choose actions that build credibility, competence, and character, even when they require effort, patience, or delayed gratification. How do you know if you have personal discipline? Ask yourself if you are doing the small things every day: preparing before you are asked; managing emotions under pressure; following through on commitments; investing in learning when no one is looking; holding yourself accountable when no one is looking. If we zoom out a bit, you will see that personal discipline becomes the following: time discipline is prioritizing growth over distractions; behavior discipline

DOI: 10.4324/9781003728849-3

is professionalism, reliability, and follow-through; emotional discipline is composure, maturity, and resilience. As an early professional, we want to seek out how to be confident first, but in reality, confidence is a byproduct because discipline can create competence. Competence builds confidence. Confidence earns opportunity.

Next, there is *self-awareness and purpose*. Being self-aware extends your disciplined practice to include understanding your strengths, limitations, values, emotional patterns, and impact on others. Before you can lead anyone else, you must learn and understand yourself—your triggers and your blind spots. Did you know that many promising professionals stall in their careers not because of a lack of skills, but because of unexamined behaviors of self. The ways you can stay self-aware is knowing how it shows up: reading a room and adjusting your communication; regulating your emotions under stress, managing ego and staying coachable; recognize your skills gaps and work to close them; and seek feedback without defensiveness. When you look from a strategic perspective, strengths awareness accelerates confidence and contribution; gap awareness directs learning investment; emotional awareness builds trust and credibility; impact awareness strengthens influence.

Purpose shifts the perspective from chasing titles, promotions, or validation to "What am I here to build or contribute?" It is so important to ask yourself, "Why am I doing this?" That answer becomes your anchor when things get tough because knowing what drives you keeps you focused and helps you avoid burning out.[2] But it also creates direction when choices feel overwhelming; gives you that motivation during difficult seasons; clarity about which opportunities to say yes or no to; resilience when progress feels slow, and integrity in decision-making. It also helps set goals aligned with values, not just visibility; persist through setbacks because the work matters and helps you lead with service rather than status. Thinking about your purpose helps answer a different, bigger question: "What difference do I want my leadership to make?"

And finally, there's a *service mindset*. What is a service mindset? It is the intentional commitment to use your skills, talent, position, and influence to support the success, well-being, and growth of others. It is simple: real leadership is rooted in serving others. The reality is that most organizational leaders promote people they trust to elevate others, not just high performers focused on themselves. You have an opportunity through service to transform your competence into credibility. Through service, you can reframe leadership as contribution versus just visibility. It shows up in how you share knowledge freely, help teammates succeed, take ownership of outcomes, volunteering for hard or unglamorous work, removing obstacles for others and thinking "we" before "me." Leaning into a service mindset is a force multiplier and strengthens leadership capacity building relational capital in how you make people feel supported and respected; reputation capital as you become known as dependable and team-oriented; influence capital when others willingly follow and opportunity capital when leaders see you as promotable. In many ways, a service mindset is the culture-setting habit of strong leaders.

DEFINING LEADERSHIP IN THE FIRST STAGE OF YOUR CAREER—FROM FRONTLINE TO SUPERVISION

Leadership in the early stages of a public safety career is often misunderstood. Many of us grow up in an organization believing that leadership arrives with the stripe, badge, or a title, that somehow authority is handed to you the day your rank changes. But that is not how it really works. Real leadership does not show up all at once. It is built long before anyone pins something on your collar or you are given the piece of paper with the framed matting. Not many will share with you that it evolves over time with maturity, exposure, and experience, but it also happens with intentional effort through stewardship, consistency, competence, and how you show up for the people around you.

Whether you are a new criminologist learning the rhythms of investigations, a forensic analyst behind the scenes, a dispatcher fielding call after call, a police officer or corrections officer holding order in difficult environments, or a probation aide walking alongside someone trying to rebuild their life, you are already standing in leadership territory. The opportunity is there. The question is simply: will you step into it?

And if you are wondering where to begin, here is the good news—it is not complicated. It is being intentional. Earlier, we talked about three building blocks that anchor your early career: personal discipline, self-awareness and purpose, and a mindset rooted in service. Those are not abstract ideas. They show up in practical ways—how you show up to work and are willing to take on the extra shift, not for the money, but because your team needs help. It feels like choosing others over self; responsibility over recognition. They may seem like small actions, maybe so. But they speak loudly. Because every action tells a story about who you are becoming. Over time, these repeated choices shape your leadership identity and your personal brand. People begin to notice how you respond under pressure, how you behave when things change, and whether they can depend on you when it matters most. That narrative, built quietly and consistently, becomes your credibility. And credibility is the currency of leadership.

You will also start to notice something else: mindset matters. Change is going to happen; it always does. You can either be the one who adds stress or the one who stabilizes the room. Being an anchor for your team is a leader who chooses constructive, solutions-oriented approaches—that model of leadership influences morale, culture, and trust. Sometimes, influence at this stage rarely looks dramatic or feels like it is even happening. It can actually look simply ordinary. Long before you carry formal authority, people will already be deciding whether they trust your judgment. That is leadership.

As your experience grows, there is another shift that happens, one that Kouzes and Posner describe as "Modeling the Way."[3] You begin moving from being only a doer to becoming a developer of others. You still perform your job well, but the aperture on your lens widens. You start paying attention to the team. Who needs support? Who's overwhelmed? You may not notice the shift; it will be subtle but powerful when it is happening. It signals maturity. It may be a sign that you are ready for more responsibility. But realize, leadership also asks you to connect daily to something bigger. Those mission statements are not just wall décor. They are guideposts. So, every choice, how you allocate resources, how you treat other people, the public, how you balance those competing demands, should reflect your agency's deeper purpose of service, justice, and accountability.[4,5] In other words, leadership is not about commanding people. It is about embodying purpose. Remember, leadership is not about a title. It is about posture. It is the quiet willingness to step forward, support others, and keep growing, especially when no one is watching. The rank may come later. But the leader? That is being built right now.

The Shift from Peer to Supervision

Perhaps the most jarring transition occurs when you shift from being a peer to someone responsible for supervising them. It seems like just yesterday you were part of the group, sharing the beat, water-cooler talk, swapping stories, and venting about policy changes. Now, you are evaluating their performance, holding them accountable, and making decisions that affect those same colleagues. The dynamics shift so quickly, and some may doubt your readiness silently or audibly. The antidote to skepticism is consistency. When you can stay consistent in your actions and words, apply standards fairly despite personal history, and maintain transparency in your decisions, confidence and trust will grow.[6]

One of the most challenging transitions is leading peers, especially your friends. Understand that relationships shift, and without clear expectations, perceptions of favoritism can creep in and quietly damage trust. Setting boundaries early, applying standards consistently, and treating people equitably align with what Tyler (2006) calls procedural justice.[7] Fairness is not just ethical; it is stabilizing. While friendships with colleagues enrich the workplace, you must strike a balance early. As a leader, you can acknowledge this change by articulating, "I value our friendship, but in this role, you have to understand my responsibility is creating fairness in my decisions first," demonstrating integrity that fosters respect. Early missteps in managing these boundaries can have long-lasting repercussions, affecting relationships and team dynamics.

Being someone who supervises others, at all levels of leadership, also means facing heightened accountability. Mistakes made by the team can reflect on your leadership, making humility a vital trait, not often easy in the moment, but with practice, it becomes a pattern. The moral philosopher of leadership practice, James MacGregor Burns, approached leadership not as a position, authority, or management technique, but as ethical, human, and transformational.[8] He anchored it in moral grounding, and that taking ownership of your errors publicly demonstrates the transformation of visibility in your growth, while building credibility and reinforcing trust amongst your team.

When examining, for example, the frontline supervisor role, it has a key dual function in organizational communication, as described by Dr. Matthew Loeslie: "New supervisors are tasked with effectively communicating the administration's directives to their team while also conveying the officers' perspectives to upper management."[9] While advocating on behalf of your team to organizational power holders can be empowering and endear a new frontline supervisor to the group, the opposite might not always be true. Often, this dual communication role requires frontline supervisors to communicate, and sometimes support, mandates, and initiatives from the organization that may not be popular with their team. Relaying negative information can be done tactfully, but it can also be a stark and sometimes unwelcome reminder that the frontline supervisor is an authority figure in the organization, which can damage or at least alter previously strong interpersonal relationships and friendships.

To help mitigate the challenge of this new role, in Next-Gen leadership, Dr. Gene Reid argues that situationally defined communication strategies are essential when mastering peer leadership in law enforcement. More specifically, he "reinforces that adaptability in communication and consistent value contribution are key to maintaining trust and authority."[10] Moreover, when transitioning from "buddy" to "boss," experts recommend holding intentional and scheduled individual meetings with team members to discuss transparently how the relationship and friendship dynamics in the team will inevitably change, but can be preserved with good situational communication, flexibility, and evident respect for the boundaries established by the new position.[11] Therefore, standard leadership best practices such as communication, transparency, and proactivity are especially critical for new frontline supervisors and should be carried out with intention.

Communication also transforms and takes on a newfound significance. Silence can be mistaken for indifference or disengagement, while careless words can fracture trust. Supervisors are expected to provide context and clarity, explain not just what needs to be done but why it matters. Effective leaders learn to delicately balance authority while also embracing curiosity, embodying openness that invites dialogue, while still upholding essential standards. Kouzes and Posner emphasize the importance of "Inspiring a Shared Vision," reminding us that leaders must connect mundane daily tasks to broader organizational goals that resonate with the team's values and aspirations.[12] Again, this is not easy but it is necessary. Building values-based influence through your leadership allows you and your team to rise together, not separately. Real sustainability and change happen when you appeal to purpose and meaning, not compliance. Burns argues essentially that leadership succeeds when both the mission and the people are stronger because of the process.[13]

As we close out this chapter, there is a whimsical book titled *Like Likes Like* by Chris Raschka.[14] The story illustrates relationships, loneliness, and a natural "laws of attraction" when a cat finds another cat like itself. Stay with me here. Although the cat encounters several other types of animals, it is not until it finds the other cat that it finally feels comfortable with someone like itself. This children's story symbolizes a pattern of leadership behavior that is interwoven into organizational culture and cultivates a landscape of "like likes like" in many industries, but which is even more prevalent in law enforcement.

This dynamic reflects a well-established concept in social science known as social identity theory, which explains how individuals naturally categorize themselves and others into groups, identify with those groups, and compare their group favorably against others.[15,16] In organizational settings, these cognitive processes can quietly influence professional relationships, access to mentorship, and leadership opportunities, as individuals may gravitate toward those who share similar backgrounds, experiences, values, or perspectives because those similarities create a sense of familiarity and psychological comfort. While this tendency is a common human behavior rather than a deliberate act of exclusion, most of the time its cumulative impact within organizations can reinforce homogeneous leadership networks and limit opportunities for individuals outside those informal circles of similarity. Over time, this pattern can unintentionally reproduce the very leadership structures already in place, making it more difficult for organizations to cultivate diverse perspectives, innovative thinking, and inclusive leadership development.

Concept Bootcamp: Theories that Shape Early Leadership

- *Concept Bootcamp Introduction*: Effective, forward-thinking law enforcement leaders must have a functional grasp of the dynamic field of public safety. Regardless of role, a macro-level understanding of the current challenges and opportunities in the profession will help any and every leader be more impactful in their assignment, organization, and society as a whole. A leader who executes their role in a vacuum, isolated from and ignorant of broader dynamics in the field, is destined to fail. By staying informed about emerging trends and best practices, leaders can be proactive in leading their teams and serving the collective needs of the community.

This is the first installment of the Art of Career Advancement "Concept Bootcamp," focusing on leadership theory. These sections are intentionally designed to be efficient, digestible, and non-exhaustive summaries of key concepts, always keeping the promotion-centric mission of the book at the forefront. A full history and overview of leadership theory is outside the scope and purpose of this book. Instead, this section provides concise summaries of several key leadership theories that may be most applicable and useful for law enforcement professionals, both in the promotional process and in the execution of their duties.

- *Leadership Theory*: Leadership theories are broad frameworks that attempt to explain the essence of leadership. More specifically, they focus on how and why individuals become effective leaders. These perspectives have evolved dramatically over nearly two centuries. Some leading scholars in the field divide the history of leadership into four main eras: trait, behavioral, situational, and new leadership.[17] A pragmatic law enforcement leader striving for promotion will want to locate their own leadership approach, strengths, and weaknesses in the context of these larger leadership paradigms. It's commonplace for leadership theories and personal leadership philosophies to be components of the promotional process.
- *Leadership Is a Skill*: A near consensus of contemporary leadership experts, both academics and practitioners, argue that leadership is a skill that can be taught and learned. Contrasting early perspectives on leadership, such as the Great Man Theories of the mid-1800s and Trait Theories of the 1930s, leadership science has evolved and now strongly argues that leadership is an ability that can be developed and mastered through education and practice. While there are innate elements to all human characteristics, leadership is not primarily innate. Thus, leadership skills are perishable and must be continually refined, practiced, and developed.[18,19]

Most experts, whether they are researchers or people working in the field, agree that leadership is not just something you are born with. It is a skill you can learn, practice, and get better at over time. In the past, people thought leaders had certain traits or were just "natural-born," but today we know that anyone can build leadership abilities with effort and the right mindset. Like any skill, if you stop working at it, you can lose your edge.

Leadership is not something you are simply born with; it is a skill you have to keep sharpening. Leadership shows up in how you manage your preparation, the discipline you bring to your training, the integrity you demonstrate in your daily choices, and the service orientation you cultivate in every interaction. By recognizing leadership as a skill, not a position, those in any stages of their careers can begin building their foundation.

- *Servant Leadership*: Servant leadership is a popular and impactful perspective on leadership within the law enforcement profession. Coined by servant leadership guru Robert Greenleaf in the 1970s, it is a leadership approach that focuses on prioritizing growth, well-being, and development of others.[20] When you embrace this mindset, you will strengthen others, cultivate healthier organizations, and contribute to more compassionate and equitable communities. In practice, the primary goal of a servant leader is to elevate the team and those that you lead both in terms of their individual capacity and organizational outcomes. A servant leader is not primarily focused on your own career advancement or career goals in favor of making a collective impact.[21] Within this perspective, humility in leadership, building trust, and a people-first perspective are fundamental. Proponents argue that servant leadership is best demonstrated with concrete action from the leader, not hollow and unsubstantiated claims about being a servant leader. Moreover, some argue this may be the single most impactful way to elevate the performance of public safety and other organizations .
- *Transactional Leadership*: Transactional leadership is a pragmatic, almost economic viewpoint on the relationship between leaders and followers. Proponents of this perspective argue that by creating goals, objects, standards, rewards, and consequences for underperformance, leaders use both positive and negative reinforcement to shape the performance of those they lead. Kuhnert and Lewis[22] emphasize this pseudo-economic emphasis of transactional leadership: Transactional leadership represents those exchanges in which both the superior and the subordinate influence one another reciprocally so that each derives something of value (Yukl, 1981).[23] Simply stated, transactional leaders give followers something they want in exchange for something the leader wants.

Some may argue that transaction leadership is a natural fit for military and paramilitary style organizations, due in part to its clarity and emphasis on policy and procedure.

Critics of this perspective argue that is focuses on management, not leadership. There is an emphasis on the accomplishment of day-to-day tasks, instead of innovation, vision, soaring and imaginative personal or organizational growth.

- *Transformational Leadership*: Building from the momentum of Servant Leadership, transformational leadership posits that leaders should not only inspire and invest in those they lead, but that they should continually emphasize the macro-level mission of the organization. Servant leaders create more servant leaders who collectively drive the organization toward its mission. Thus, through acts of leadership, entire institutions are transformed to be more effective and more impactful.[24]

The idea of transformational leadership was first described by Burns in 1978 and later expanded by Bass in 1985. Unlike transactional leadership, which focuses on exchanges and rewards, transformational leadership is all about inspiring people and keeping the organizations bigger mission front and center. Leaders who take this approach invest, encourage others to become servant leaders, and help them to move the entire organization forward.[25] Through their influence, transformational leaders can turn agencies into places that are more effective and make a greater impact. Bass sums it up: transformational leaders help their teams see beyond their own interests, embrace the group's mission, and feel motivated to work together in the greater good.

Bass (1985) sums up the soaring potential of transformational leadership in a particularly impactful way:

> Superior leadership performance—transformational leadership—occurs when leaders broaden and elevate the interests of their employees, when they generate awareness and acceptance of the purposes and mission of the group, and when they stir their employees to look beyond their own self-interest for the good of the group. Transformational leaders achieve these results in one or more ways: They may be charismatic to their followers and thus inspire them[26]

- *Situational Leadership:* This perspective on leadership dovetails with the dynamic complexities of modern law enforcement and public safety by emphasizing the importance of adapting one's leadership approach to individual contexts. There is not one single best way to lead. Rather, different individuals, situations, organizations, and teams require different leadership approaches to be most impactful. Thus, an effective leader must have a broad, deep and well-honed arsenal of leadership and communication skills that can be strategically deployed in different situations.[27]

  Developed by Hersey and Blanchard (1969), this model illustrates that a leadership style should adapt to the readiness of followers. New supervisors often rely too heavily on directing; learning to switch between coaching, supporting, and delegating can lead to stronger developmental outcomes. Arguably, one of the most challenging transitions in the leadership journey of a public safety professional is moving from a peer to a frontline supervisor.
- *Situational Leadership: Peer to Supervisor*: Arguably, one of the most challenging transitions in the leadership trajectory of a public safety profession is the transition from a peer to a frontline supervisor. Well-honed and intentional strategies, often with situational leadership in the forefront, position a new supervisor to succeed and to navigate these new group and interpersonal dynamics effectively. The frontline supervisor role has a key dual role in organizational communication, as described by Dr. Matthew Loeslie: "New supervisors are tasked with effectively communicating the administration's directives to their team while also conveying the officers' perspectives to upper management."[28] While advocating on behalf of your team to power holders in the organization can be empowering and endear a new frontline supervisor to the group, the opposite may not be true. Often this dual communication role requires frontline supervisors to communicate, and often support, mandates and initiatives from the organization that might not be popular with their team. Relaying negative information can be done tactfully, but can be a stark and sometimes unwelcomed reminder that the frontline supervisor is an authority figure in the organization, which can damage, or at the very least change, formerly strong interpersonal relationships and friendships.

  To help mitigate the challenge of this new role, in *Next-Gen Leadership: Mastering peer leadership in law enforcement* Dr. Gene Reid argues that situationally defined communication strategies are key. More specifically, he "reinforces that adaptability in communication and consistent value contribution are key to maintaining trust and authority."[29] Moreover, when going from "buddy" to "boss,"[30] experts recommend holding intentional and scheduled individual meetings with team members to transparently discuss how the relationship and friendship dynamics in the team now will inevitably change, but can be preserved with good situational communication, flexibility, and clear respect for the boundaries created by the new position. Thus, the standard leadership best practices are particularly acute for new frontline supervisors—communication, transparency, and proactivity—and should be executed with intention.

- *Adaptive Leadership*: Many cite Ronald Heifetz's 1994 *Leadership without easy answers* as the defining piece on adaptive leadership.[31] This perspective emphasizes leadership behaviors in a dynamic environment, over dated and more rigid hierarchical models of leadership that historically have been prominent in many organizations, especially military and paramilitary organizations often associated with public safety.

In this paradigm, Heifetz argues that leaders have historically over-relied on technical leadership. Technical leadership is described as leadership responses and resolutions to tangible and largely static problems. These largely static problems may be technically new to the organization, but will resemble past challenges and feel familiar in many aspects to all parties involved. In contrast, truly impactful leaders must nurture skills related to adaptive leadership. While technical leadership is largely mechanical and organizational in nature, adaptive leadership is disproportionately about people and disproportionately about solving emerging and largely novel problems without a directly related historical precedent. According to Heifetz and Laurie in the *Harvard Business Review* (2001), modern-era effective leaders must be skilled at guiding creative, human-centric responses to adaptive change, "[t]he sort of change that occurs when people and organizations are forced to adjust to a radically altered environment—they challenge the traditional understanding of the leader-follower relationship."[32] Accordingly, skilled adaptive leaders are likely to be found at all levels of the organization, and can sometimes be seen as disruptive and challenging the status quo.[33]

This perspective on leadership has had a significant and enduring impact on policing. As a result, understanding adaptive leadership concepts, and demonstrating adaptive skills in the field and in the organization are likely key to successful promotion. Professor of Criminal Justice Philip Mancini puts it powerfully and directly in Police One, "Promotion doesn't prepare you for moral gray zones, fractured teams, or public pressure — adaptive leadership does."[34] More specifically, Mancini reiterates the key Heifetz mantra to "get on the balcony"; to take a step back from the ground-level mechanics of the situation, gain elevation and perspective. Only from that slightly removed and elevated vantage point can a leader truly understand the bigger picture and the complexities involved. Thereafter, skilled adaptive leaders can "empower your team to think, solve and lead"[35] with an understanding of the larger organization and political context, and with an emphasis on cocreating a solution with those you lead.

Arguably, adaptive leadership is a quintessential example of bridging theory and practice. To their credit, many adaptive leadership theorists have focused on the utility and applicability of the theory in the real world. This is evidenced by adaptive leadership being the cornerstone theory used in prominent state-mandated frontline supervisor trainings in the field of policing,[36] and an essential leadership skill.

- *The Five Practices of Exemplary Leadership*: The Leadership Challenge by Kouzes and Posner offers a practical, field-tested leadership framework that translates well to the realities of career leadership. At its core, the model reinforces that leadership is not about authority or title; but consists of practices and behaviors that guide leaders. The five practices of exemplary leadership are modeling the way, inspire a shared vision, challenge the process, enable others to act, and encourage the heart.[37] The first practice, Model the Way, is demonstrated when leaders align their actions with clearly stated values. The second, Inspire a Shared Vision, occurs when leaders help others understand how their work contributes to larger purpose.[38] Third is Enable Others to Act, which emphasizes trust, collaboration, and empowering people to do their best work. Challenging the process refers to the attitude of transformational leaders who are willing to question the status quo and take action on their ideas. It also involves individuals who actively seek opportunities to test their skills and abilities and constantly strive to find new and innovative ways to improve themselves and their organizations.[39] The last is Encourage the Heart, reminding leaders that recognition, appreciation, and human connection are not soft skills; they are performance multipliers.[40] Therefore, for an emerging leader, the strategic advantage of this model is scalability and you really do not need positional authority to apply it. Think about how you can create high-impact micro-moments: how you run a briefing or meeting, how you debrief or discuss after an incident, how you give feedback during a one-to-one, or how you support a friend, peer, or colleague under pressure or during time of need. Over time, these small, intentional leadership behaviors compound your credibility, trust, and influence.

- *Emotional Intelligence (EI)*: Goleman identified emotional intelligence (EI) as the foundation of effective leadership, which comprises self-awareness, self-management, social awareness, and relationship management.[41] For new supervisors, EI is particularly essential for managing conflict and building credibility with both subordinates and command staff while regulating your own emotions, empathize with others, and effectively navigate relationships.[42] Proponents of emotional intelligence in public safety argue that it enhances communication skills both in the field and among colleagues, increases empathy, facilitates effective decision-making, and helps de-escalate tense situations. A workplace culture that prioritizes advanced EI skills offers numerous advantages, including improved recruitment, retention, and succession planning. Furthermore, like all core leadership competencies, evidence shows that EI can be actively taught and learned at both individual and organizational levels.[43]

Voices from the Field Installment One: Methodology

This book is not an abstract theoretical discussion of best practices for promotion. Rather, it is a tangible and actionable playbook, in large part because it leverages the collective wisdom of approximately 1,500 public safety professionals from across the United States and beyond. As previewed in the introduction, we surveyed a diverse array of public safety professionals from across the United States and beyond. These public safety professionals are all graduates, faculty, or current students in the

University of San Diego's 100 percent online Law Enforcement and Public Safety Leadership Master's Degree.

The methodology employed in this book may best be described as an informal survey. The goal of this feature of the book is systematically to review, analyze, and report the survey data. However, there was no intention to adhere to the standard qualitative research methodology conventions or draw traditional social-science-based qualitative conclusions. Rather, the goal was simply to provide a vehicle for a uniquely positioned series of law enforcement professionals to share promotional best practices, pitfalls to avoid, and their own lived experience navigating the successes and failures inherent in the promotional process.

The survey results, best practices, and guidance presented throughout this book are derived from a striking array of strikingly experienced public safety professionals. Approximately 72 percent of respondents work in local municipal police departments. Approximately 17 percent represent county sheriff's departments. But there are a notable number of respondents from state, tribal, military, and federal law enforcement agencies as well.

Given that the University of San Diego is located in the state of California, our students, and thus our survey respondents, are disproportionately from that state. In all, 61 percent of respondents serve an agency in California. Other states with significant representation include: Colorado, Florida, Illinois, Nevada, New York, Pennsylvania, Texas, Washington State, and Arizona. Moreover, respondents represent other states from across the Midwest, the Northeast, and Hawaii.

Our respondents also represent a comparatively even distribution across rank levels. Approximately 18 percent are currently serving as chiefs of police, assistant chiefs, sheriffs or undersheriffs. 19.5 percent self-describe their role as captains or commanders, 18.5 percent as lieutenants, and 17 percent as sergeants. The remaining respondents span corporals, frontline officers and deputies, detectives, field training officers, and several different types of professional staff roles.

Survey respondents also represent the full career trajectory and thus can provide insight and guidance to every reader, regardless of where they are in their leadership journey. Approximately 44 percent of respondents have twenty-five or more years of professional experience. 30 percent have between twenty and twenty-five years of experience. 16 percent have between fifteen and twenty years of experience, while 7 percent have between ten and fifteen years of professional experience. All remaining respondents have between two and ten years of public safety work history.

There is also a notable variety in the size of the agencies represented in this book. Approximately 34 percent of respondents represent very large agencies, defined as agencies with 501 or more total personnel. An additional 17 percent represent large agencies, with 201 and 500 total personnel. Respondents representing medium agencies, with total personnel between 51 and 200 personnel, constitute the largest body of respondents by a narrow margin at approximately 35 percent. Lastly, about 13 percent of respondents represent small departments with personnel totals ranging from one to fifty.

Lastly, the career guidance the is presented throughout this book is derived from public safety professionals that serve a diversity of types of communities across the United States and beyond. 37 percent self-describe their communities as urban and densely populated; 24 percent as suburban on the residential outskirts of a city; 18 percent represent fairly large metropolitan areas that span both city centers, suburban, and residential areas. 13 percent of respondents serve small towns, with an additional 3.5 percent representing rural areas.

As these data clearly illustrate, the forthcoming career guidance does not over or underrepresent one particular pathway, or one particular perspective, on the profession broadly or the promotional process specifically. We are deeply appreciative that these students, alumni, and faculty members invested their time in providing the insights captured in the *Voices from the Field* segments throughout this book.

Voices from the Field Installment One, Part Two: Creating A Solid Foundation for Promotability

As established in the opening of this chapter, leadership is not a destination reached upon the receipt of a new rank, role, or accolade. Rather, our respondents consistently advocate that leadership is a mindset. Moreover, this mindset must be intentionally and deliberately nurtured long before one begins actively seeking promotion.

With that guiding mantra in the forefront, we begin our *Voices from the Field* qualitative feature focused on the transition from frontline operator to supervisor. One could argue that this transition represents the most significant shift in one's public safety career. Building on themes from our respondents, one's mindset must broaden, expanding from focusing on one's own individual competence to a larger collective responsibility overseeing a team or small group. While the following section focused on this first promotional step, these foundational habits, mindsets, and career-planning strategies have powerful applicability throughout one's public safety career and across the entire hierarchical spectrum within a law enforcement or public safety organization.

The "Informal Leader"

A recurring truth among our respondents is that the promotional process is often the culmination of attitudes, behaviors, and skills that have already been firmly established by an individual. Many respondents have argued persuasively that the first step in promotion is, to paraphrase colloquially, to lead from where you are; that every individual—regardless of rank and position—has the opportunity to infuse a growth mindset in those around them and have a positive impact on their team and thus the organization as a whole.

As an undersheriff of a county sheriff's department in a Metropolitan Area put it:

> Be an unofficial leader where people respect your integrity, knowledge, and leadership abilities. Be the second voice in the room, either in support or articulating caution to new proposals. Be the person who provides the moral compass when there is misconduct occurring. When people describe you, they should say: "They would never stand for that type of behavior."

A very similar message was reaffirmed by a sergeant from a small town municipal police department in California:

> Start acting like the position I wanted long before I had the badge or the title. I took on extra responsibilities, especially the ones nobody volunteered for. I became someone others came to for help, guidance, and direction. I didn't complain, didn't make excuses, and didn't blame people; I focused on solutions.

A detective from a medium-sized municipal police department in California echoes the importance of taking tangible steps daily to build your leadership skill set, not just passively waiting for others to provide you these opportunities: "Work hard, get involved, develop relationships, and continue to build your resume as your career moves on. Taking on special projects and extra work. Volunteering for extra training to gain more experience."

A captain from a very large municipal police department in California adds that developing your own leadership skill set and leadership dossier should focus on a selfless dedication to the betterment of others: "Volunteer for special assignments. Help out others and be selfless. You are one of the most important people (like an FTO) who sets standards and must lead by example."

Avoid Career Stagnation

In any organization, becoming specialized or hyperspecialized is tempting. While excelling in a narrow category of expertise may be beneficial in many fields, according to our respondents, modern public safety professionals must intentionally cultivate a diverse skill set, especially if they have the goal to promote. Moreover, many argued that true and impactful organizational leadership by definition requires a broad understanding of the agency, the people within it, and living its mission, vision, and values by executing many types of roles.

According to a lieutenant from an urban municipal police department:

> Do everything you want to do as a line level employee. Once you promote, the ability to get operational line level experience in various assignments is over. This makes it difficult to get supervisory roles in specialty assignments, which can lead to career stagnation.

A sergeant from a county sheriff's department in a metropolitan area echoes those sentiments: "Work different positions. Take uncomfortable assignments or tasks that others may avoid. You will learn from them, and be able to pull from your experience when faced with a similar situation. People will come to you for guidance."

A deputy chief from a small municipal police department in Illinois highlights the "non-glamorous" side of avoiding stagnation: "Taking on special projects and extra training that may not seem glamorous. I took on projects that no one else wanted to do. Those projects helped me learn administrative skills that I otherwise would not have gained."

A lieutenant from a very large municipal police department in California emphasizes that becoming a successful leader requires intentional diversification of your skill set:

> I always looked at promotion in three aspects. There is merit, education, and experience. The promotional process was always on a 2-year cycle, which meant candidates could look for opportunities to expand their resumes. I would always look for opportunities to gain experience in areas others shy away from. Too many people in law enforcement focus solely on street work and forget that leadership and management are far more than that. When looking at the next rank, I would advocate for myself an interest in any leadership opportunities. As a patrol officer, I looked for Acting Sergeant positions. If I could not locate one of them, I would look for a job that would challenge me and give me a much more diversified resume. For instance, I volunteered to become a Juvenile Officer, which was not a sought-after position, but was valuable experience. As a sergeant, I volunteered for administrative projects and assignments to gain experience in administration.

Aside from that, every day in my career was a job interview. An officer's reputation and integrity are everything that gives an individual merit. Doing the best job where I was always was important. I spent many years doing street-level work and had an unblemished, solid reputation as a man of honor and integrity. I was also known as someone who would always be there to help. The merit I earned was important in gaining a reputation before I sat in any interview.

Lastly, but not least important, was to educate myself continually. I took leadership courses whenever I had the opportunity through the state or POST. I obtained a B.A. in Organizational Leadership, followed by an M.S. in Law Enforcement Leadership. I believe that education is vital for gaining knowledge. That knowledge, combined with the merit and experience, assists in decisions based on wisdom.

Field Training Officers and Instructor Positions

Throughout the survey, respondents emphasized the importance of serving in Field Training Officer (FTO) and other instructor-type roles, for both the betterment of the organization and to prepare oneself for promotion. Thematically, respondents argue that these training and instructor roles help facilitate the mindset shift that your own career development is no longer exclusively about mastering skills yourself. Rather, you are a critical teacher and mentor sharing knowledge and developing the skills of others.

A lieutenant from an urban municipal police department explained the importance of mentorship, with these organizational and personal goals in the forefront:

> Apply for FTO and spend time learning to train. Be a mentor, and share your experiences, merit, and education with your trainees. This is a start to develop your reputation as a leader. If you are a good FTO, your reputation will precede you when you seek promotion.

A captain, also from an urban municipal police department provided nearly identical advice: "You are one of the most important people (like an FTO) who sets standards and must lead by example."

Leadership Is a Skill

A cornerstone of modern leadership theory that is echoed and discussed in depth in this book is that leadership is a skill. While some aspects of effective leadership may be inherent in an individual, the evidence strongly suggests that leadership is something that needs to be actively developed and nurtured throughout one's career, and potentially throughout one's lifetime. Our respondents' positions dovetail with these leadership theories, often spotlighting that leadership is not only a skill but a perishable skill. Moreover, those seeking promotion must proactively seek out training and education opportunities both inside and outside one's agency.

It is noteworthy that proactive skill development was also seen as a force to overcome organizational politics and roadblocks. Anecdotally, it is clear that an entrenched culture of cronyism may still be an influential presence in some public safety organizations. These networks may unduly influence the promotional process. In these organizational contexts in particular, our respondents urge investigating in one's own professional development as a way to overcome these structural barriers and be successful in the face of these obstacles.

Finally, our respondents emphasize that leadership is a "perishable skill." To end-run these insular networks that still haunt some agencies, one must create a margin of excellence through advanced education and critical thinking.

A response from a professional staff member of a suburban municipal police department with more than twenty years of professional experience reaffirms that, unfortunately, the promotional processes in some agencies do in fact remain broken, highly political, and far from meritocracy. According to this respondent, the key to promotion is to "[i]ngratiate yourself with command staff ... be fake, do the minimum, and kiss a lot of rear ends and be very, very political."

While this response should serve as a sobering reminder of the presence of toxicity and internal politics in many organizations, many respondents argue that skill building can often overcome challenging circumstances.

For example, a captain from a metropolitan county sheriff's department argued that actively seeking out candid feedback is critical for promotion. They point out that we need to develop trusted allies in our professional walk that will give us the critical feedback that we may not see introspectively ourselves. They offered the following nine-point strategy:

> Line level supervision is the most important position in a department. You directly influence the culture and are responsible for messaging the direction of the chief and executive staff. The vision and mission is supported or disparaged by you and your team will follow you. You must be a good leader and exemplary follower:

1. Be patient—promote when you are truly ready. Too many people worry about timing, trying to get promoted early in their career. My best bosses were those with broad experience and could explain how what I did as a patrol officer or sergeant impacted others across the organization. In the organization where I grew up it was not uncommon for a new sergeant to have ten years' experience. Of course, that is changing too as many of my generation have retired.
2. Get outside your comfort zone and take hard "dirty" assignments that many steer away from—crimes against children, financial crimes, community relations, etc. The goal is to develop a broad range of experiences to see LE holistically while also proving you are not afraid of hard work.
3. Similar to the above, do an honest inventory of your patrol deficiencies and seek to improve. For example, if you are a great investigator and weak in tactical management, attend training or speak with subject matter experts. If you are weak on certain types of calls,

volunteer for them to improve your skills. As a boss your people will look to you. You should have a broad understanding of policing to properly guide them to find the answers, or lead in a crisis.
4. Be a good follower for your boss now. That does not mean be a yes person or suck up. Study followership. It is critical to your success.
5. Related to the above, be a leader now. Be willing to make the hard decisions within your purview. Lead younger officers in a positive way and build the department culture to match chief's vision. Do not engage in the gossip or toxic complaining.
6. Get a mentor!
7. A chief once told me to put mentors around myself. These are people you trust who will always tell you the truth. We do not always see our flaws and we need trusted people that will honestly tell us.
8. Be a lifelong student of leadership and coaching. Seek formal education and read! I was once told, "A reader is a leader!" Each book give you the opportunity to take away the best tools to put into your tool kit. Each promotion level requires greater people skills, organizational awareness, and being politically savvy therefore you have to continually grow. Do not get stuck into a single mindset.
9. The goal of most of the above advice is to become a critical thinker. LE has evolved that simple checklists for how to handle a call are not useful. We have to be able to think on our feet, adapt to changing circumstances, and make good decisions under pressure. If you are a checklist person you have to develop your ability to think within broad policy guidelines. The overuse of AI is negatively impacting humanity's ability to research and think critically.

Another captain from a suburban county sheriff's department reaffirms the importance of seeking out both education and training: "Earn an undergraduate and subsequently a graduate degree to ensure quality writing and critical thinking skills and attend every leadership training possible to always improve on your ability to create both team and organizational success."

A captain from a very large county sheriff's department in Florida emphasizes the holistic nature of a modern leadership skills set, including policy expertise, decision-making and emotional intelligence:

> The most crucial skills when preparing for promotion were a deep understanding of agency policies, strong decision-making under pressure, and the ability to communicate clearly … Combining

> technical knowledge with emotional intelligence was essential to being ready for the next level.

A detective from a large county sheriff's department in California reiterates the mindset shift necessary for leadership roles, and the identity and camaraderie impacts of that mindset shift:

> With my department and my 20 years of experience, I found that people who promoted to supervisory roles in patrol, often found success when they acted as leaders and not friends. Often new supervisors in positions of patrol blur the line between being one of the troops and being a leader, and although having friendships is important in law-enforcement, I think it's important for a supervisor to maintain a supervisor mindset and realize that although they're part of patrol [but also] have oversight and help guide the younger deputies. And as I've said several times already, it's important to understand what you're position your promoting to and what goals you have when you get to that position.

In summary, the collective wisdom of these practitioners reveals a clear, albeit rigorous, roadmap for working toward that first frontline supervisor position. This goal clearly requires a mindset shift, which may be the most important element of preparing oneself for promotion. Moreover, our respondents reaffirm the importance of becoming an informal leader long before a formal position is earned. By intentionally seeking to avoid career stagnation via training, professional development and serving in an array of professional capacities, you ensure that you are poised to embrace the wider viewpoint necessary to be an effective frontline supervisor. Field training officers and instructor positions are critical steps in making this mindset shift and investing in the success of others.

More broadly, we learned that all aspiring leaders must acutely understand that Leadership is a Skill that demands continuous nurturing throughout one's career. While we acknowledge the sobering reality of agencies where the process remains highly political, the collective wisdom of this cohort suggests that often, but likely not always, professional development can overcome toxic environments. By seeking out mentorship, especially those willing to provide candid and growth-oriented feedback, you are creating that foundational skill set that will set you apart for promotion. Promotion simply becomes recognition for the leader you have already become.

APPLIED LEADERSHIP AND CRITICAL THINKING QUESTIONS

1. How are you currently demonstrating leadership in your role without relying on title, authority, or formal position?
2. Which of the three foundational elements—discipline, self-awareness\ purpose, or service mindset/requires the most intentional development in your leadership, and why?
3. How do your daily habits and decisions contribute to, or detract from, your long-term credibility as a leader?
4. In what ways does your current behavior reflect the type of leader you aspire to become and where is their misalignment?
5. How can leadership theories (e. g., servant, transformational, situational, adaptive) be translated into specific behaviors in your current environment?
6. As you prepare for reflect on the transition from peer to leader, how would you establish trust, fairness, and boundaries while maintaining professional relationships?

Leadership Tools: Building Leadership Before the Title

The Leadership Identity Audit[44]

Purpose: This self-assessment audit is integrated with a leadership readiness index (LRI) and designed to help emerging professionals—and those transition into new roles—to assess and measure your internal leadership readiness before formal authority is granted. Assessing your readiness for leadership roles and promotion are an area that helps to set the foundation of your journey. As has been mentioned, leadership credibility begins long before the title is ever obtained. The goal is by using this tool it may help you evaluate and become aware of the habits, posture, and patterns that shape you, your reputation and you as a leader.

Step 1: Leadership Identity Self-Assessment

Rate each statement from 1–5

1 = Rarely
2 = Inconsistent
3 = Sometimes Demonstrated
4 = Frequently Demonstrated
5 = Consistently Demonstrated

Domain 1: Personal Discipline and Reliability

- I prepare before I am asked.
- I follow through without reminders.
- I meet deadlines consistently.
- I hold myself accountable without being told.
  Subtotal (Max 20) _____

Domain 2: Emotional Regulation and Self-Awareness

- I regulate my emotions under pressure.
- I respond rather than react.
- I ask for feedback without defensiveness.
- I admit mistakes quickly and correct them.
  Subtotal (Max 20) ________

Domain 3: Confidence and Growth Orientation

- I actively invest in skill development.
- I seek stretch opportunities.
- I believe in my own abilities while remaining coachable.
- I reflect on my behavior and adjust my behaviors intentionally.
  Subtotal (Max 20) _________

Domain 4: Service and Purpose Alignment

- I contribute to others and the organization without needing recognition.
- I prioritize team success over personal acknowledgment.
- I connect routine work to larger purpose and mission.
- My actions align with my stated values.
  Subtotal (Max 20) _________

Step 2: Calculate Your Leadership Readiness Index (LRI)

Maximum Score = 80
Formula:

(**Your Total Score/80**) x 100 = Leadership Readiness Index
LRI = _____ percent

Step 3: Interpret Your Results

90–100% | Advanced Internal Readiness
You demonstrate consistent discipline, emotional maturity, and service alignment. You are building promotable credibility before promotion.

75–89% | Strong Readiness
You show solid leadership patterns. You need to focus on strengthening one or two weaker domains to increase consistency.

60–74% | Emerging Readiness
Leadership potential is present, but your patterns fluctuate. Assess the domains closely for areas of improvement as they require intentional reinforcement.

Below 60% | Foundational Development Needed
This is not to discourage you but to reinforce the importance of focusing on strengthening internal leadership habits so you can be more successful in your next promotional or role expansion.

Step 2: Self-Awareness Mapping

Identify:

Highest Domain: ________
Lowest Domain: _________

Now assess which of the questions in the domain lowered your score. Once you identify, these become areas of self-awareness and improvement.

NOTE: It is a good idea to retake the audit occasionally and chart your LRI score over time. Your leadership readiness trend should show visible growth over time and if not, it may be time to seek additional training, feedback from your mentors or supervisors, and additional self-reflection.

Leadership Development in Practice

Optional Journaling Exercise: Building Leadership Before the Title

While the audit measures behavior, journaling your reflections can help with better clarity, navigate your thoughts, emotions and awareness. There are a few questions for you to consider to jumpstart you, but this is also a space for you to journal freely and start to build a habit or practice of journaling your own observations and based on your needs.

1. Do my routines or habits support my leadership and career advancement ambitions or goals? Or do they quietly, or loudly, undermine them?
2. What are my behavioral blind spots that contradict my values?
3. What kind of leader do I refuse to become?

KEY TAKEAWAYS

1. Leadership Begins before Rank/Position.
   In this chapter, the emphasis was on how leadership is not activated by the promotion, it is cultivated through daily habits, character, and consistency long before authority is granted with several examples.
2. Discipline Builds Competence. Competence Builds Confidence.
   Understanding that disciplined preparation, emotional regulation, and reliability helps to build confidence and that it takes intentional work.
3. Self-Awareness Accelerates Growth.
   The reality is that most careers stall not because of lack of skill, but because of unexamined or changed behaviors. When you understand your strengths, blind spots, and emotional triggers, you can strengthen credibility and influence.
4. Purpose Anchors Leadership.
   Take time to know your "why" because when you do, and it is clear, you are less dependent on titles, recognition, or external validation. Quite often, when your progress feels slow or you feel stuck, your purpose sustains your resilience.
5. Selfless Service is a Leadership Amplifier.
   When you choose to serve others before yourself, it is transformative to your individual competence which equates to your greater collective impact.
6. Reputation is Built in Small Moments.
   Reputation, reputation, reputation. How you respond under pressure, not under pressure, criticize, and show up messy, you are quietly shaping your leadership reputation, your brand. Others are watching.
7. The Shift from Peer to Supervision Requires Intention.
   Promotion can alter relationships. Essential to building trust and being more effective in the transition is consistency, communication, fairness, and transparency.

8. Leadership is a Skill—And It Is Perishable.
   Like physical fitness, leadership requires continual practice, humility and renewal.

CONCLUSION

Leadership does not begin the day a title changes: that has been said repeatedly throughout this chapter. Actually, it begins the day you decide to take responsibility for who you are becoming and who you will be. Long before stripes, insignia, or executive authority, you are building a leadership identity through discipline, through service, through how you show up when no one is watching. Every shift, every conversation, every small decision adds another layer to your credibility. Over time, those layers become your reputation. And reputation becomes the currency of your leadership.

In the early stages of a career, it is tempting to focus on visibility and advancement. But the professionals who rise stronger and resilient are those who first build internal alignment. They've developed those habits that support growth and regulate their emotions under stress. They intentionally seek feedback without defensiveness and choose service over status. They work hard daily to connect tasks to the larger purpose and mission, even on the hard days.

This is a stark reminder that transitioning from peer to supervision will test your consistency and that authority will test your humility. In that same vein, responsibility will test your emotional discipline, but if your foundation has been built intentionally, those tests will not destabilize you: they will refine you.

Remember, leadership is not about posture; it is about preparation. Stay ready. It is not about title, but about trust. It is not about status, but about stewardship. When the promotion eventually comes, it does not create a leader—it reveals one. Will that be you? The rank and the position may come later, but the leader is being built right now.

KEY TERMS

Adaptive Leadership—A leadership approach focused on navigating complex, evolving challenges by adjusting strategies and engaging others in problem-solving.

Chain of Command—The formal hierarchy within an organization that defines authority, communication pathways, and decision-making structure.

Deliberate Practice—Structured, feedback-driven effort focused on improving specific skills through repetition, evaluation, and refinement.

Emotional Intelligence (EI)—The capacity to recognize, manage and influence emotion in yourself and others.

Field Training Officer (FTO)—A designated officer responsible for training, evaluating, and mentoring new personnel, often serving as a foundational model for skill development and performance standards.

Five Practices of Exemplary Leadership—A leadership framework developed by James Kouzes and Barry Posner describing the five core behaviors of effective leaders: modeling the way, inspiring a shared vision, challenging the process, enabling others to act, and encouraging the heart.

Frontline Leadership—Leadership demonstrated at entry or operational levels, often without formal supervisory authority, through influence and behavior.

Firstline Supervisory Leadership—The first level of formal leadership (e.g., sergeant or supervisor) responsible for direct oversight of personnel, operation execution, and communication between command staff and the line staff.

Procedural Justice—A leadership and organizational principle emphasizing fairness, consistency, transparency, and respectful treatment in decision-making processes to build trust and legitimacy.

Servant Leadership—A leadership philosophy that prioritizes the growth, well-being, and development of others as the primary objective.

Situational Leadership—A leadership approach that adapts style and strategy based on the needs of individuals, teams, and specific circumstances.

Transactional Leadership—A leadership approach based on structured exchanges, including rewards and consequences, to influence performance.

NOTES

1 Simon Sinek, Leadership Has to Be Learned, YouTube video, June 11, 2025, https://youtu.be/VOXrpW-rotE.
2 Daniel Goleman, Emotional Intelligence: Why It Can Matter More Than IQ (New York, NY: Bantam Books, 1995).
3 James M. Kouzes and Barry Z. Posner, The Leadership Challenge: How to Make Extraordinary Things Happen in Organizations (6th ed.) (Hoboken, NJ: Wiley, 2017).
4 James MacGregor Burns, Leadership (New York, NY: Harper & Row, 1978).

5 Bernard M. Bass, Leadership and Performance Beyond Expectations (New York, NY: Free Press, 1985).
6 Paul Hersey and Kenneth H. Blanchard, Management of Organizational Behavior: Utilizing Human Resources (4th ed.) (Englewood Cliffs, NJ: Prentice Hall, 1982).
7 Tom R. Tyler, *Why People Obey the Law* (2nd ed.) (Princeton, NJ: Princeton University Press, 2006).
8 James MacGregor Burns, Leadership (New York, NY: Harper & Row, 1978).
9 Loeslie, M. (2024, January 17). Peer to boss: Avoiding the pitfalls. American Police Beat.
https://apbweb.com/2024/01/peer-to-boss-avoiding-the-pitfalls/
10 Reid, G. (2024, April 23). Next-gen leadership: Mastering peer leadership in law enforcement. Police1.
https://www.police1.com/police-leader-playbook/next-gen-leadership-mastering-peer-leadership-in-law-enforcement
11 Sargent, C. (2018). From buddy to boss: Effective fire service leadership (2nd ed.). Fire Engineering
Books & Videos.
12 Kouzes, J. M., and Posner, B. Z. (2017). *The leadership challenge: How to make extraordinary things happen in organizations* (6th ed.). Wiley.
13 James MacGregor Burns, Leadership (New York, NY: Harper & Row, 1978).
14 Raschka, C. (2019). *Like likes like*. Atheneum Books for Young Readers.
15 Tajfel, H., and Turner, J. C. (1979). An integrative theory of intergroup conflict. In W. G. Austin and S. Worchel (Eds.), The social psychology of intergroup relations (pp. 33–47). Brooks/Cole.
16 Cherry, K. (2023). *Social identity theory: Definition, examples, and key concepts.* PositivePsychology.com. https://positivepsychology.com/social-identity-theory/
17 Benmira, S., and Agboola, M. (2021). Evolution of leadership theory. *BMJ Leader, 5*(1), 3-5.
18 Benmira, S., and Agboola, M. (2021). Evolution of leadership theory. *BMJ Leader*, 5(1), 3-5.
19 Willink, J. (2020). *Leadership Strategy and Tactics: Field Manual.* St. Martin's Press.
20 Greenleaf, R. K. (1977). *Servant leadership: A journey into the nature of legitimate power and greatness.* Paulist Press.
21 Hickman, G. R. (2016). *Leading organizations: Perspectives for a new era* (3rd ed.). Sage.
22 Kuhnert, K. W., and Lewis, P. (1987:649). Transactional and transformational leadership: A constructive-developmental analysis. Academy of Management Review, *12*(4), 648–657.

23 Yuki, G.A. (1981). Leadership in organizations. Englewood Cliffs, NJ. Prentice-Hall.
24 Bass, B. M. (1985). *Leadership and performance beyond expectations.* Free Press.
25 James MacGregor Burns, Leadership (New York, NY: Harper & Row, 1978). Bernard M. Bass, Leadership and Performance Beyond Expectations (New York, NY: Free Press, 1985).
26 Bass, B. M. (1985:11). *Leadership and performance beyond expectations.* Free Press.
27 Hersey, P., and Blanchard, K. H. (1969). Life cycle theory of leadership. *Training & Development Journal, 23*(5), 26–34.
28 Loeslie, M. (2024, January 17). *Peer to boss: Avoiding the pitfalls.* American Police Beat. https://apbweb.com/2024/01/peer-to-boss-avoiding-the-pitfalls/
29 Reid, G. (2024, April 23). *Next-gen leadership: Mastering peer leadership in law enforcement.* Police1. https://www.police1.com/police-leader-playbook/next-gen-leadership-mastering-peer-leadership-in-law-enforcement
30 Sargent, C. (2018). *From buddy to boss: Effective fire service leadership* (2nd ed.). Fire Engineering Books & Videos.
31 Heifetz, R. A. (1994). Leadership without easy answers. Belknap Press of Harvard University Press.
32 Heifetz, R. A., and Laurie, D. L. (2001:131, December). The work of leadership. Harvard Business Review, *79*(11), 131–141
33 Loren, G. (2005, August). Thought leadership: Ronald Heifetz - The challenge of adaptive leadership. New Zealand Management, 46–48.
34 Mancini, P. (2025, June 25). Leadership development series: Why adaptive leadership is essential for modern police supervision. Police1. https://www.police1.com/police-leader-playbook/leadership-development-series-why-adaptive-leadership-is-essential-for-modern-police-supervision
35 Mancini, P. (2025, June 25). Leadership development series: Why adaptive leadership is essential for modern police supervision. Police1. https://www.police1.com/police-leader-playbook/leadership-development-series-why-adaptive-leadership-is-essential-for-modern-police-supervision
36 Police Officer Standards & Training (n.d.) Sherman Block Supervisory Leadership Institute. https://post.ca.gov/Portals/0/post_docs/SBSLI%20Network/SLI%20Journal.pdf
37 Kouzes, J. M., and Posner, B. Z. (2017). *The leadership challenge: How to make extraordinary things happen in organizations* (6th ed.). Wiley.
38 Kouzes, J. M., and Posner, B. Z. (2017). *The leadership challenge: How to make extraordinary things happen in organizations* (6th ed.). Wiley.
39 Redick, J. (2024). *The factors that influence and nurture women law enforcement officers to promote into leadership roles within law enforcement.*

California Baptist University. Proquest. https://www.proquest.com/docview/3065843306?sourcetype=Dissertations%20&%20Theses

40 Kouzes, J. M., and Posner, B. Z. (2017). *The leadership challenge: How to make extraordinary things happen in organizations* (6th ed.). Wiley.

41 Goleman, D. (1995). *Emotional intelligence: Why it can matter more than IQ.* Bantam Books.

42 TalentSmartEQ. (2025). Emotional Intelligence Programs & EQ Skills Training. Retrieved from https://www.talentsmarteq.com/

43 Police1. (2025). Emotional Intelligence: The Hidden Skill Every Police Officer Needs. Retrieved from https://www.police1.com/police-training/emotional-intelligence-the-hidden-skill-every-police-officer-needs.

44 Portions of this self-assessment and related exercises were generated or adapted using generative AI tools and reviewed by the author for accuracy and context.

REFERENCES

Bass, B. M. (1985). *Leadership and performance beyond expectations.* Free Press.

Benmira, S., and Agboola, M. (2021). Evolution of leadership theory. *BMJ Leader, 5*(1), 3–5.

Burns, J. M. (1978). *Leadership.* Harper & Row.

Cherry, K. (2023). *Social identity theory: Definition, examples, and key concepts.* PositivePsychology.com. https://positivepsychology.com/social-identity-theory/

Goleman, D. (1995). *Emotional intelligence: Why it can matter more than IQ.* Bantam Books.

Greenleaf, R. K. (1977). *Servant leadership: A journey into the nature of legitimate power and greatness.* Paulist Press.

Heifetz, R. A. (1994). *Leadership without easy answers.* Belknap Press of Harvard University Press.

Heifetz, R. A., and Laurie, D. L. (2001, December). The work of leadership. *Harvard Business Review, 79*(11), 131–141.

Hersey, P., and Blanchard, K. H. (1969). Life cycle theory of leadership. *Training & Development Journal, 23*(5), 26–34.

Hersey, P., and Blanchard, K. H. (1982). *Management of organizational behavior: Utilizing human resources* (4th ed.). Prentice Hall.

Hickman, G. R. (2016). *Leading organizations: Perspectives for a new era* (3rd ed.). Sage.

International Association of Directors of Law Enforcement Standards and Training. (n.d.). Sherman Block Supervisory Leadership Institute. California Commission on Peace Officer Standards and Training. https://post.ca.gov/Portals/0/post_docs/SBSLI%20Network/SLI%20Journal.pdf

Kouzes, J. M., and Posner, B. Z. (2017). *The leadership challenge: How to make extraordinary things happen in organizations* (6th ed.). Wiley.

Kuhnert, K. W., and Lewis, P. (1987). Transactional and transformational leadership: A constructive-developmental analysis. *Academy of Management Review, 12*(4), 648–657.

Loeslie, M. (2024, January 17). Peer to boss: Avoiding the pitfalls. American Police Beat. https://apbweb.com/2024/01/peer-to-boss-avoiding-the-pitfalls/

Loren, G. (2005, August). Thought leadership: Ronald Heifetz - The challenge of adaptive leadership. *New Zealand Management*, 46–48.

Mancini, P. (2025, June 25). Leadership development series: Why adaptive leadership is essential for modern police supervision. Police1. https://www.police1.com/police-leader-playbook/leadership-development-series-why-adaptive-leadership-is-essential-for-modern-police-supervision

Police1. (2025). Emotional intelligence: The hidden skill every police officer needs. https://www.police1.com/police-training/emotional-intelligence-the-hidden-skill-every-police-officer-needs

Raschka, C. (2019). *Like likes like.* Atheneum Books for Young Readers.

Redick, J. (2024). The factors that influence and nurture women law enforcement officers to promote into leadership roles within law enforcement [Doctoral dissertation, California Baptist University]. ProQuest Dissertations and Theses Global.

Reid, G. (2024, April 23). *Next-gen leadership: Mastering peer leadership in law enforcement.* Police1. https://www.police1.com/police-leader-playbook/next-gen-leadership-mastering-peer-leadership-in-law-enforcement

Sargent, C. (2018). *From buddy to boss: Effective fire service leadership* (2nd ed.). Fire Engineering Books & Videos.

Sinek, S. (2025, June 11). Leadership has to be learned [Video]. YouTube. https://youtu.be/VOXrpW-rotE

Tajfel, H., and Turner, J. C. (1979). An integrative theory of intergroup conflict. In W. G. Austin and S. Worchel (Eds.), The social psychology of intergroup relations (pp. 33–47). Brooks/Cole.

TalentSmartEQ. (2025). Emotional intelligence programs & EQ skills training. https://www.talentsmarteq.com/

Tyler, T. R. (2006). *Why people obey the law* (2nd ed.). Princeton University Press.

Willink, J. (2020). *Leadership strategy and tactics: Field manual.* St. Martin's Press.

Yukl, G. A. (1981). *Leadership in organizations.* Prentice-Hall.

CHAPTER TWO

Strategic Career Planning

Mapping Your Path to Success

Mapping your career path in today's world requires a mindset shift. Career development is no longer handed down from organizations; it is an individualized journey driven by personal ambition, values, and a definition of success where adaptability and self-direction are key.[1] This new landscape empowers individuals to take control, chart a course that fits their life-work boundaries, and embrace the flexibility of ownership that comes with it. To map out your path, it is important to reflect on how you evaluate your self-awareness and develop ways to grow in this area before you can fully discern what goals you will be setting. Understanding your motivations, ambitions, and desires for your career and how they align with your personal and family dynamics is valuable for establishing a solid foundation to support your progress.

Assessing one's readiness for promotion is a critical endeavor requiring profound introspection and deliberate evaluation. The journey toward leadership positions within law enforcement demands a comprehensive understanding of personal and professional aptitude and a keen awareness of the demands inherent in assuming higher roles of responsibility.

Central to this assessment is what may be termed "Evaluating Self." This transcends mere superficial introspection, delving instead into a holistic appraisal of one's readiness from all angles. Reflecting on personal experiences, it becomes evident that the impetus for promotion often arises prematurely, driven by an external perception of capability rather than an internal acknowledgment of readiness. Embarking on a premature path to promotion is frequently a result of youthful enthusiasm but lacking experiential maturity, and that is why there is importance in emotional preparedness as a foundational pillar of readiness. Interrogating one's emotional landscape becomes imperative, as it directly correlates with the arduous journey toward promotion. Questions concerning aligning personal aspirations with the demands of elevated roles,

DOI: 10.4324/9781003728849-4

the impact on familial dynamics, and the fortitude to withstand the crucible of competition and potential failure permeate this reflective process.

ASSESSING PERSONAL READINESS FOR PROMOTION

When discussing what is needed for promotional readiness, the areas that surface for examination involve examining the job descriptions, examination eligibility, and scope of the position to meet the criteria and gaining a fundamental understanding of the position. Once taking a superficial glance, there is a second layer of evaluating performance, experience, skills, and consideration of whether the position is a good fit. These will be covered later in this chapter.

While these variables are valuable to assessing overall readiness, there are still corridors of consideration that might have been overlooked: specifically, the part about evaluating "self," not stuff. When we pause and allow ourselves to explore our motivations, desires, feelings, fears, and perceptions, there is an opportunity to reveal greater self-awareness, which can generate more authentic outcomes. For example, if the assessment of your readiness for promotion is based on comparison to "others," you may feel like you should be promoted simply because you think you are more equipped than supervisors in your organization or "others" who have been promoted recently, which may or may not be accurate.

To better understand your status, consider if you are to be promoted tomorrow, again because you think you are ready, how would that change the balance of your personal priorities and family responsibilities? Examining your family dynamics and value system is a vulnerable space, especially when assessing your work-life boundaries for the balance you may need or hope to achieve. You may want to ask yourself if you are willing to start over and work unfavorable shifts, oversee challenging personnel, and interact with colleagues and leaders with different perspectives or approaches. Moving into leadership roles without considering these factors can lead to unrealistic expectations. When creating work-life boundaries, it is important to consider your current comforts and the potential changes that could challenge your values, mindset, and mental health. By grounding your boundaries in thorough self-assessment, tangible and intangible boundaries can support your goals and aspirations, minimize disruptions for you and your family, and help you cope with and manage stress.

How do you feel about conflict management and difficult conversations with others on your team, supervisors, or management? Are those conversations constructive or destructive? When considering transitioning into a new leadership role and interacting more with personnel, especially those you work alongside as a peer, this situation can be challenging if you have little or no experience. It would be beneficial to start monitoring your interpersonal interactions in the workplace and see where you can improve or seek guidance on gaining more experience navigating those opportunities. Evidence shows that self-perception of your emotions is more "effective in navigating the social and relational aspects of management in the work environment, which can be uncertain and highly pressurized."[2] Developing your emotional resilience will be valuable by becoming more self-aware about the areas you need to balance, further grow, and improve emotional intelligence early in your career with a level of emotional agility. For example, emotional intelligence is the ability to "perceive, understand, integrate and manage one's own and other people's feelings and emotions, and to act upon them reflectively and rationally."[3]

Taking the step to embark on promotional endeavors calls for navigating the promotional examination process and understanding the organizational resources and support needed or even offered. When you don't know what you don't know, it can be overwhelming and emotionally exhausting to figure it out and compete. Sometimes, you may struggle with feelings of self-doubt when considering whether you are worthy of pursuing a promotion. This struggle might stem from a perceived lack of support from your organization, such as not feeling supported by your direct supervisors, not being recognized for your contributions, or not having access to leadership development opportunities beyond your current responsibilities.[4]

Additionally, the absence of clear guidance on advancing your career may contribute to these feelings. Leadership should prioritize identifying high-potential (HiPo) employees and progressing them through the talent pipeline.[5] However, many employees may not receive this support from their supervisors, managers, or executives due to favoritism, group dynamics, personal relationships, biases, and sometimes discrimination.[6] The phrase "It's not what you know, it's who you know" often plays a significant role in career advancement.

WORK AND LIFE EXPERIENCE INVENTORY

While there are very valid points of consideration for how the organization should provide a supportive environment and equitable access to opportunities and treatment to help you advance in your career, there are individual factors that have to be evaluated. What does your work experience look like? Are there gaps in your road to promotion that need to be filled? This can get tricky when discussing what is missing in your experience inventory as you seek to promote into leadership positions. The gaps could be in your specific skill sets that are needed; it could be in your experiential exposure to those opportunities that could demonstrate and show your leadership potential; it could be the lack of opportunities in job rotation to see how different assignments work.

For example, if you are in patrol and interested in any investigative or detective positions, how are those job shadowing or short-term opportunities available to you? It is important not to minimize any experience you might have from other jobs before coming into your current profession because you want to make sure that you are translating that very tangible and intangible work experience to correlate to your readiness before the next promotional opportunity you seek. In addition, when you are looking at your inventory, what type of training have you received that is outside of the required perishable skills retraining or training needed for your technical position? Are you also getting training that will help you grow in areas toward the future leadership role that you are seeking? Are you seeking leadership development training, or is specific skills training needed? Are you exposing yourself to individuals in the organization who could be looking at you for future jobs to gain knowledge and understanding from them while researching and learning about that potential leadership role you seek? Are you balancing the development of tactical skills with human skills and experience? Some may feel they need to be overly trained in law enforcement tactics and can overlook the human side of leadership. Real leadership effectiveness is people-centric.

These are just a few ideas of how you can begin to inventory and look at your experience to see the gaps that need to be filled. Suppose your next promotional examination or opportunity for leadership role advancement is a long way off. In that case, you have an excellent opportunity to fill those gaps in your work experience. Remember, your organization may not be best suited financially to provide all the additional training and development you seek, so you may have to invest in yourself. Investing in yourself pays off with great dividends in the end. Due to the size of your organization, you may not have as many opportunities for job rotations, job shadowing, or exposure to different assignments. Therefore, you must be creative in finding ways to gain these experiences. Consider collaborating with partner agencies and be open to volunteering your time to your agency without compensation to pursue these opportunities. Are there opportunities for you to engage in the community and develop those community engagement leadership skills and knowledge?

CREATING A ROAD MAP WITH A CAREER DEVELOPMENT PLAN

A career development plan is a great way to provide a structured strategy designed to help you set career goals and identify the steps and resources needed to achieve them.[7] It is a roadmap that outlines skills, experiences, training, and actions necessary for professional growth and career advancement. When researching to determine the factors that influence and support female law enforcement officers with less than five years of career experience, many participants expressed a sense of unawareness or lack of access to organizational leadership development planning for their careers.[8] They planned their career advancement mostly based on informal expectations that were understood based on established patterns and practices within the agency. These expectations included the expected length of time needed for the job, the types of assignments they should have, and factors such as maintaining a good reputation. Although these expectations were not formally documented in policy, they have seen how they play a significant role in promotions to leadership roles or selection for specialized assignments.

According to Adams (2021), the workforce is undergoing a significant transformation, and younger generations are bringing a fresh set of expectations to the table that stands in contrast to the differential attitudes of older generations;[9] this was also evident in the responses from the participants. When discussing career development, participants expressed a sense of individual commitment to preparing for leadership roles because they felt the onus was on them due to a lack of supportive practices, policies, or programs. Despite acknowledging the supportive nature of their supervisors, these participants often felt they had to proactively seek support on career advancement interests, such as considering specialized assignments or leadership roles, rather than being noticed by their supervisors and approached proactively.[10] In addition, one of the participants for this book project, a sergeant with ten to fifteen years on from a midsized agency in California, shared there is a lot of talk about support but it all comes down to how much effort you put into it. Many mid-management and executive leaders talk about leadership development, but only when it helps them with their career advancement. It is unfortunate that is still happening and the model of leadership in some agencies. But here is the good news, organizational leadership has a great opportunity, a real opportunity. For example, leadership can collaborate with human resource departments to create a career development plan for employees that matches the employee's career goals. Within the plan, it should involve both the supervisors and employees, fostering a supportive and guiding relationship for access and accountability. If your organization lacks these resources or programs, you can develop your plan strategy.

A well-crafted career development plan helps you with these critical components:[11]

1. Self-assessments that help you evaluate where you need to develop and can include your skill sets, areas for improvement, areas of strength, interests, and values.
2. Set goals for both performance, career ambitions and vision. These can be designed for immediate or short-term objectives or longer-term

considerations that align with job roles or specific professional milestones and tailored to your particular needs.

3. Make a plan that breaks down your career goals into doable steps, such as learning new skills, getting specific exposure and experiences, or pursuing certifications, continued education or training. The plan should also help you set deadlines for each step to monitor progress and stay on track. Accountability matters.
4. Developing your skills, or sharpening your edge, involves identifying the technical and human skills you need to achieve your goals and aligning your progress. It also involves figuring out how you will acquire these skills, such as through training, mentorship, workshops, education, job rotation, or other opportunities.
5. Beyond the resources listed in number 4, identify opportunities for networking, career coaching, and seeking out employee development programs through your organization, or seek those outside of the organization if not available. Attend conferences, virtual workshops and learning labs. What's key is learning how to leverage those resources will be beneficial to grow your knowledge, gain valuable feedback and wise counsel to guide you.
6. Create a reasonable timeline and realistic milestones for reaching your career goals. Remember to set a cadence that works for your lifestyle and any need for potential sequencing of your career plans. Make sure that you create a review system to evaluate your progress and to be able to make modifications.
7. As with all things, they shift. Ensure you have included the ability to adapt to the evolution of your profession and your change in desired goals. Always be a continuous learner, keep your plan flexible, but stick to it.

A career development plan's benefits help you provide clear direction for that sense of purpose and clarity regarding where you want your career to go. It also helps you establish a level of engagement in your professional trajectory instead of waiting for someone within your organization to do it for you. In addition, setting specific goals can increase motivation and focus as you work towards achieving them. The skill enhancement you have identified through your career development plan can help encourage continuous personal and professional development in these areas so your progression throughout your career does not feel random or fragmented. Instead can be intentional and purposeful. In addition, your career progression, when it is aligned with your actions and development efforts, will provide better opportunities for promotional readiness and promotion or new career paths. It is a valuable tool when well-constructed for both employees and employers, fostering growth, engagement, and accountability for both the employee and the employer to work together as a shared responsibility for the success of your career advancement. Remember, it is a living document to modify, update, and review regularly with your supervisor or manager to ensure growth and adaptability.

Here is an example of a career development plan for ascending into an executive management position (modify based on your current position):

Step 1: Write down your primary career interest.

Primary Career Interest:

- Reach the level (rank/classification) of ***Executive Management*** within the organization.

Step 2: Identify long-term professional goals (including positions desired)

Long-term professional goals *(include tentative goal dates):*

1. Promote to Sergeant or Supervisor
2. Promote to Lieutenant or Manager
3. Promote to Captain or Commander
4. Promote to Executive Management

Step 3: Identify the short-term goals that will contribute to long-term interests.

Short-term professional goals*:*

1. Be an acting supervisor or manager.
2. Be a team leader for a special assignment, detail, or project.
3. Join external community or non-profit organizations.
4. Participate in a leadership council, internal or external.

Step 4: List 2–3 activities to help you reach each goal.

Short-term Goal 1: Be an acting supervisor or manager

Activity 1:

Action: Enroll in training programs such as leadership or management courses that enhance supervisory or management skills.

Resources: Internal or external training platforms and professional development budgets.

Start Date: March

Completion Date: Continuous, with regular evaluations.

Activity 2:

Action: When available, express interest to current supervisors about acting manager roles.
Resources: Meetings with supervisors and cover performance evaluations and career development plan.

Start Date: June

Completion Date: Ongoing.

Short-term Goal 2: Be a team leader for a special assignment or project

Activity 1:

Action: Volunteer for projects outside your regular daily duties, like participating in internal task forces or community outreach programs.
Resources: Internal communications with supervisors/managers for opportunities.

Start Date: Ongoing

Completion Date: Leave open for future opportunities.

Activity 2:

Action: Engage with cross-departmental teams to offer insights and leadership during special assignments.
Resources: Networking opportunities and team collaboration tools.

Start Date: August

Completion Date: Leave open.

Step 5: Write down additional skills, knowledge, or experience you want to acquire.

Additional skills, knowledge, or experience desired:

1. Enroll in conflict management and problem-solving courses.
2. Complete a Master of Science in Law Enforcement and Public Safety Leadership from the University of San Diego by (include date).
3. Build analytical skills through exposure to incidents and investigations by job shadowing.
4. Increase knowledge in critical incident management.

Step 6: Identify when you will meet with your supervisor or manager and what will be discussed.

Progress Report Meetings:

- Progress Meeting 1:
    - Date and Time: Monday, April 5 at 10:00 a.m.
    - Purpose: Discuss opportunities to participate in initiatives to build leadership experience and foster community relations.
- Progress Meeting 2:
    - Date and Time: Friday, May 7 at, 10:00 a.m.
    - Purpose: Review insights gained from recent leadership training and job shadowing opportunities.

SETTING SMART CAREER GOALS

Whether it is a promotion or a particular assignment, it is crucial to consider your career goals and develop a plan for your career journey. When considering career goals, it is essential to correlate your readiness self-assessment due to true motivations for promotion, desired career progression, and how the organization's lack of skills, experience, confidence, or feedback mechanisms might impact those goals. Remember, career progression may not necessarily involve immediate promotion to a supervisory or managerial role; all career advancement opportunities can be non-linear in unexpected advantageous ways.

It is crucial to set smart career goals that align with your career development plan or leadership development plan, regardless of what your agency calls it or—if they do not have one—what you choose to call it. Remember to keep your goals 'Specific, Measurable, Achievable, Relevant, and Time-bound' (SMART). This acronym is a helpful way to set effective goals and objectives. When you are setting your smart goals, think about what you want to achieve in your career. For instance, when setting goals in a career development plan within a paramilitary organization, you have to evaluate the rank structure and then identify the next progressive promotion level, as well as subsequent ranks. This will allow you to formulate a goal statement: "I aim to achieve the rank of Sergeant by the year ____." To achieve this goal, I needed to outline the necessary steps, measure progress, and ensure I possessed the requisite skills. This involved assessing my skills, identifying gaps, and taking steps to fill them. By setting clear and achievable goals, you can effectively map your career progression and take the required steps to advance. The key is starting. Start by asking yourself what comes next and how you are progressing toward those goals. Be open to feedback and take an honest look at where you can improve and what gaps need to be filled.

STRATEGIC NETWORKING FOR ADVANCEMENT

Networking is not just a buzzword but a powerful tool that can propel your career forward. It is a great way to gain access to professionals who can provide wisdom in your career planning. Having a diversified professional network can give you access to a better understanding of the promotional role you are seeking and a broader understanding of your organizational infrastructure and operations. Leveraging your professional network helps grow your leadership and business acumen by exposing you to different perspectives and problem-solving approaches.

Networking is not just about making connections but about building relationships that can significantly impact your career. Numerous studies demonstrate that professional connections increase job and business prospects, broader and deeper knowledge, enhanced innovation capabilities, quicker career progression, and higher status and authority. Cultivating professional relationships also elevates work quality and boosts job satisfaction.[12] Cultivating a strong professional network will provide opportunities for mentorship and sponsorship by increased visibility and access to information that will help in overall professional development and toward career advancement. You no longer have to be the one who doesn't know what you don't know.

Professional networking allows you to connect with others doing similar work and those in elevated positions who can provide valuable insights, information, and sponsorship. Remember that having sponsors can expand your professional network, as they use their networks to create opportunities for you. Finding a robust and reliable sponsor with the time to invest in you can be challenging, but remember that sponsors are influential individuals, not just a high rank or position. They can be from within your organization or from another.

Networking may feel uncomfortable, especially if you are not used to connecting with unfamiliar people or those in higher positions. However, in an interesting article by Matthew Meade, professional connections can increase job and business prospects, broader knowledge, enhanced innovation capabilities, quicker career progression, and higher status and authority.[13] Building professional relationships also improves work quality and job satisfaction. It is important to remember that networking is not just about connecting with higher-ups; it also involves connecting with peers and breaking down awkward interpersonal dynamics, especially for women in male-dominated work environments. Recognizing the significance of social skills and emotional intelligence in successful social interactions can help you build a solid professional network. Bolman and Deal discuss the importance of social skills for effective teamwork and collaboration and the significance of emotional intelligence (EI) in successful social interactions.[14]

As you work to build your professional network, recognize that you will need different networking opportunities throughout your career advancement to keep you ahead of the arc of your career. Overall, networking is essential for career advancement, and it is important to seek out different networking opportunities throughout your career to stay ahead. For organizational leaders, there is a great opportunity to create healthier cultural norms and break down limiting social constructs to promote professional growth opportunities for women. To create structured networking activities to reduce concerns about stigmas in professional relationships and create equitable opportunities for women to connect to peers and mentors consider cross-role mentorship circles. These circles are small, diverse groups of professionals at different ranks and roles that meet regularly in a structured setting to discuss career development, leadership, and professional growth. Meetings can be scheduled monthly, facilitated by a senior professional, and each month a different participant can lead the discussion to build leadership skills. By creating space for professionals to foster professional connections, discussing career development openly helps to build trust and a stronger sense of team unity.

Networking can accelerate professional development at any stage, especially at the student or academy stage. It is important to identify good instructors, adjunct faculty, or other co-workers who model good values, character and professionalism, and seek them out for guidance to create the bridges into or within the profession. These conversations do not need to be formal; networking can start with a single conversation or a shared story. At the same time, networking is an ongoing process that happens through individual interactions whether you are in a professional association, attending business or stakeholder meetings, or with peer groups. All those opportunities expand visibility and begin to open opportunity that formal processes may not yet provide. So, remember the power of networking and how if you start early, it the exposure gives you more access to opportunities, illuminates career paths and builds a rapport system that will serve you as you grow. But the power of networking only works if you do it.

VOLUNTEERISM

When evaluating your readiness for promotion, it is crucial to consider both internal assessment and tangible contributions in your professional sphere. Simply being proficient in your job responsibilities is not enough. You should also assess how you have gone beyond your routine obligations by seeking opportunities for professional growth and expanding your expertise and professional network. This involves actively contributing to organizational objectives, taking on extra responsibilities, and fostering a proactive attitude that aligns with leadership roles. Consider reframing your approach to taking on additional opportunities that may not offer compensation, or it may, and it is possible it might disrupt your personal time. When you are assessing your capacity to volunteer, this is where you have to establish healthy boundaries for yourself and your personal time, but it is also where you need to challenge yourself to be a contributor to your organization outside of your regular duties. There is an example where an officer volunteered to work overtime, which is not uncommon, but they did it intentionally when they selected the overtime assignment. They chose to work a different assigned area than their regular beat, work for a different supervisor and manager which exposed them to other leaders in their large department, and they gained new knowledge in the experience.

Volunteer experiences also build practical leadership competencies that often mirror supervisory responsibilities such as collaboration, communication, and problem-solving.[15] It is also a chance to coordinate projects, engage with community partners, and mentoring others, all of which are essential for leadership roles. These experiences expand your perspective beyond your assigned position and demonstrate initiative, service orientation, and a willingness to contribute to the broader mission of the organization. Volunteerism is an opportunity if you see it that way.

THE IMPORTANCE OF MENTORS, SPONSORS AND COACHES

Mentoring is a powerful personal and professional growth tool, offering guidance, support, and insight. It fosters development by connecting less experienced individuals with seasoned leaders who can share knowledge, offer feedback, and help navigate challenges. In law enforcement and public safety, mentoring enhances skills, builds confidence, and creates a path for career advancement and can promote a culture of continuous learning, ensuring that personnel feel supported and valued, improving performance and job satisfaction.[16] The expectation is that a mentor imparts wisdom and guidance, while the mentee reciprocates with receptivity and humility, or that is how it should happen, and mentors are incredibly valuable in your assessment process and have an indispensable role in navigating this intricate journey with you. However, having a clear and nuanced understanding of mentorship is essential, as it involves a unique symbiotic exchange between mentor and mentee.

Pursuing mentors requires proactive engagement, transcending conventional barriers of gender and hierarchical dynamics. For example, research indicates that mentorship helps women feel more legitimate in leadership roles and promotes behavioral changes that improve leadership effectiveness.[17,18] There is a reality to this dynamic in law enforcement and a pattern of leadership behavior mentioned in Chapter 1 around Social Identity Theory. It is important to reemphasize these relationships on this theory for better understanding. Social Identity Theory includes three cognitive components: social categorization, social identification, and social comparison.[19] Mentorship dynamics can be shaped by these social and cultural perceptions, as well as available advancement opportunities.

In a 2010 study from the Center for Talent Innovation, it was found that nearly two-thirds of senior male leaders reported pulling back from one-on-one mentoring relationships with junior female employees because of concerns about how the relationship might be perceived, while 50 percent of women reported similar concerns.[20] It is important to be aware that when mentorship and sponsorship opportunities becomes constrained by these dynamics, leadership pipelines may unintentionally narrow and yes, leadership at all levels matters, but the responsibility to create social exchanges that shape the perceived ethical values within an organization rests heavily within all levels of leadership, especially executive leadership. It is time for organizations to move beyond cultural norms rooted and outdated standards that foster ethical standards that work for some and not for others. Organizational cultures built around "like likes like" can unintentionally stifle growth, innovation, and meaningful change and can create silos of similar leadership styles that perpetrate themselves through further succession planning.

Therefore, you must be ready to approach those individuals, in leadership, or that you may perceive to be unapproachable if you want to be proactive and not wait for them to come to you. For example, as a lieutenant, I observed an assistant chief from a distance and watched how they interacted with other people and his leadership style. I never had any opportunities from his mentorship, but others did, primarily men, but he also did not know me very well. One day, we were at an event, and I approached this assistant chief, and directly asked if he'd be willing to mentor me as I desired to be promoted not only to the next rank of captain but also to the long-term goal of promotion to chief. He looked at me with a side nod, unsure how to answer, but he eventually said "sure." I took that brief sure as a yes and held him accountable for what I needed. It wasn't that he did not want to be helpful; he shared with me later that he wasn't sure how to be beneficial and comfortable, as I was a female. But what I did that day was shift the hierarchy role dynamic and those gender barriers that can create awkward social interactions, as well as the ability to have mentorship from those higher up in the organization by creating a safe mentorship bridge for us.

In addition, when you are looking for mentorship, you have to be willing to go outside of your comfort zone, possibly even be dismissed, perhaps even be told no the first time, and be persistent in getting the mentorship you need. But you also have to do the work when asked or selected. It may not always be optimal those special assignments or committees. Howevetr, they demonstrate your willingness to contribute back to the organization, to stretch and grow your leadership acumen, and they will remember it. So, I encourage you not to wait for someone to tap you on the shoulder: it may never happen. It is okay to bravely go and find mentors who work for what you need and your aspirational career advancement journey.

The mentoring relationship also served as a sponsorship for me, creating a dual role. When you are looking at mentors to identify, it is a good idea also to leverage the potential for their sponsorship of you to help grow the awareness for others of who you are and what you can bring to the organization as a high-potential employee that they can see fit into the talent management pipeline for succession planning. The sponsorship that this assistant chief provided was someone to become familiar with who I was as a professional in my work experience, my character, and my inner personal skills and 'fit' or 'likability,' factors that influence leaders' decisions to select you for opportunities for training, opportunities for assignments, or to consider you for future promotional opportunities. Having the sponsorship elevated my existence to other leaders in the organization. I had opportunities to participate on large committees that exposed me to a broader number of leadership executives in the organization and also elevated my level of autonomy in a different space than where I was assigned to grow my more significant body of knowledge around strategic vision and planning for the organization, having input into the development of organizational policies, practices, processes, networking and collaborating with a broader community and other public safety stakeholders, and exposing me to a more extensive understanding of risk management, liability, and the importance and value of relational leadership when it comes to working with key contacts in our local and state legislators and government.

A side note on mentoring: I also want to encourage you to consider peer mentors. Some of them may have more time than you, different life experiences, and diverse skill sets due to other assignments. When choosing peer mentors, prioritize those with the right mindset and your best interest at heart, avoiding individuals with hidden agendas, negativity, or personal agendas that conflict with your own. Remember, friends may not be the best mentors, and some friends may not endure the career advancement ride with you, and that is okay.

Lastly, coaching. When most of us think of coaching, we reflect on any experience we've had in a team sport, and a coach would be the person that was hardest for us to do our best. Reflecting on the coaching we received as athletes, some may have positive experiences and feelings, while others may recall negative memories. However, the coach's role is to bring out the best in you by using a well-designed strategy and plan to help us improve, develop the skills needed, and be resilient in the process. In today's sports, the coaching staff has evolved beyond just a head coach and an assistant coach. Most professional athletes now have a team of specialized coaches to address various aspects of their development. This holistic coaching approach covers physical training and emotional, spiritual, wellness, and financial aspects. Coaching now goes beyond mentoring, offering specific attention and planning to help athletes achieve their goals.

For career advancement, coaching is leveling up from mentorship. Coaching is often a more structured and goal-oriented process that aims to enhance an individual's performance and skills through tailored guidance and feedback[21] with the ability to help address challenges in real-time, not just to listen but to help develop strategies for better outcomes. The elevated benefits of coaching are personalized attention to skill enhancement, increased accountability, and a focus on achieving measurable outcomes to reach your career goals and promotional leadership roles. Research shows that leadership development, mentoring and coaching opportunities play a critical role in advancing women's careers, particularly when organizations intentionally create an environment that supports sponsorship, inclusive leadership networks, and equitable career development pathways.[22] Some of those outcomes include strengthening your communication, negotiation, and strategic thinking skills while improving overall performance and career satisfaction and addressing self-limiting behaviors.[23]

APPLIED LEADERSHIP QUESTIONS AND CRITICAL THINKING

1. How aligned are your current career goals with your personal values, life priorities, and long-term vision—and where are there gaps?
2. Are you pursuing advancement based on internal readiness or external comparison—and how might that influence your decision-making?
3. What gaps exist in your experience, skills, or exposure that could limit your readiness for your next role, and what is your strategy to address them?
4. How effectively are you taking ownership of your career development versus relying on your organization to create opportunities for you?
5. In what ways are you intentionally building relationships (mentors, sponsors, peers) that expand your visibility, growth, and access to opportunity?
6. How are you balancing technical expertise with human-centered leadership skills such as communication, emotional intelligence, and influence?
7. If you were promoted tomorrow, how prepared are you to manage the personal, professional, and leadership demands of that role—and what would need to change immediately?

KEY TAKEAWAYS

Networking with Intention: Key Stakeholders

Intentional networking means taking the initiative to connect with people who can really help you move forward in your career. These might be industry leaders, colleagues, decision-makers, or experts whose experience lines up with where you want to go. Try to build genuine relationships with those who share your values and have similar goals. When you do this, you create a network that not only gives you helpful advice and opens up new possibilities, but also supports your growth. Plus, this kind of networking is not just good for you, it creates a team spirit that lifts everyone up.

How to Build Mutually Beneficial Relationships

Building meaningful professional relationships really comes down to give-and-take and trust. Instead of networking just to get ahead, think of it as a chance to help others and add value wherever you can. Share your knowledge, lend a hand, and be authentic in your interactions. By focusing on helping each other grow, you create connections that last and benefit everyone involved.

The Role of Mentors, Coaches, and Sponsors in Career Success

Mentors, coaches, and sponsors each play a distinct role in helping you move forward in your career. A mentor is someone who offers advice and encouragement, guiding you through challenges and helping you grow professionally. Coaches, on the other hand, work closely with you in real time, listening to your concerns and helping you come up with practical strategies to tackle obstacles. This hands-on support not only improves your problem-solving skills but also builds your confidence when facing tough situations, making it easier for you to reach your goals. Sponsors are the ones who go to bat for you; they use their influence to open doors and connect you with valuable opportunities and resources. When you tap into all three types of support, you create a powerful network that can truly accelerate your career and help you achieve your ambitions.

CONCLUSION

In closing, mapping your career path is an intentional process that starts with self-awareness and evolves through purposeful goal-setting and strategic action. By taking the time to evaluate your personal and professional readiness, aligning your ambitions with your values, and utilizing tools such as career development plans, SMART goals, and strategic networking, you position yourself to navigate your journey with clarity and confidence. Remember, mentors, sponsors, and coaches can serve as invaluable allies, while volunteerism and meaningful connections expand your influence and opportunities. Embracing this holistic approach ensures that your career map is not just a plan but a dynamic guide that empowers you to achieve a fulfilling and sustainable future, balancing both work and life aspirations.

KEY TERMS

Self-Assessment (Evaluating Self)—a deliberate and holistic process of examining one's skills, experiences, motivations, values, emotional readiness, and life alignment to determine true readiness for leadership and advancement beyond surface-level qualifications.

Promotional Readiness—the combination of self-awareness, experience, skill development, emotional intelligence, and preparation required to successfully compete for an perform in a higher role.

Promotional Examination Process—the formal, structured system used by public safety organizations to assess and select candidates for advancement, often including written exams, oral boards, and assessment centers.

Career Development Plan—a strategic, structured roadmap outlining goals, actions, timelines, and resources needed for career progression.

Professional Networking—the intentional development of relationships that provide access to knowledge, opportunities, mentorship, sponsorship, and influence.

High-Potential Employees (HiPo)—individuals identified as having the capacity, aspiration, and readiness to assume greater leadership responsibilities.

Talent Pipeline—an organizational system for identifying, developing, and advancing employees into future leadership roles.

Professional Visibility—the degree to which an individual's skills, contributions, and leadership potential are recognized by decision-makers and organizational leaders.

Volunteerism—intentional engagement in additional assignments or initiatives to build skills, exposure, and leadership experience.

Career Adaptability—the capacity to adjust career strategies in response to changing personal goals, organizational dynamics, and industry trends.

Voices from the Field Installment Two: Skill Set Development, Communication, and Promotional Readiness

In this section of *Voices from the Field,* we shift from a focus on mindset to a focus on tangible skills. We leveraged the collective expertise of our respondents to disaggregate tangible skills into two conceptual categories. First, we explored the process of personal and professional growth, actually identifying and building knowledge and skills within yourself for promotional readiness. We asked our respondents: "What specific skills or knowledge did you find most crucial when preparing for a promotion?"

Second, we wanted to unearth more about how our respondents effectively communicate their professional growth to decision makers in their organization. More specifically, how do those seeking promotion broadcast their skills to influential figures within their agency, without being self-aggrandizing and making sure to continue to focus on the betterment of the organization itself, not just themselves? With this goal in mind, we asked: "What actions or behaviors did you find most effective in demonstrating your readiness for the next level? What specifically did you do to show your organizational leadership that you were ready for the next step?" As you can see, the array of tactics and strategies employed by our respondents, and the attendant advice they share, reaffirms the importance of intentionally cultivating a broad base of skills to prepare for leadership roles. Many argued that a more subtle, service-oriented approach to broadcasting these skills up the chain of command may be more effective than a more overt, self-focused one.

Developing the "Next Steps" Skills

A near-universal theme among our respondents is the necessity of "stepping into the shoes" of the rank you are seeking well before you begin the formal promotional process. Respondents often recommended mastering the skills necessary to execute your current role effectively. But thereafter, intentionally seek out opportunities to practice bigger picture skills, often mimicking the approach of effective leaders in your organization, and learning lessons about skills and approaches to avoid from leaders who you perceive as less effective, or downright counterproductive. According to our respondents, bigger-picture leadership skill sets often include a broader lens for identifying and addressing problems and how you communicate with your peers, as well as how you communicate with those above and below you in the chain of command.

As a deputy chief from a large municipal police department in Colorado put it: "Answer the questions from the perspective of the rank you are testing for and not your current position."

A captain from a very large municipal police department in Washington State expressed a very similar sentiment: "Mentally putting myself in the position to which I was aspiring. I needed to answer the questions as the sergeant, not answer 'If I got promoted, I would ...' "

Much like a professional interview process in any field, a critical task is demonstrating your readiness for the next level by highlighting the specific skills, duties, and responsibilities you have already executed that translate directly to the requirements of the role you are seeking.

A detective from a large municipal police department in California makes this point powerfully: "You must know and learn the position you want to promote to. Then you can start identifying how you've already been working in that capacity and what you need to start doing to prepare for the role."

Communication: A Key Leadership Competency

The ability to communicate effectively is arguably the single most important leadership skill in any field. The central importance of communication is a major theme in the leadership literature,[24] public safety-specific research,[25] and a prominent sentiment across our survey responses. Building from our survey results, respondents articulated that communication is a broad and encompassing concept and a broad and encompassing skill set. As evidenced below, communication can mean the ability to synthesize and effectively communicate complex dynamics. Communication can mean making challenging decisions under pressure and clearly relaying that directive to those around you. Moreover, communication may also encompass the array of so-called soft skills that dovetail with the emotional intelligence skills demonstrated by many highly successful leaders.

Specific to the promotional process, many respondents argued that presentation skills are essential. Moreover, they explained that this is an area where otherwise qualified candidates can struggle.

A chief of police from a large municipal police department in California articulated just this position:

> Candidates first need the real-world experience to be prepared to step into the new role, but I often see candidates fail to work on their presentation skills and fail during the promotional process. You must have the confidence and skillset to present the facts of why you are best for the job during the oral board presentations.

A sergeant from a medium-sized municipal police department in California provided further guidance on skills to develop for those seeking promotion. "Public speaking, but in a manner that is tact, concise, and effective."

Master the Minutiae

Many respondents argued that the foundation for leadership success is first developing technical public safety skills. Someone can possess sophisticated leadership skills and strategies, but they often ring hollow within a law enforcement organization unless they are coupled with an obvious mastery of the daily tasks and technical competencies required in a modern law enforcement organization. The core technical skills include a sophisticated understanding of policy, guiding case law, and internal administrative processes. In combination, mastering these technical skills provides an aspiring leader credibility, which is necessary not only to be promoted, but also to be successful in the new role.

An undersheriff from a large County Sheriff's Department in California noted that the technical skills-leadership skills paradigm is a sliding scale that evolves throughout one's leadership arc:

> This breaks into two parts. The first is technical skills, such as policies, laws, and procedures. The second is leadership's soft skills. Most people are promoted due to technical skills. But the higher one rises, the less critical technical skills become, and leadership skills reign supreme. Problem-solving is a vital skill, especially in leading others to provide solutions. Promotion skills involve managing more than just patrol. Being able to step into new roles and be successful is essential.

A lieutenant from a very large municipal police department in California emphasized the combination of communication skills with technical knowledge in a leadership role:

> Being able to organize my thoughts, speak clearly, and articulate my decisions on why and how I came to my decisions. It was also important to truly know and understand the general orders, procedures, and rules and regulations of the department.

The Balance of Support and Assertiveness

Lastly, many respondents pointed out that when building skills for promotional readiness, there is a fine line between support and more decisive actions required in a leadership role. As argued throughout this book, a mainstay of leadership is possessing a diverse skill set of leadership approaches that can be strategically deployed based on each individual situation. Our respondents emphasized that this array of skills is something to be honed intentionally in advance of promotion.

A chief of police from a small town in Texas captured the importance of adaptive leadership:

> The most crucial skill I developed was understanding when to lead with a servant mindset and when to step forward with a warrior mindset. Preparing for promotion required learning how to balance humility, service, and support for my officers with the ability to act firmly and assertively when the situation demanded it.

In sum, those seeking promotion must develop multifaceted communication skills, master the technical elements of their roles, and cultivate a diverse set of leadership tools to utilize intentionally and strategically. However, simply developing this diverse array of technical and leadership skills is only the first step.

Ascending the law enforcement ladder requires individuals seeking promotion to demonstrate those leadership skills to key stakeholders and decision-makers within their organization. As noted, this is a delicate process. A high-achieving, growth-minded public safety professional must demonstrate their effectiveness and promotional readiness, but do so in a manner that enhances their credibility within the organization, and avoids possible resentment from peers and superiors alike.

Undesirable Work Tasks as an Opportunity

Respondents argued that taking on unwanted or less-desirable tasks is an effective way to demonstrate your promotability. Not only does the effective execution of less desirable tasks show off your own diverse professional skill set, but it also shows a commitment to the mission of the organization.

A deputy chief from a small municipal police department in Illinois powerfully articulates this strategy, and how it helped him develop a macro-level understanding of local organizational dynamics:

> I took on projects that no one else wanted to do. Those projects helped me learn administrative skills that I otherwise would not have gained. It gave me perspective on how things came together from beyond just the police department. It also helped me learn to both network and collaborate well with others.

A sergeant from a small town municipal police department in California made a nearly identical point, with an emphasis on being solutions oriented:

> I started acting like the position I wanted long before I had the badge or the title. I took on extra responsibilities, especially the ones nobody volunteered for. I became someone others came to for help, guidance, and direction. I didn't complain, didn't make excuses, and didn't blame people, I focused on solutions. Over time, that spoke louder than any resume. I was always a firm believe about reputation, take it seriously and you will make a name for yourself.

Dovetailing with taking on less desirable assignments is cultivating an intentional diversity in your professional roles. A captain from a medium-sized municipal police department in California outlines several specific avenues for demonstrating the breadth of your skill set: "Demonstrating that you are a well-rounded candidate. This can be accomplished by spending time in a special assignment, becoming an in-house instructor, or taking informal leadership roles on your respective teams."

Modeling Leadership

Many respondents argued that a powerful way to demonstrate you are ready for a leadership position is to take on training and mentoring roles at your current rank. Recommendations included serving as a formal or informal trainer in your area(s) of expertise and making it a point not just to identify problems but to provide several evidence-based and data-driven potential solutions for your superiors to evaluate.

A captain from a very large county sheriff's department in Florida described this approach as "operating above your rank":

> The most effective actions in demonstrating my readiness for the next level were consistently taking ownership, seeking out responsibilities beyond my current role, and focusing on developing the people around me. I made it a point to solve problems instead of simply elevating them, and I regularly provided thoughtful recommendations supported by data and policy. I also worked to model calm, steady leadership in high-pressure situations and maintain strong communication with both supervisors and peers. By demonstrating reliability, initiative, and the ability to think strategically, I showed

> organizational leadership that I was already functioning at the next level before ever holding the title.

The Importance of Relationship Building

Promotional readiness is surely about tasks and organizational betterment, but it is also about relationships. Many respondents echoed a key theme from this book by encouraging the active solicitation of mentors. More specifically, many argued to actively seek out mentors who are willing to provide well-reasoned praise, advice, as well as the constructive criticism that is a necessity for professional growth.

A chief of police from a small municipal police department in California echoes this advice, encouraging being proactive in seeking out mentors:

> Don't be afraid to use the resources around you. Request to meet with individuals in the rank you are seeking or the rank above to learn the supervisor's expectations. For example, if you are in the promotional process for lieutenant, talk to other lieutenants to get their perspectives, and also talk to captains to find out what they expect of their lieutenants.

A lieutenant from a very large municipal police department in California outlines several ways to seek out mentorship and be a mentor, both formally and informally:

> Find someone who many consider a great front-line supervisor and work for them. If you cannot work for them, then set up an appointment and have a cup of coffee with them. The skills needed are all part of what I mentioned above. The importance of gaining merit, experience, and education is vital … Apply for FTO and spend time learning to train. Be a mentor, and share your experiences, merit, and education with your trainees. This is a start to develop your reputation as a leader. If you are a good FTO, your reputation will precede you when you seek promotion.

A captain from a medium-sized municipal police department in California notes that an effective leader in contemporary public safety must cultivate relationships across all elements of the department, including professional staff and sworn personnel:

Establishing relationships. Good leaders have developed relationships both internally and externally. In the case of sworn personnel, they must remember that relationships with professional staff members (non-sworn) are equally as important.

This installment of *Voices From the Field* has demonstrated empirically that the journey towards promotion is in part about developing one's professional skill set and in part about effectively communicating that skill set to decision-makers within the organization. The array of public professionals featured here argue that the foundation for promotion depends on mastering the technical aspect of your current role and building an array of leadership skills and tools. The next iteration of professional growth involves developing a wider lens to serve the organization by seeking out challenging assignments that others avoid, and executing them with skill, vigor and a positive attitude. Moreover, many advised to seek out formal and informal training roles to demonstrate a leadership skill set prior to seeking any formal title or rank. Lastly, respondents reaffirmed the importance of relationship building and connecting with mentors. In combination, this advice should help build the skills and demonstrate the skills necessary to promote and be a long-term asset to your organization and the profession as a whole.

NOTES

1 Jacobs, S., De Vos, A., Stuer, D., and Van der Heijden, B. I. J. M. (2019). "Knowing Me, Knowing You" the Importance of Networking for Freelancers' Careers: Examining the Mediating Role of Need for Relatedness Fulfillment and Employability-Enhancing Competencies. *Frontiers in Psychology, 10*, 2055. https://doi.org/10.3389/fpsyg.2019.02055

2 Singh, A., and Dubey, A. (2015). Role of trait emotional intelligence in prosocial behavior of managerial personnel. *Journal of Psychosocial Research, 10*(2), 439–447.

3 Singh, A., and Dubey, A. (2015). Role of trait emotional intelligence in prosocial behavior of managerial personnel. *Journal of Psychosocial Research, 10*(2), 439–447.

4 Redick, J. (2024). *The factors that influence and nurture women law enforcement officers to promote into leadership roles within law enforcement.*

California Baptist University. Proquest. https://www.proquest.com/docview/3065843306?sourcetype=Dissertations%20&%20Theses

5 Valentine, S. R., Meglich, P., Mathis, R. L., and Jackson, J. H. (2019). *Human Resource Management* (16th ed.). Cengage Learning.

6 Valentine, S. R., Meglich, P., Mathis, R. L., and Jackson, J. H. (2019). *Human Resource Management* (16th ed.). Cengage Learning.

7 Hedge, J. W. and Rineer, J. R., (2017). Improving Career Development Opportunities Through Rigorous Career Pathways Research. RTI Press Publication No. OP-0037-1703. Research Triangle Park, NC: RTI Press. https://doi.org/10.3768/ rtipress.2017.op.0037.1703

8 Redick, J. (2024). *The factors that influence and nurture women law enforcement officers to promote into leadership roles within law enforcement.* California Baptist University. Proquest. https://www.proquest.com/docview/3065843306?sourcetype=Dissertations%20&%20Theses

9 Adams, L. (2021). *HR disrupted: It's time for something different* (2nd ed.). Practical Inspiration Publishing.

10 Redick, J. (2024). *The factors that influence and nurture women law enforcement officers to promote into leadership roles within law enforcement.* California Baptist University. Proquest. https://www.proquest.com/docview/3065843306?sourcetype=Dissertations%20&%20Theses

11 Redick, J. (2022). *Survival Guide to Law Enforcement Promotional Preparation.* Curry Brothers Publishing.

12 Gino, F. (2024, March 7). *Learn to love networking.* Harvard Business Review. https://hbr.org/2016/05/learn-to-love-networking

13 Meade, M. C. (2025, December 16). The Power Of Networking With Purpose. Forbes. https://www.forbes.com/sites/matthewmeade/2025/12/16/the-power-of-networking-with-purpose/

14 Bolman, L. G., and Deal, T. E. (1991). Leadership and management effectiveness: A multi-frame, multi-sector analysis. *Human Resource Management, 30*(4), 509–534. https://doi.org/10.1002/hrm.3930300406

15 Forbes Nonprofit Council. (2026, February 18). *Volunteerism is a skill set: Why it belongs on every résumé.* Forbes.

16 "The Power of Mentorship," *Police Chief Magazine*, International Association of Chiefs of Police, December 20, 2023, https://www.policechiefmagazine.org/power-mentorship/

17 de Haan, E., Bertie, C., Day, A., and Sills, C. (2010). Clients' critical moments of coaching: Toward a "client model" of executive coaching. *Academy of Management Learning & Education*, *9*(4), 607–621. https://doi.org/10.5465/amle.9.4.zqr607

18 Lavender, L., and Todak, N. (2022). Exploring the value of mentorship for women police officers. *Policing*, *45*(6), 1064–1081. https://doi.org/10.1108/pijpsm-06-2022-0082

19 Cherry, K. (2023). *Social identity theory: Definition, examples, and key concepts.* PositivePsychology.com. https://positivepsychology.com/social-identity-theory/
20 Lebowitz, S. (2015). *Why women are still less likely to be promoted than men*. Business Insider.
21 Valentine, S., Hollingworth, D., and Fleischman, G. (2020). Ethical climate, ethical leadership, and employee well-being in organizations. *Human Resource Management, 59*(2), 195–210. https://doi.org/10.1002/hrm.21995
22 Van Oosten, E. B., Buse, K., and Bilimoria, D. (2019). Advancing women's careers through leadership development programs: The role of organizational context and mentoring. *Human Resource Management, 58*(2), 207–226. https://doi.org/10.1002/hrm.21953
23 Van Oosten, E. B., Buse, K., and Bilimoria, D. (2019). Advancing women's careers through leadership development programs: The role of organizational context and mentoring. *Human Resource Management, 58*(2), 207–226. https://doi.org/10.1002/hrm.21953
24 Fairhurst, G. T., and Connaughton, S. L. (2014). Leadership communication. In L. L. Putnam and D. K. Mumby (Eds.), The SAGE handbook of organizational communication: Advances in theory, research, and methods (pp. 391–413). SAGE Publications.
25 Fitch, B. D. (2015). Law enforcement interpersonal communication and conflict management: The IMPACT model. SAGE Publications.

REFERENCES

Adams, L. (2021). *HR disrupted: It's time for something different* (2nd ed.). Practical Inspiration Publishing.

Bolman, L. G., & Deal, T. E. (1991). Leadership and management effectiveness: A multi-frame, multi-sector analysis. *Human Resource Management, 30*(4), 509–534. https://doi.org/10.1002/hrm.3930300406

Cherry, K. (2023). Social identity theory: Definition, examples, and key concepts. PositivePsychology.com. https://positivepsychology.com/social-identity-theory/

de Haan, E., Bertie, C., Day, A., & Sills, C. (2010). Clients' critical moments of coaching: Toward a "client model" of executive coaching. *Academy of Management Learning & Education*, *9*(4), 607–621. https://doi.org/10.5465/amle.9.4.zqr607

Fairhurst, G. T., & Connaughton, S. L. (2014). Leadership communication. In L. L. Putnam & D. K. Mumby (Eds.), *The SAGE handbook of organizational communication: Advances in theory, research, and methods* (pp. 391–413). SAGE Publications.

Fitch, B. D. (2015). *Law enforcement interpersonal communication and conflict management: The IMPACT model*. SAGE Publications.

Forbes Nonprofit Council. (2026, February 18). Volunteerism is a skill set: Why it belongs on every résumé. *Forbes*.

Gino, F. (2024, March 7). Learn to love networking. *Harvard Business Review*. https://hbr.org/2016/05/learn-to-love-networking

Hedge, J. W., & Rineer, J. R. (2017). *Improving career development opportunities through rigorous career pathways research* (RTI Press Publication No. OP-0037-1703). RTI Press. https://doi.org/10.3768/rtipress.2017.op.0037.1703

International Association of Chiefs of Police. (2023, December 20). The power of mentorship. *Police Chief Magazine*. https://www.policechiefmagazine.org/power-mentorship/

Jacobs, S., De Vos, A., Stuer, D., & Van der Heijden, B. I. J. M. (2019). "Knowing me, knowing you" the importance of networking for freelancers' careers: Examining the mediating role of need for relatedness fulfillment and employability-enhancing competencies. *Frontiers in Psychology*, *10*, 2055. https://doi.org/10.3389/fpsyg.2019.02055

Lavender, L., & Todak, N. (2022). Exploring the value of mentorship for women police officers. *Policing*, *45*(6), 1064–1081. https://doi.org/10.1108/pijpsm-06-2022-0082

Lebowitz, S. (2015). *Why women are still less likely to be promoted than men*. Business Insider.

Meade, M. C. (2025, December 16). The power of networking with purpose. *Forbes*. https://www.forbes.com/sites/matthewmeade/2025/12/16/the-power-of-networking-with-purpose/

Redick, J. (2022). *Survival guide to law enforcement promotional preparation*. Curry Brothers Publishing.

Redick, J. (2024). *The factors that influence and nurture women law enforcement officers to promote into leadership roles within law enforcement* [Doctoral dissertation, California Baptist University]. ProQuest Dissertations and Theses Global.

Singh, A., & Dubey, A. (2015). Role of trait emotional intelligence in prosocial behavior of managerial personnel. *Journal of Psychosocial Research*, *10*(2), 439–447.

Valentine, S., Hollingworth, D., & Fleischman, G. (2020). Ethical climate, ethical leadership, and employee well-being in organizations. *Human Resource Management*, *59*(2), 195–210. https://doi.org/10.1002/hrm.21995

Valentine, S. R., Meglich, P., Mathis, R. L., & Jackson, J. H. (2019). *Human resource management* (16th ed.). Cengage Learning.

Van Oosten, E. B., Buse, K., & Bilimoria, D. (2019). Advancing women's careers through leadership development programs: The role of organizational context and mentoring. *Human Resource Management*, *58*(2), 207–226. https://doi.org/10.1002/hrm.21953

PART II

The Competitive Edge

CHAPTER THREE

Sharpening Your Edge

Skill Mastery and Professional Visibility

In the field of law enforcement and public safety, continually enhancing your skills is essential; it is not just an option, but a critical mission. As emphasized throughout this book, leadership is a skill that requires practice, refinement, and ongoing development. Skills can diminish over time if not reinforced through disciplined training. Therefore, continuous learning and skill enhancement are vital for career advancement in the ever-changing landscape of law enforcement and public safety. The demands faced by police and public safety professionals are constantly evolving, influenced by new technologies, shifting community expectations, and complex legal frameworks. This requires a proactive approach to professional growth.

Moving up in your career is not just about wanting it; it is about purposefully building the right skills for the job you want next. If you do not have a clear picture of what the next role requires, your efforts to grow can end up scattered and unfocused. The most successful professionals take the initiative to figure out exactly what skills, knowledge, and behaviors they will need to excel in future positions. By preparing ahead of time, they make sure they are ready and stand out as the obvious choice when new opportunities come along.

The first thing you want to do when figuring out what skills you need is to really dive into what the job expects, both officially and unofficially. Sure, you can start with the basics like job descriptions, exam announcements, and leadership guidelines; these spell out the technical requirements. But do not stop there. Pay close attention to people who are already thriving in the role. Talk to them, watch how they handle tricky situations, and read through after-action reports to pick up on the subtle habits and decision-making styles that set successful leaders apart: details you will not always find written down. It is also important to remember that the skill set you need is always changing. New

DOI: 10.4324/9781003728849-6

technology, shifts in how communities interact, evolving leadership demands, and fresh operational strategies all shape what is expected. So, staying sharp means you have to keep scanning the environment—not just to understand what is needed now, but to anticipate where the profession is headed. Great leaders make it a point to stay on top of these changes; they know that success comes from being connected and informed, not from working in silos.

When approaching skill development, consider categorizing necessary competencies in three domains:

- Technical skills (e.g., data-driven decision-making, report writing, tactical proficiency)
- Leadership skills (e.g., emotional intelligence, team building, strategic communication)
- Organizational skills (e.g., project management, resource allocation, cross-functional collaboration).

Breaking skills down into categories makes it a lot easier to put together a solid development plan, instead of just staring at a long, intimidating list. You do not have to be an expert in everything right away. Focus first on the skills that matter most for your current goals and what your organization really needs.

In building new skills, habits play a pivotal role. Forming small, consistent behaviors aligned with new skill development accelerates proficiency. Behavioral research shows that automaticity—the ability to perform skills effortlessly—emerges from repeated exposure and intentional practice. This is why creating an activation habit loop—where specific cues trigger immediate practice or study—can bridge the gap between motivation and sustained action.[1]

Therefore, just knowing which skills are important is insufficient; purposeful, disciplined action is required. Action must often precede motivation, and embedding quick activation triggers ensures that learning and practice become embedded in daily routines. Without deliberate action, motivation fades into inertia.

One of the first steps in career advancement is assessing the skills and knowledge required for your current position versus those needed for the next promotion or specialized role. As we discussed in the last chapter, setting specific, measurable, achievable, relevant, and time-bound (SMART) goals is instrumental in guiding your career development and assessing your skills. To sharpen your edge, it is crucial to understand the fundamental ways to identify what skills and knowledge you need to develop for those future roles. Thoughtfully and strategically reflecting on your work experiences, life experiences, training, and education is key to this process.

THE SHARPEN FRAMEWORK: A PRACTICAL APPROACH TO LASTING SKILL MASTERY

The concept of the SHARPEN Framework stemmed for the work done over many decades to help others prepare for promotional opportunities where I found that having a structured approach with deliberate and reinforced learning processes helped candidates be more successful in making their promotional lists. Over time, there were other strategies that were integrated to even strengthen the ability to what some would consider mastering the skills needed to do well in promotional examinations and also deepen the level of understanding for the roles they were seeking. As we know, mastering a skill is not something that happens overnight; it is something you work on every day. If you want to keep growing and stay sharp, you need a system that supports your progress. That is where the 'Structure, Habit Formation, Activation Triggers, Repetition with Reflection, Practice Under Pressure Deliberately, Embodied Learning, and Neurological Reinforcement' (SHARPEN) framework comes in. For this approach, neuroscience was explored with real-world learning to find ways to make sure they were building skills, and knowledge, in a way that sticks, rather than just memorizing or responding. Let's break down what SHARPEN stands for: seven practical elements that help you grow retention, using recognition and recall.

Structure

We all know that having a clear structure for your learning makes a huge difference. When you set goals and create an environment where you can focus, you are much more likely to stay on track and keep improving. Bandura's Social Cognitive Theory shows that people learn best when they are surrounded by good examples, get feedback, and face new challenges regularly. Basically, structure is the backbone of skill mastery.[2] Many candidates seeking help with promotional preparation find this is the area they struggle with the most because they simply do not know where to start or how to begin. But it also has a significant impact when you are already in your leadership role and you need to have organization, time management, and boundaries—structure gives you a framework, guideposts.

Habit Formation

The next element is creating a habit because showing up consistently is the secret to getting really good at something. When you build small, everyday habits that connect to your growth, the process feels less overwhelming and more like who you are—similar to the saying that if you are trying to eat an elephant it seems insurmountable, but if broken down into small manageable pieces, it is possible. What is also important about building a habit, as James Clear points out in *Atomic Habits*, is that real change happens when your habits match up with your values and goals. You have to want it for yourself. It is not about forcing yourself, but about making growth part of your daily life.[3]

Activation Triggers

Motivation is fickle: it comes and goes, but action is what matters. Charles Duhigg talks about using triggers, such as certain cues in your environment, to prompt you to practice new skills automatically. These activation cues help turn your intentions into real, regular behaviors, so you are not just waiting for a burst of motivation.[4] For example, motivation wanes incessantly for me to get a daily walk in, so placing my shoes at the front door is an activation cue for taking the next literal step to getting out the door. Jim Cathcart wrote The Self-Motivation Handbook and he actually talks about this ideas of just getting out the door but he also ask the reader the question, "What do you want?"[5] He shares that self-motivation is not simply a personality trait but a learned discipline that requires intentional goal setting, self-awareness, and the ability to sustain personal momentum even when you are not going to receive any external recognition or reward.[6] It really is up to you.

Repetition with Reflection

Just repeating something is not enough because with pausing to feel and think about what happened, what worked, and what did not, we do not get the change to take in our emotions, experiences, or consequences to improve our practices. Kolb's Experiential Learning Cycle recommends mixing practice with reflection through activities like reviewing your actions, keeping a journal, or having quick "what did I learn?" sessions. This helps you adapt and get better with each try.[7] Reflection is an extra step in your practices, but it is worth it. It is where you get to debrief yourself and reinforce learning.

Practice Under Pressure Deliberately

It is one thing to perform well when everything's calm, but the real test comes when things get intense or theirs tension, friction, or chaos. Anders Ericsson discovered that the best way to truly strengthen your skills is to practice in real, high-pressure situations; this kind of focused, "deliberate practice" means intentionally working on specific areas to improve your performance over time.[8] In law enforcement and public safety, you are often forced to make quick decisions in stressful and unpredictable environments, so learning how to train under pressure is not just a nice-to-have: it is absolutely essential. It is the same when you are preparing for career advancement, promotional processes or leading in your new roles. Practice like it is real every day.

Embodied Learning

Skills really stick when you do not just read or think about them; instead, you get up and actually try them out. The idea behind embodied learning is that the more you physically practice and experience a skill, the more natural and automatic it becomes which is very different than when you have not had the exposure or experience. Work to get included in activities like role-playing, hands-on exercises, and real-world simulations to help you pick things up faster and remember them longer, turning new skills into second nature. An immersive learning curriculum is highly engaging but it helps with memory retention, personalization, frees up mental space and allows for self-efficacy. According to George Lakoff and Mark Johnson's embodied cognition theory, professional growth is most powerful when it goes beyond just learning concepts in a classroom and includes real, physical experiences. Since our thinking is shaped by what we do and feel, you become truly skilled when you get out there and practice, thereby making what you learn a natural part of how you act.[9]

Neurological Reinforcement

Dopamine—the brain's reward system—kicks in when we reach small or big milestones, or improvement, which reinforces our motivation and encourages us to continuing with our efforts.[10] Getting better at something is not just about practice; it is also about recognizing progress along the way and it feels good to know we are doing something well or right. Celebrate those small wins—they matter. In tough jobs like law enforcement and public safety, where praise is not always frequent, recognizing your own wins helps you reframe your motivation and keeps you moving forward. So whether you are working on your leadership skills, mastery of your craft, career advancement, or those promotional processes, a neurological backup helps to get over the hump on the days you lack motivation.

Remember, in law enforcement and public safety, keeping your skills sharp is not optional; it is essential. Skills fade if you do not keep working at them, even the ones you have already mastered. When you incorporate the SHARPEN framework every day, you are not just getting better at your job; you are building confidence, deepening your knowledge, and becoming the kind of leader who is ready for whatever comes next. Be intentional about putting time into learning new technical skills, such as crisis response, investigations, and data analysis. By balancing these with human skills like listening, compassion, and emotional intelligence, you make yourself invaluable to your team. These sharpened abilities help you shine in your current job and stand out when you are ready for promotion—or once you are in the position—it is in some ways a continuous loop for sharpening. Showing that you are constantly learning proves you are proactive and future-focused, ready for bigger challenges. Maybe you are working on conflict resolution, stepping up your leadership game, or staying on top of new trends in policing. The more you learn, the stronger you will lead and the more respect you will earn from your co-workers, your leaders, and the community. Keep sharpening your skills, and you will stay ready when the next opportunity comes your way.

One of the first things to do when you are thinking about moving up is to check what skills and knowledge you have now, and compare them to what you will need for your next step. As we talked about in Chapter 2, setting SMART goals gives you a roadmap for your growth and helps you see where you need to focus. If you want to sharpen your edge, get clear on what skills and knowledge you will need for the future, and take some time to reflect on everything you have learned from your work, your life, and your training so far.

IDENTIFYING NECESSARY SKILLS FOR THE NEXT ROLE

Skills gaps can happen due to several factors, including a lack of professional development training from your agency, a lack of interest in the training provided, and the recency and frequency of use of some of those skills and knowledge if not used consistently. They dull over time. Complacency in feeling that you have mastered the skill and do not need any additional development. With that in mind, let's consider whether a habit is a skill. While often conflated, habits and skills are distinct yet interwoven constructs. A habit is an automatic behavior triggered by cues, while a skill is a learned capability requiring deliberate practice to reach proficiency.[11] Yet, the relationship is symbiotic—habits build the foundation upon which skills are formed, reinforced, and retained.

Some skills are often overlooked but are essential. These include active and empathetic listening, practical and compassionate communication, the ability to resolve conflicts, critical thinking, and making sound decisions to solve problems. Social skills are also crucial because they are used to interact with others, build effective relationships, and find solutions to problems.[12] One of the main shortcomings of leaders and managers is their lack of strong social skills.[13] When you think about effective communication, it should ideally be transformative, creating meaning that extends beyond simply sharing information, issuing orders, or engaging in superficial interactions.

Highlighting the skill of communication is crucial for your leadership growth and professional development, paving the way for future career advancement. As leaders, you must reconsider how you perceive the world within an organization as you transition or consider transitioning into leadership positions. Our perspective can have tunnel vision based on our silo of work and limited experience and exposure, which limits our ability to see beyond our immediate scope of work responsibilities and duties. Instead of seeing individual parts, we should learn to see the whole picture. Rather than focusing on linear cause-and-effect chains, we should consider the interconnectedness of everything.[14] Instead of perceiving static entities, we should recognize the processes of change, which include ourselves. Challenge yourself to step out of your comfort zone, engage in diverse conversations, and meet with people you are unfamiliar with who perform various roles in and outside your organization. Go beyond the default comfortable light banter and be curious about their work and how they feel about it. Creating opportunities for a robust exchange of information and ideas enhances your communication skills, strengthens professional relationships, and improves your overall communication process. For example, what do you know about the work of your professional staff, whether it is administrative professionals, custodians, automotive technicians, dispatchers, or analysts? What do you know about them and their daily functions if you do not directly lead any of these people? Ascending to leadership roles requires you to identify and understand the skills you need to lead effectively.

Cross-cultural communication is essential. Today, those you lead are considered the most multicultural and generational generation. This means they will learn differently, connect, and communicate differently.[15] You must be intentional with your communication and interactions to ensure that everyone feels seen, heard, and valued within the organization. You must understand the value of seeing their view and allow them to share their thoughts, concerns, and curiosity by creating psychologically safe environments. It can sometimes be uncomfortable if the moments are personally or professionally unfamiliar to your lived experience. However, as you cultivate the environment, be vulnerable, and ask your questions, you will discover that the walls of self-protecting may come down on both sides. Within these moments, you will begin to tap into the numerous benefits of your team's contributions toward innovative ideas and improve misunderstandings for a healthier work environment.

Next is building your confidence in *problem-solving and decision-making.* Mark Cuban, the billionaire entrepreneur and investor, believes that people who can decrease stress versus create it through the ability to "analyze a situation, find a solution, and not make a big deal of it" are the number one soft skill employees need to have.[16] Research on learning and decision-making suggests that strong problem-solvers develop the ability by learning to think through complex or even contradictory situations. When you wrestle with ambiguity rather than rushing to simple answers, you strengthen metacognition skills—the ability to examine assumptions, reflect on reasoning, and adjust decisions as new information emerges.[17] Developing strategies and skills to increase decisiveness and confidence in solving problems at higher levels of responsibility will help you reduce stress and uncertainty in your decisions, ultimately reducing stress for those you lead because research shows how stress has increased liability costs and decreased how employees engage in the workplace and are not enjoying their work, which reduces their performance.[18]

When considering decision-making processes, it is important to understand the concepts of System 1 and System 2 thinking. System 1 involves quick, intuitive decision-making that is fast and automatic.[19] System 1 can be sufficient, but it can also be impulsive and emotion-driven when we feel rushed or busy, making us prone to errors. System 2 is more deliberate and slower, allowing for more thorough decision-making when you have more discretionary time, and allows you to apply more logic.[20] Practice slowing yourself down when you have the discretionary time and know that it is okay to review the policy, seek guidance from others who may be more knowledgeable, and weigh all your alternatives before making a final decision.

Another consideration is how we often use mental shortcuts, also known as heuristics, to simplify our complex decisions. While these shortcuts can be helpful, they can also lead to biases based on available information, distorting our decision-making process and preventing us from considering all relevant factors.[21] There needs to be consideration for multiple perspectives; anticipate potential outcomes, and carefully weigh the implications of your decisions. For example, when implementing a new program or creating organizational change, slowing down helps identify the critical criteria necessary for successful implementation. It is not just about the program's goals and objectives; you need to consider what resources will be required, budget implications, how the program aligns with existing policies, who needs to be involved in the design and implementation, collective bargaining union concerns, how success will be measured, and how the program will be sustained. Even with all these elements outlined, you must prioritize them, evaluating each based on its benefits, risks, and implications. This methodical approach will also increase your focus on evidence-based research, which helps inform decisions and proposals for change while slowing down your thought processes.[22]

When working one-on-one with someone toward a decision, frame your approach through communication partnerships with others in the organization. Gaining buy-in and creating synergy for a shared vision is crucial for the success of any initiative. Sometimes, we can get ahead of ourselves, driven by passion or certainty in an idea, and overlook the need for a structured process. Slowing down allows us to cultivate a "slow burn" approach to our emotions and focus on achieving small wins. These early successes demonstrate to others what is possible. As others begin to see progress, they get motivated, inspired, and even rethink their approaches.[23]

One of the biggest challenges in decision-making is how past decisions, particularly poor ones, can haunt us. Many of us carry the emotional trauma of a bad decision and hold onto the feelings associated with it, almost as if reliving the experience. This is not easy to overcome.

A colleague shared a situation where they made a quick decision during a tactical incident that did not turn out well. At first, they described the experience as overwhelming, believing their decision was a massive failure. However, as we discussed it further, it became clear that the decision was not as bad as they initially thought. While it may not have been the best possible decision, it was not a catastrophe. They were more embarrassed and concerned that others might see them as less competent. As we discussed the incident, they realized that slowing down, gathering information from reliable sources, asking for clarification when uncertain, bringing others into the process, and considering the potential consequences (both intended and unintended) would have led to a better decision.[24] Kristen Hadeed is the CEO of Student Maid, an all-student cleaning company that provides students with the opportunity to earn money while pursuing their education. She has cultivated a culture that fosters the development of essential life and leadership skills among her employees. In her book, *Permission to Screw Up*, she reflects on her early leadership experiences and shares valuable lessons about vulnerability, learning mistakes, and creating environments where growth and accountability can coexist. Hadeed states: "Trust people with enormous responsibilities, allow room for mess-ups, then give them the chance to fix their mistakes so they can learn from them."[25] Essentially, she encourages us to recognize that we will make mistakes, which in turn will help us become better leaders. This process will occur repeatedly, but each time, we will learn and grow. Additionally, granting permission to those we lead to make mistakes, and guiding them through those experiences, fosters the development of better leaders, enhances leadership, and builds trust.

When building your confidence, problem-solving, and decision-making skills, it is essential to get exposed to various opportunities to challenge your decision-making process in a space you have not been able to or had the chance to. When you have an opportunity to be in a temporary leadership role, for example, being an officer in charge of a shift for the day or being an acting supervisor or manager, those are great opportunities to practice improving your decision-making. These opportunities allow you to receive valuable feedback, helping you gain confidence in making decisions beyond your usual responsibilities and comfort zone. If you do not have the chance to take on leadership roles or temporary positions, try to pay attention to your peers' situations. You can participate in debriefings and discussions to understand the decisions that were made and the issues that were addressed. You can also ask for feedback from your supervisors on specific incidents to gain insight into their perspectives and ask any questions you may have.

A helpful approach, and one that encourages curiosity outside of your role and responsibilities, is to examine the headlines in the daily newspapers or social media to understand what is happening in law enforcement agencies nationwide, or any sector of the workforce. There are numerous examples of both leadership failures and successes. Each instance offers valuable lessons to be learned. Consider how you can role-play these scenarios or bring them to the attention of your immediate supervisors, managers, or executive leadership. Discuss how they would respond or how you should respond, allowing for a collective understanding of these incidents. For instance, active shooter incidents and mass casualty incidents occur across the country, but it is possible that your agency has not experienced one or that such events are infrequent. Mental training and situational scenarios that are infrequent or rare help prepare you for crisis management during stressful decision-making moments.

In addition, do not forget to integrate the use of decision trees or checklists, which many organizations have created for officer-involved shootings (OIS), civil disturbance, or other critical incidents and when there is a need for unified commands. There are checklists for handling equal employment opportunity (EEO) investigations or other employee misconduct that require supervisors and managers to take immediate action and ensure they follow policy guidelines and collective bargaining union memorandums of understanding (MOUs), among many others, and you can create your own. It is essential to practice expanding our decision-making process, being comfortable with making mistakes, and learning from them to grow and improve as influential leaders.

Remember, even though you will be faced with intense and highly scrutinized problems to solve and decisions to make, and it is always wise to be prepared for large-scale incidents, it is also just as important to have clear decision-making processes for smaller-scale matters, such as guiding your team in their daily responsibilities. Sometimes, our daily decisions can challenge our confidence and make us hesitant about taking action. Imposter syndrome may surface but remember that you will feel more confident when you are prepared and intentionally sharpen your edge. You are encouraged to reflect on your decision-making process, whether you are a first-line supervisor, middle manager, commander, or executive staff member. Consider how you approach decisions, how you involve others, and how you might refine your methods to make better, more informed decisions.

KNOWLEDGE

Sharpening your knowledge as you move up in rank or responsibility is important. This may require a shift in mindset to understand and embrace your new role. You will need to balance the demands of leadership with the practical aspects of your work. Keep in mind that leadership is not always straightforward; some days will be peaceful, while others will be chaotic, and sometimes you will experience both on the same day, and you still need to show up and lead. Mastering key policies, processes, and protocols is critical for leadership roles and understanding organizational risk management and legal considerations. When you build your knowledge competency, it will help to give you better resilience on those high-voltage days when you can feel like you are stretched from all sides. It also enhances credibility and fosters trust with your teams and organizational leaders.

Inventory your knowledge and identify the gaps in your confidence in your abilities. Spend time reviewing policy and procedural manuals to strengthen understanding. As you transition into a new leadership role, it is essential to have a "leadership readiness kit"—a modern, streamlined version of the traditional "go bag" used in the field. Just as your operational go bag evolved throughout your career, this leadership readiness kit will serve as a dynamic toolkit, tailored to your new responsibilities. It is a personal, portable resource that ensures you are always equipped with what you need to lead effectively in any situation. This kit can take many forms, whether it is a well-organized briefcase, a digital folder on your tablet or phone, or even a cloud-based reference system. Regardless of the format, it should contain key materials, such as (list is not all inclusive):

- *Essential Policies*: Quick-reference guides for specific policies and procedures you will frequently encounter in your role.
- *Common Forms*: Digital or hard copies of frequently used forms, ready for immediate use or distribution.
- *Contact Directory*: A curated list of essential contacts, including key personnel, partner organizations, and community stakeholders.
- *Critical Notes*: Summaries of recent meetings, critical incidents, or high-priority tasks that require follow-up or monitoring.
- *Leadership Tools*: Checklists, briefing templates, and notes on best practices or decision-making and communication.

Today, many agencies have digital access to policies through mobile apps and within consolidated patrol car environments (CPVE), so be sure to create digital files or folders with all necessary checklists and references for easy access.

In addition, being a continual learner is essential as you move into leadership roles. Leverage your educational experience in your new role and seek training that enhances your skills, technical knowledge, and leadership competencies by any means necessary. It is a reality that organizational budgets and waiting lists can create challenges for accessing training opportunities. Do not get discouraged if your organization lacks the budget or prioritizes other needs over your development. Instead, focus on investing in yourself. A mentor once recommended that the most effective way to ensure your success is to take initiative and pursue it yourself. When you are determined to achieve your goals, no one will advocate for you more than yourself.

You should consider the following list to categorize and build toward enhancing your skill development and knowledge. Identify the areas where you feel you need improvement, and then develop strategies to increase your exposure and experience:

- Organizational awareness and communication: Understanding the chain of command and the importance of hierarchical structures and communication channels, especially those you will be a part of in your next leadership role.
- Effective communication and techniques for handling difficult conversations, de-escalation, and resolving conflicts.
- Mastering written communication (e.g., memos, reports, evaluations, research, white papers) for administrative and leadership roles.
- Emotional intelligence: self-awareness, self-regulation, motivation, empathy, and social skills. Managing stress, burnout, and emotional responses to high-stakes situations.
- Innovative and forward-thinking leadership that embraces technology and modern policing techniques (e.g., data-driven policing and community engagement strategies). Encouraging artistry, creativity, and adaptability in solving complex problems.
- Strategic thinking and vision: Operational leadership, understanding the organization's broader goals, and aligning team efforts.
- Developing strategic and tactical plans that support both short and long-term objectives.

Ultimately, identifying and cultivating the necessary skills for the next role is an act of leadership itself, an expression of foresight, adaptability, and personal accountability. It is not enough to be ready when called upon; true professionals sharpen their edge in advance, ensuring they are the clear and confident choice when opportunity arrives.

STEPPING INTO THE SPOTLIGHT—PROFESSIONAL VISIBILITY

As you cultivate the art of your career advancement, you will find that if you haven't already done so, you need to develop a comfort level by stepping into the spotlight to increase your professional visibility. Professional visibility is a critical yet often overlooked component of career advancement. Employees who consistently demonstrate their contribution, communicate their ideas, and engage in meaningful organizational conversations are more likely to be recognized for leadership opportunities.[26] Remember, visibility is not about self-promotion for its own sake; rather, it involves strategically sharing work, building relationships across the organization, and ensuring the decision makers understand the value of your contributions. When individuals remain silent about their accomplishments or limit their engagement to a small circle, the work can easily go unnoticed, regardless of its quality or impact.[27] It is important to develop visibility through intentional communication, collaboration, and participation in organizational initiatives that allow you to build credibility and position yourself for future leadership roles.

Part of crafting your personal brand and how to shape and promote your professional identity when the organization hinges on how you approach your visibility. Oftentimes, we can be so focused on mastering our craft and doing our work and doing it well that we make the assumption that those in influential positions are noticing and that we do not have to do anything extra. In reality, some of that occurs; however, if you want to ensure that your visibility is noticeable, then you want to make sure to do certain things consistently. Visibility will require you to intentionally communicate the value of your contributions and demonstrate leadership through your actions and engagement across the organization. Part of your branding is who people know you to be as a leader. In your daily interactions, decision-making, and work performance, as well as your interpersonal skills, you are continually shaping the reputation and leadership identity that others associate with you over time.[28]

Recall when you did the self-assessment of your readiness for career advancement and when you looked at all the things that you have done and identified the gaps where you needed to build and grow; there might have been space that emerged where you find yourself in need of increasing your volunteerism to the organization, your proactive interest in getting involved in additional responsibilities outside of your daily duties and taking on additional leadership responsibilities in an acting or interim capacity. These are ways to increase your professional visibility and not just be in the status quo of the silo of your regular duties for the day. Although you may meet standards or be above in some categories, remember your brand is also the culmination of all these things, and your reputation, so guard it well. You want to have those supervisors, mentors, coaches, and peers be able to speak to your brand, enhance the organizational culture, and establish you as a strong leader, so remember the value and importance of those social exchanges and those interpersonal dynamics between all groups as you navigate your career advancement. You never know who you will run into again that might influence or change your career trajectory, and it is not what you say. It is what you do that they will remember most.

The next thing to consider is positioning yourself as a subject matter expert in your field and being recognized as a thought leader. Reflect on your investigations, presentations, collaborative projects, and any written work you have produced for your organization. Think about how these experiences contribute to establishing you as a thought leader. For those of you who have specialized positions, you are already building your space as a thought leader and subject matter expert in that specialized area, but remember, as you advance in your career, your primary focus will not be that specialized area; it will become broader so you do not want to pigeonhole yourself into that specialized position only so think about how you can evolve your subject matter expertise into something broader and with more significant implications.

One experienced supervisor with fifteen to twenty years' experience from a large municipal department of over 200 personnel described it this way: to build expertise in a variety of fields whether it is investigative work, tactical proficiency, legal processes, or training, the expertise backs your credibility. Expanding on that insight, also consider thinking about not only how the knowledge that you have and expertise help your role in your position and addressing duties and outcomes based on procedure and law but also think about the implications beyond your organization to the broader policing and public safety community and those impacts that it can have for more significant policy development and greater organizational change and how it impacts the communities that you serve.

Growing your professional visibility also includes expanding networks and influencing decision-makers. Identifying opportunities to connect with key leaders and influencers in your organization becomes one of your primary focuses. As we mentioned earlier, the value of mentors and coaches is exponential. So, it is for enhancing your visibility to those influential decision makers within the organization and other stakeholders outside the organization. There is a great opportunity when you get involved in different assignments that connect you externally to the organization, like being involved in community engagement and working with other key leaders in the community to reduce crime and solve problems that enhance the quality of life for citizens. Those individuals that you often connect and build relationships with become advocates for you and influence the decision-makers within your organization for your benefit. These relationships become mutually beneficial as you work on common concerns on improving safety and collaboration in the community.

You will notice that there is a strong connection between visibility and volunteerism in leadership roles. This includes participating in committees, working on special projects, and taking on temporary assignments for task force missions outside of your usual work. For example, suppose you are a supervisor aiming to become a manager. In that case, you should express your interest in participating in investigations such as employee misconduct, internal investigations, EEO investigations, or task forces that require personnel from different units. If these opportunities are not readily available, you can suggest to your leadership the benefits of having field supervisors play adjunct roles in investigations, which can broaden their leadership skills in accountability, operations, risk assessment, and personnel matters.

GROWTH THROUGH FEEDBACK—PERFORMANCE AND CONTINUOUS IMPROVEMENT

As you strive to enhance your professional visibility, seeking feedback and working on continuous improvement are essential. A survey conducted by Police 1 in 2020, which included over 4,300 law enforcement officers from urban, suburban, and rural areas across the country, highlighted some valuable insights.[29] Officers, regardless of their experience ranging from under five years to over 30, agreed that performance expectations are often too vague, not communicated, and unclear on how their performance was measured.[30] In addition, according to Gordon Graham, there are four common mistakes public safety agencies make with personnel assessments: reusing last year's evaluations, inflating employee performance rates, endorsing mediocrity, and increasing risk and retaliation claims.[31] These errors can add to how functional or practical evaluations are for career advancement or special assignments because they do not allow for their input during the review process.[32] In addition, employees can feel their contributions are unrecognized, which can erode the relationships and trust between personnel and their supervisors and managers as the support needed to succeed in their career aspirations.

Performance feedback is not just about annual reviews; it is an ongoing process that helps you understand where you stand, what is expected, and how to improve. It is important for you to understand your role in growth and development and how you can be active in that process. Here are some things to consider:[33]

- You need to understand expectations early by asking questions before your annual review to ensure you understand the expectations for your role. Do not wait until review time to ask your supervisor; ask early and often.
- Know your responsibilities by clarifying your duties and what "meeting" or "exceeding" standards look like. If something is unclear, request specific examples from your supervisor because asking those questions is okay.
- Stay engaged throughout the year and record your achievements, challenges, and areas where you have gone above and beyond. This can even include training, special projects, commendations, and other criteria that can fit under tracking your performance for the year.
- Provide input, and do not wait for your supervisor to bring up your performance. Be proactive in sharing your successes and contributions throughout the year. Highlight things that may not have been noticed, such as handling a challenging situation or even assisting inside the office with interpersonal things that have helped a colleague.
- Be open to feedback and ask for regular feedback. If you are unsure how you are doing, ask your supervisor for feedback, even outside of formal reviews. The more you ask, the more you can adjust and improve.
- Accept constructive criticism. Not all feedback will be positive, but constructive criticism is valuable. It helps you grow, so listen closely and work on the suggested improvements. Constructive criticism can be challenging for some people if they do not develop the ability to receive it and make improvements, rather than reacting emotionally to the person delivering the feedback. When that happens, we miss the opportunity to grow. It is true that some supervisors and managers may not offer constructive criticism; they may simply be critical. However, it is important to discern the difference. If the criticism is valid, you should make the effort to implement the necessary improvements.
- Request clarification if any feedback is unclear or unfair; ask for specific examples and ways you can improve. Understanding the "why" behind feedback helps you develop the right skills.
- Preparing for the annual review is an excellent idea by gathering your own input. Before your review, list your accomplishments and areas where you feel you have improved or could use more support. This will also ensure your contributions are recognized and that it is okay to highlight your good work.
- Think about your career aspirations and the goals you have set. Do you want to advance into leadership roles or a higher leadership role? Do you want to specialize in a particular area? Bring these up during the review and ask your supervisor for guidance on what skills or training are needed and how you can get the training. Do not forget that important question.

- During the review, listen carefully to the feedback, both positive and critical period, take notes on areas of improvement, and ask for clarification where needed. Discuss developmental opportunities and use this time to ask about training promotions or special assignments. Seek advice on how to enhance your skills and grow professionally. If you disagree and feel your evaluation is unfair, ask for specific examples of your performance and seek guidance on addressing these concerns. If further action is needed, follow your agency's policies and your memorandum of understanding.
- Develop a long-term plan. Work with your supervisor to collaborate on a career development plan that aligns with both your goals and the agency's needs. This can include leadership training, specialized roles, or other professional growth opportunities.
- Review your progress throughout the year. Check in with your supervisor to see how you are progressing, adjust your goals as needed, and ask for feedback to stay on track.
- And lastly, own your growth and be proactive. Do not wait for opportunities to come to you. Seek out assignments, volunteer for new roles, and invest in your professional development by attending training, continuing your education, and expanding your skill set.

It is important to maintain open communication with your supervisor regarding your progress, challenges, and career goals. This demonstrates your engagement and commitment to your success. In summary, performance reviews serve as a tool for improvement, but your growth ultimately relies on your active involvement. By understanding expectations, tracking your achievements, seeking feedback, and setting clear goals, you can effectively use the performance review process to advance your career and contribute more meaningfully to your agency.

APPLIED LEADERSHIP QUESTIONS AND CRITICAL THINKING

1. What specific skills—technical, leadership, or organizational—are most critical for your next role, and how intentionally are you developing them today?
2. How are your daily habits either reinforcing or undermining your long-term skill development and Leadership growth?
3. What ways are you practicing under pressure to prepare for real world decision-making, rather than relying solely on theory or low stakes environments?

4. How do you balance fast, intuitive decisions (System 1) with deliberate, analytical thinking (System 2) and high-stake situations?
5. What feedback have you received recently, and how have you translated that feedback into measurable improvements?
6. How are you increasing your professional visibility while maintaining authenticity and a service oriented leadership approach?
7. Where might complacency be limiting your growth, and what intentional actions will you take to continue sharpening your edge?

KEY TAKEAWAYS

Developing Strong Communication Skills

It is important to explore the importance of clear and effective communication in leadership roles; for example, regularly practicing active listening by paraphrasing what the other person is saying and asking follow-up questions, providing timely specific feedback, such as "I appreciated how you handled that incident by staying calm and offering solutions." When facing difficult conversations, using a structured approach like the SBI (Situation—Behavior—Impact) model can defuse tension and focus on facts, not personalities. These practices strengthen relationships, improve team cohesion, and make resolving conflicts more straightforward.

Mastering Organizational Awareness

Understanding your agency's structure and culture can set you apart. Take time to map out your department's chain of command and identify key decision-makers. For example, attending cross-departmental meetings or shadowing a supervisor for a day can reveal unwritten norms and priorities. Aligning your persona goals—such as developing a new community policing initiative—with broader organizational objectives ensures your contributions are recognized and valued.

Fostering Social Skills

Empathy, adaptability, and collaboration are not just buzzwords—they are daily practices for effective leaders. For instance, after a challenging incident, making a point to check in with each team member individually demonstrates empathy and builds trust. These actions foster a supportive environment when everyone can thrive.

Embracing Feedback for Continuous Improvement

Seek regular feedback from peers, supervisors, and direct reports. For example, after leading a briefing, or providing a presentation, ask a trusted colleague, "What's one thing I could have done better?" Encourage your team to do the same by creating a "feedback moment" at the end of meetings to create a culture of feedback. Reflect on the feedback received and set specific improvement goals, such as improving clarity in written communications, acknowledging others, body language, or delegating more effectively.

Stepping into the Spotlight

Explore strategies for increasing professional visibility, such as public speaking, contributing to organizational initiatives, leading small team projects and participating in community events. Volunteering can increase your professional visibility so think about the ways you can build your personal brand and positioning yourself as a thought leader can open doors to new opportunities.

Positioning Yourself as a Thought Leader

This takes time. So think about the steps to establish thought leadership, You could begin by sharing insights or lessons learned during after-action reviews, or contribute short articles to your agencies intranet, or even external opportunities that might be available. Consider adjunct teaching or even mentoring at your local junior college or offer to host a lunchtime discussion on trending topics important to your agency. Sharing knowledge and expertise not only builds your credibility but also benefits the organization.

Committing to Lifelong Learning and Skill Enhancement

Stay current with evolving best practices by enrolling in webinars, pursuing relevant certifications, or reading the latest research in your field. Set a personal goal to attend at least one professional development event every quarter. Adopting a growth mindset—being open to learning from successes and setbacks alike—will help you remain adaptable and innovative throughout your career.

Transforming Challenges into Opportunities

When faced with setbacks, approach them as learning opportunities. For example, after a project stalls, gather your team to brainstorm alternative solutions rather than getting frustrated and assigning blame. Practice resilience by maintaining a positive outlook and encouraging creative problem-solving.

CONCLUSION

Throughout my career in public safety, I have seen firsthand how those who make time for skilled development and learning stand out as leaders. For example, when you pursue training in the latest evidence-based practices, or step outside of your comfort zone to volunteer and grow, you often find yourself better equipped to handle your current challenges and for those that will come. Beyond technical skills, building strong relationships within your organization, your teams and with the public fosters trust and cooperation—essentials for effective policing. When you actively seek feedback and adapt to new situations, you not only grow personally, but you also inspire those around you to do the same. So commit to ongoing growth—whether it is becoming more proficient with new technology, practicing emotional intelligence in daily interactions, or taking the lead on innovative projects—you position yourself as a valued, adaptable professional ready for the future of law enforcement and public safety.

KEY TERMS

After-Action Report (AAR)—a structured review process to evaluate decisions, actions, and outcomes following an incident or operation, identifying strengths, gaps, and opportunities for improvement.

Officer in Charge (OIC)—a temporary leadership role assigned to oversee a team or operations, providing practical opportunities to develop supervisory decision-making and leadership skills.

Standard Operating Procedures (SOPs)—established guidelines that direct routine operations, ensuring consistency, accountability, and alignment with organizational expectations.

Incident Command System (ICS)—a standardized, scalable framework used to manage emergencies and critical incidents through clear structure, roles and communication.

Early Intervention Systems (EIS)—a data-driven system used to identify patterns in employee performance that may require intervention, coaching, or corrective action.

Situational Awareness—the ability to perceive, understand, and anticipate evolving conditions in dynamic environments which is critical for both tactical and leadership decision-making.

CompStat—a data-driven management system used to analyze crime trends, allocate resources, and hold leaders accountable for performance outcomes.

SHARPEN Framework—a structured system for sustained skill mastery emphasizing, habit formation, activation triggers, repetition with reflection, practice under pressure, embodied learning, and neurological reinforcement.

System 1 and System 2 Thinking—a dual-process model of decision-making where System1 is fast, intuitive, and automatic, while System 2 is slower, analytical, and deliberate.

Heuristics (Mental Shortcuts)—cognitive strategies used to simplify decision-making, which can increase efficiency.

Voices From the Field Installment Three: Strategic and Impactful Preparation

This installment of *Voices From the Field* bridges from conceptual preparation, mindset foundations, and broad advice to a detailed focus on the tangible process to prepare for the promotional process. We asked our respondents to describe the single most effective approach or strategy that they used to prepare for the promotional process at any point in their career. The following data will illustrate that there is no single best practice for success and promotion. Rather, successful candidates employ an intentionally diverse approach, including cultivating relationships, seeking out professional development, and nurturing the operational skill sets necessary to promote. The thematic takeaway from these respondents is that promotional preparation is not a discrete endeavor. Rather, promotion is the culmination of a career-long daily investment in one's own professional and personal growth.

The "Leadership Lifestyle"

A striking and prominent theme emerged from our most senior respondents on this topic, that leadership development is a daily practice.

Individuals who saw promotion as seasonal were far less successful than those who strive for excellence in every task, in every meeting, and who conceptualized every day as a job interview for promotion.

As a chief of police from a large municipal police department in California explained:

> I think there is an opportunity to be intentional in your desire to grow and lead BEFORE the promotional process. We often see candidates begin to prepare once the promotional announcement hits. We need to be better oriented to understand that leadership is not seasonal—it is a "lifestyle" and one cannot step in and out of their leadership walk. All to say, the preparation should be in the practice of leadership and then we are continually working to better our craft.

A nearly identical point was echoed by a lieutenant from a medium-sized municipal police department in California:

> One, intentionally seeking mentorship from people already performing at the rank I aspired to. I asked them to critique my thinking and approach to problem-solving. That helped me understand what decision-makers were truly looking for: sound judgment, accountability, and the ability to lead people through ambiguity. Two, I focused on daily leadership practice. Rather than preparing only when the promotion vacancy was announced, I focused on performing at the next rank every day. This meant taking ownership, supporting others, and making sound decisions. When the process came, the preparation felt natural because the behavior was already in practice.

Lastly, a professional staff supervisor from a very large municipal police department in Nevada summed up the thematic takeaway on this section with a masterful phrase, "Treat every day as if it were an interview."

Exams and the Assessment Center

Many respondents cited written exams and the oral assessment center as the most daunting aspects of the promotional process. This concern was particularly acute for those in agencies governed by civil service requirements. To overcome these concerns, respondents emphasized a consistent, long-term, and disciplined approach. Those who were intentional and persistent in their test preparation strategy were far more successful than those who were less systematic in their approach. Moreover, preparation should include both studying for the substantive elements of the exam, and also preparing a strategic test-taking and test-execution strategy.

Persistence and Practicality

The data clearly demonstrated that "winging" the promotional process is a recipe for disaster. Respondents consistently emphasized that advanced preparation over a long period of time was an advisable best practice. While this may seem intuitive in theory, having the self-discipline to execute a rigorous long-term study strategy can likely be challenging for some.

A chief of police from a medium-sized municipal police department in Delaware offered some practical advice, in the context of the relative scoring systems inherent in the promotional process:

> In my case, studying for written exams. Civil service system. If you got into the resource books 6 to 9 months ahead of time, and got up to speed on how standardized tests are constructed, you could post a written score that often made it mathematically impossible for anyone to surpass you with the other weighted components of the process.

A lieutenant from a very large municipal police department in Nevada added an important nuance to a sound study strategy: "Understanding the importance of catering answers on written tests and assessment centers to 'what they want to hear' as opposed to how policy, procedures, and protocol are handled in real-world applications." One could argue that this response suggests that memorization and regurgitation of information are not sufficient. Rather, an operational and applicable understanding of complex substance is key to demonstrating your readiness for the next level of leadership and being successful in the testing process.

Other respondents echoed that the testing process is about both substance and process. Preparing for the conceptual elements of the test is only one aspect. Successful candidates must also develop and practice for the mechanical aspects of the actual assessment center. A captain from a medium-sized municipal police department in California offered some very practical advice on this topic: "I have used a consultant to prepare for the assessment center. Navigating the assessment center is a skill in itself."

Mentorship: A Consistent Theme

Across the entire survey, one theme was as prominent as any: the importance of quality mentors. According to our respondents, quality mentors are truly invested in the success of others, good coaches, and have the ability and courage to provide meaningful constructive criticism when warranted.

A sergeant from a medium-sized municipal police department in California provided some candid advice about proactively seeking out feedback:

> Honestly, the most effective thing I ever did was ask for real, honest feedback, especially the kind that's uncomfortable to hear. I sat down with people I trusted and asked them what I needed to work on, and then I actually did the work. It grounded me, kept me humble, and gave me a roadmap for where to improve. That changed everything for the better and professionally.

Quality mentors should not be limited to one's own organization. As a lieutenant from a medium-sized municipal police department in California shared: "I met with Captains and Chiefs outside of my organization throughout all my promotions."

Finally, a sergeant from a very large County Sheriff's Department in Washington succinctly summed up this theme. What was the single best approach or strategy you used to prepare for the promotional process at any point in your career? "Having mentors."

The Leadership Narrative

Finally, successful candidates intentionally developed the ability to synthesize their own experiences into concise, impactful narratives. Public safety is inherently complex, and the professionals who execute these roles will have an archive of layered, intricate experiences that demonstrate their readiness for promotion. Our respondents consistently emphasized the importance of crafting succinct and compelling examples that streamline these complex experiences into digestible messages that will resonate with the audience. Like any leadership skill, this succinct messaging should be practiced and developed long before the actual promotional process begins.

A commander from a medium-sized municipal police department in California shared advice that captures these messaging best practices: "Staying focused and concise in all public speaking engagements. For example, speaking to everyone everywhere in a concise, polished manner as if you're speaking to a member of your promotional board. Do this months prior to any promotional process."

A chief of police from a small municipal police department in Colorado echoed nearly identical advice, "Developing short vignettes to have at memory recall to answer situational or behavioral questions with specific examples."

A captain from a medium-sized municipal police department in California explained how they intentionally practiced these skills, "I created a list of interview questions, wrote out detailed answers, and rehearsed my responses."

In sum, the promotional process is not separate and distinct from one's career. Rather, promotion should be seen as a natural outcome of the commitment to professional growth and leadership as a daily practice. Mechanically, promotion requires substantive mastery, but also a mastery of the assessment process itself. This dual challenge can be overcome by developing an intentional preparation strategy, seeking out quality mentors, and practicing effective leadership communication at every opportunity.

Common Pitfalls to Avoid

Thus far, *Voices from the Field* has focused on mindset and tangible best practices for promotional success. Arguably equally as important, if not more important, is nurturing a systematic understanding of common pitfalls to avoid. As the following data from our respondents will demonstrate, both promotional success and success in leadership roles require both consistency and authenticity. But the evidence took this argument one step further. Not only are consistency and authenticity important for success, but being inconsistent in your approach and behavior—and inauthentic when you seek promotion—can cause long-term and significant damage to your reputation and career.

Silly Season and Performative Leadership

Respondents consistently emphasized the risk of inauthentic performative leadership. Candidates who wait for a promotional opportunity to start mentoring others, seek mentorship, take on a community-facing partnership, or volunteer for additional work or assignments can be viewed as self-serving.

A sergeant from a medium-sized municipal police department in California described this transparently self-serving approach as the "silly season": "Don't act differently because you want to get promoted. In my agency, we call it 'silly season' when it is promotion time, because some candidates will start behaving differently and try to make sure everyone notices everything they do. Just be yourself."

A deputy chief from a medium-sized municipal police department in California pointed out that agency leadership and decision-makers can often easily identify these promotion-centric behavior changes:

> A common pitfall I have observed in my current position as the Deputy Chief is officers who have showed minimum effort over the years trying to be more active right before a promotion opportunity presents itself. Officers need to realize that their hard work is taken into consideration, especially what they have done over the course of a few years, not a few months.

A chief of police from a large municipal police department in California added that this performative behavior can have enduring negative consequences for one's reputation:

> So often we see the excitement and engagement during promotional periods and then upon the results, we see the outward frustration (and sometimes disparaging of the decision makers or process) that undermines those successful candidates. I love to see when unsuccessful candidates immediately look for clarity, seek feedback, not because it is 'required' but because they want to grow. I always tell candidates that the next promotional period begins the day the current ends. And unfortunately, those who are intent on undermining or creating chaos, are long remembered as those 'leaders' who only lead for the potential for promotion. True leaders are always looking to grow and become better at their craft.

Your Promotion is a Team Effort

According to our respondents, far too many individuals seeking promotion view it as an independent endeavor. As reiterated throughout this book, and the *Voices from the Field* sections, career advancement and promotion takes a village and the failure to develop a support system is a common pitfall to avoid.

A sergeant from a small municipal police department in California reaffirmed the risks of performative leadership. But they also candidly shared the importance of seeking out opportunities to grow in underdeveloped areas, and not shying away from asking for help:

> A big mistake is thinking you can "turn it on" only when you're being watched. Leadership isn't a switch, it's a lifestyle. Another pitfall is trying to look perfect. I made the mistake early on of hiding my weaknesses instead of asking for help. That slowed my growth. Promotions come faster when you're honest, open, and willing to learn.

A detective from a large county sheriff's department in California noted that the concept of a support system should be construed broadly and include those closest to you:

> I have been single and divorced for about three years. The pitfall I would tell people to avoid is thinking you can take on a new promotion and its challenges alone. Whether you're married or have a partner, lean on them for support because any change in your career or new promotion will come with challenges and having support at home is very important. Even leaning on friendships or family can help.

A captain from a very large county sheriff's department in Florida emphasized that pursuing professional growth in isolation makes it more likely that key concepts and skill sets will be overlooked. A broad support base and broad skill set will help make you into the well-rounded professional needed in your agency and the profession as a whole:

> A common pitfall when seeking promotion is focusing too much on the test and not enough on the actual responsibilities of the

> position. Early in my career, I made the mistake of trying to memorize information instead of truly understanding how to apply policy, lead people, and make sound decisions. Another pitfall is trying to prepare in isolation, as failing to seek mentorship or feedback limits growth. Finally, many candidates overlook the importance of emotional intelligence and self-awareness. Titles do not make leaders; behaviors do. Avoiding these missteps helped me grow into the role rather than just earn it.

Ego: The Self-Inflicted Pitfall

Under the broad umbrella of pitfalls, respondents frequently spotlighted the very real danger of ego. Many organizations have longstanding and significant challenges. Many respondents discussed the dangers of thinking that one individual, regardless of that person's capacity and capabilities, can assume a new leadership position and make immediate and substantial improvements to longstanding bad processes. Even the most capable leaders typically must embrace patience, sequential, deliberate, and incremental approaches in the face of longstanding and complex organizational challenges.

A captain from a small municipal police department in New York reaffirmed this message with some sobering advice:

> Believing YOU are the answer to all the problems facing your department and YOU can fix them all. Believing your current level of training, knowledge and experience will get you through the interview process. You MUST, talk and inquire about other positions within the department that you have not held or know little about. Talk with your Professional Staff members and learn what they are doing every day, what issues they are facing. Remember, when you get promoted to surround yourself with members that have knowledge in all the things you think you do, be humble to recognize, YOU DON'T KNOW EVERYTHING.

A chief of police from a large municipal police department in California noted that unrestrained critiques of your agency should be avoided in the promotional process: "I have witnessed applicants in interviews lose focus and turn the interview into a complaining session about the department. That is an absolute no-no." Instead, a professional engagement of organizational challenges, grounded in reliable data and evidence, and posing well-reasoned solutions is advisable.

Building on these themes, a Chief of Police from a medium-sized municipal Police Department in Delaware reiterated the importance of preparation. Moreso, the Chief offers a stern warning to candidates who rely solely on their skill set and past job performance to be successful in the promotional process:

> Thinking that your superior technical abilities as a working police officer is enough to dispense with any other preparations. I've seen a lot of folks, good cops, who just showed up and expected to do well. After the fact, they covered their behavior by complaining that the process should not require such preparation when people have kids, busy lives, etc.

In conclusion, avoiding these common pitfalls requires a candid, introspective mentality. Successful candidates must avoid the "silly season" of performative leadership, an isolated preparation process, and the pitfall of ego-centric preparation avoidance.

Concept Bootcamp: Sharpening Cutting-Edge Knowledge and Industry Best Practices

In this installment of the *Concept Bootcamp* we focus on cutting-edge industry best practices, technology, and guiding ethical principles. This chapter focused on knowledge and skill development broadly construed. To demonstrate promotional readiness within your organization, it is advantageous to link broad knowledge and skill development with tangible, cutting-edge industry issues and dynamics that provide a real-world and relatable example of this understanding.

- *Real-Time Crime Center (RTCC)*: These innovative centers or specialized units actively integrate diverse types of technology to provide real-time information to public safety agencies. Often, but not always RTCCs combine live video feeds from both public and private sources, automatic license plate readers (ALPR), computer-aided dispatch systems, gunshot detection tools, and other technology to provide an intelligence and situational awareness force multiplier for law enforcement in public spaces. RTCCs may also include facial recognition technology, geolocation data, and possibly information on probationers and parolees in the area. According to Police One: "Real-time crime centers are rapidly expanding across the U.S., growing by 148% over the past four years; around 150 police agencies have adopted these units."[34]

While RTCCs are undeniably powerhouses of high-utility information, privacy rights and community expectations are important considerations. Best practices suggest that when an agency is developing or expanding technological tools that could be considered surveillance, the community is well-integrated into the process from an early stage. Depending on the expectations and societal dynamics of the region, communities may appreciate the opportunity to cocreate a vision for technology-enhanced public safety in the area. Moreover, many jurisdictions have legal restrictions, including surveillance ordinances, that attempt to formalize a technology oversight process. Surveillance ordinances in the cities of Seattle, Portland, San Diego, Madison, New York, and others[35] codify particularly stringent oversight that may have been in part the byproduct of advocacy from privacy-rights groups such as the Electronic Frontier Foundation[36] and American Civil Liberties Union.[37]

- *Drone as First Responder Program*: Unmanned Aerial Vehicles (UAVS), often colloquially referred to as drones, have become increasingly common in modern public safety. UAVs have a long history of successful application for search and rescue scenarios sand situational awareness during fires and other natural disasters.[38] Modern applications of UAVs include cutting-edge Drone as First Responder (DFR) programs pioneered by the Chula Vista Police Department in San Diego County.

  Launched in 2018, "[t]he mission of the Chula Vista Police Department's Drone Program is to provide airborne support to police operations in a safe, responsible, and transparent manner to preserve the peace, reduce response times, and increase the quality of life in Chula Vista."[39] Co-created with the community, the Chula Vista DFR program has used UAVs to respond to nearly 22,000 calls for service to date, with an average response time of 93.47 seconds when the UAV is the first police presence at the scene and a total average response time of 113 seconds.[40]

- *Data-Driven Policing*: Since the 1970s, data and evidence-based policing strategies have become increasingly prominent and often a de facto expectations in public safety. From budget requests, to operational strategies, to personnel decisions, and community engagement strategies grounding decisions and approaches in data and evidence is a mainstay approach. Moreover, increasingly law enforcement organizations and the community expect apolitical, carefully gathered, and relatable data to demonstrate whether or not a particular initiative or strategy is effective and having its intended effect.

  Many trace the origins of modern data-driven policing to the New York Police Department's pioneering Compstat program in the mid-1990s. Compstat formalized regular meetings and held law enforcement managers accountable for not only understanding crime data, statistics, and trends in their jurisdiction, but having devised comprehensive strategies to address them. Proponents of data-centric approaches often cite Compstat as one of the main drivers of a significant decrease in crime in New York City during this era.[41] Over the next quarter century, data-driven policing now encompasses artificial intelligence technology, predictive policing, and real-time crime centers.[42]
- *Problem-Oriented Policing (POP)*: Dovetailing with data-driven policing, is the uber-impactful concept of problem-oriented policing. This perspective broadens the vantage point of policing professionals and tasks them not only with managing their organizations and responding to the problem of crime, but thinking proactively and creatively about becoming encompassing problem-solvers for the communities they serve. In Improving Policing: A Problem-Oriented Approach, a seminal piece in the field, Herman Goldstein (1979) writes:

  If the police are to realize a greater return on the investment made in improving their operations, and if they are to mature as a profession, they must concern themselves more directly with the end product of their efforts. Meeting this need requires that the police develop a more systematic process for examining and addressing the problems that the public expects them to handle. It requires identifying these problems in more precise terms, researching each problem, documenting the nature of the current police response, assessing its adequacy and the adequacy of existing authority and resources, engaging in a broad exploration of alternatives to present responses, weighing the merits of these alternatives, and choosing from among them.[43]

Goldstein argues that historic metrics of police performance, like response times, arrests, and calls for service, are inherently important in policing but limited. Progressive police departments should create initiatives, teams, and an overarching mentality that focuses on underlying problems and root causes.[44]

Relatedly, Gordon Graham encourages the profession to focus on root causes and "problems lying in wait."[45] Through the lens of risk management, he argues that far too often policing focuses on the "'proximate cause' the thing immediately preceding the tragedy."[46] Instead, embracing the principles of Problem-Oriented Policing, Graham advocates that tragedies and issues should be analyzed in a larger social, historical, and organizational context. Thereafter, organizations can respond via systematic adjustments in hiring, policy development, training, and more.

The parallels between POP and this Grahamsian concept of Problems Lying in Wait are significant in modern policing. They both encourage broader, deeper, and more systematic assessment of society's wicked problems, making organizational adjustments to address them, and arguably cocreating public safety solutions with the community, social service providers, and other key stakeholders.

- *Constitutional Policing*: The paradigm of Constitutional Policing reflects a movement in modern law enforcement to broaden its mission and goals and fully embrace procedural justice. Fundamentally, this perspective emphasizes policing while reinforcing the Bill of Rights and the core Constitutional protections that are the fabric of American society. These Constitutional protections are not just abstract concepts or hurdles that law enforcement must work around. Rather, they are fundamental to justice and tools for building trust and collaborating with the community. As police protect and reify the First, Fourth, Fifth, and Fourteenth Amendments, for example, they demonstrate a commitment to connecting police practices to civil liberties. Proponents argue that Constitutional Policing further legitimizes law enforcement in modern society and the Guardian model in the Guardian v. Warrior conceptualization of public safety. In the Police Executive Research Forum's 2015 report, Constitutional Policing as a Cornerstone of Community Policing, Retired Madison (Wisconsin) Police Chief Noble Wray sums up this concept powerfully,

What we need to understand is that 'constitutional policing' is both foundational and aspirational for the police. The Constitution, in other words, provides both the basic legal framework within which we operate and the larger ethos which we strive to embody.[47]

- *Stare Decisis*: This concept is a cornerstone of Western law. *Stare Decisis* is a term with Latin origins that translates to "to stand by things decided."[48] This legal principle grounds present legal decisions in past legal precedents. In practice, this creates a process whereby current legal decisions must consider previous courses on related substantive matters.

NOTES

1 Duhigg, C. (2012). The power of habit: Why we do what we do in life and business. USA: Random House.

2 Bandura, A. (1986). Social foundations of thought and action: A social cognitive theory. Prentice Hall.

3 Clear, James. (2018). Atomic Habits: an easy & proven way to build good habits & break bad ones (PDF ed.). New York: Avery.

4 Duhigg, C. (2012). The power of habit: Why we do what we do in life and business. Random House.

5 Jim Cathcart, *The Self-Motivation Handbook* (New York: St. Martin's Press, 1983).

6 Jim Cathcart, *The Self-Motivation Handbook* (New York: St. Martin's Press, 1983).

7 Kolb, D. A. (1984). Experiential Learning: Experience as the Source of Learning and Development. Prentice Hall.

8 Ericsson, K. A., Krampe, R. T., and Tesch-Römer, C. (1993). The role of deliberate practice in the acquisition of expert performance. Psychological Review, *100*(3), 363–406. https://doi.org/10.1037/0033-295X.100.3.363

9 Lakoff, G., and Johnson, M. (1980). Metaphors we live by. University of Chicago Press.

10 Huberman, A. (2022). *Dopamine and motivation: The science of progress and reinforcement* [Video]. YouTube. https://www.youtube.com/watch?v=-JZ9lBKg7KPA

11 Duhigg, C. (2012). The power of habit: Why we do what we do in life and business. USA: Random House.

12 Harris, T. E., and Nelson, M. D. (2018). *Applied organizational communication: Theory and practice in a global environment* (4th ed.). Routledge.
13 Harris, T. E., and Nelson, M. D. (2018). *Applied organizational communication: Theory and practice in a global environment* (4th ed.). Routledge.
14 Harris, T. E., and Nelson, M. D. (2018). *Applied organizational communication: Theory and practice in a global environment* (4th ed.). Routledge.
15 Jonni Redick, "Are You Ready to Lead Cops? The Interpersonal Skills You Need After You Promote," *Police1*, July 10, 2024.
16 Smith, M. (2024, October 10). *Mark Cuban says his best employees share this soft skill: "You need to reduce stress, not create it."* CNBC. https://www.cnbc.com/2024/10/10/mark-cuban-the-no-1-soft-skill-that-my-best-employees-share.html
17 DeGraff, J. (2026, January 20). *Want deeper thinking? Let students wrestle with paradox first.* Substack.
18 Smith, M. (2024, October 10). *Mark Cuban says his best employees share this soft skill: "You need to reduce stress, not create it."* CNBC. https://www.cnbc.com/2024/10/10/mark-cuban-the-no-1-soft-skill-that-my-best-employees-share.html
19 Bazerman, M. H., and Moore, D. A. (2012). *Judgment in managerial decision making* (8th ed.). Wiley.
20 Bazerman, M. H., and Moore, D. A. (2012). *Judgment in managerial decision making* (8th ed.). Wiley.
21 Bazerman, M. H., and Moore, D. A. (2012). *Judgment in managerial decision making* (8th ed.). Wiley.
22 Redick, J. (2024, September 29). *Leadership development series: Mastering the decision-making process.* Police1. https://www.police1.com/police-leader-playbook/leadership-development-series-mastering-the-decision-making-process
23 Redick, J. (2024, September 29). *Leadership development series: Mastering the decision-making process.* Police1. https://www.police1.com/police-leader-playbook/leadership-development-series-mastering-the-decision-making-process
24 Redick, J. (2024, September 29). *Leadership development series: Mastering the decision-making process.* Police1. https://www.police1.com/police-leader-playbook/leadership-development-series-mastering-the-decision-making-process
25 Kristen Hadeed, *Permission to Screw Up: How I Learned to Lead by Doing (Almost) Everything Wrong* (Austin, TX: Greenleaf Book Group Press, 2017), 31.
26 Rebecca Knight, "How to Become More Visible at Work," *Harvard Business Review*, August 25, 2023, https://hbr.org/2023/08/how-to-become-more-visible-at-work

27 Rebecca Knight, "How to Become More Visible at Work," *Harvard Business Review*, August 25, 2023, https://hbr.org/2023/08/how-to-become-more-visible-at-work
28 Harvard Business School Online, "Personal Branding at Work: Why It Matters and How to Build Yours," April 13, 2022, https://online.hbs.edu/blog/post/personal-branding-at-work
29 Redick, J. (2022, March 4). *LEO supervisors, the results are in. It's all about YOU!* Police1. https://www.police1.com/what-cops-want-2022/articles/leo-supervisors-the-results-are-in-its-all-about-you-9O9rSXdAYT5QhSpz/
30 Redick, J. (2022, March 4). *LEO supervisors, the results are in. It's all about YOU!* Police1. https://www.police1.com/what-cops-want-2022/articles/leo-supervisors-the-results-are-in-its-all-about-you-9O9rSXdAYT5QhSpz/
31 Gordon Graham (2019, April). *Performance Evaluations: Worth the Risk? 4 Common Mistakes.* Retrieved from https://www.police1.com/chiefs-sheriffs/articles/making-performance-evaluations-worth-it-white-paper-4hplwXiZE1y9KmCs/
32 Redick, J. (2022, March 4). *LEO supervisors, the results are in. It's all about YOU!* Police1. https://www.police1.com/what-cops-want-2022/articles/leo-supervisors-the-results-are-in-its-all-about-you-9O9rSXdAYT5QhSpz/
33 Redick, J. (2022, March 4). *LEO supervisors, the results are in. It's all about YOU!* Police1. https://www.police1.com/what-cops-want-2022/articles/leo-supervisors-the-results-are-in-its-all-about-you-9O9rSXdAYT5QhSpz/
34 Przeszlowski, K. (2021). How real-time crime centers can shorten response times and aid investigations. *Police1.* Retrieved from https://www.police1.com/tech-pulse/criminologist-how-real-time-crime-centers-can-shorten-response-times-aid-investigations
35 Texas Privacy Protection Initiative. (2025). Surveillance ordinances in five U.S. cities. *Texas Technology and Privacy Institute.* Retrieved from https://texastipi.org/surveillance-ordinances-in-five-u-s-cities/
36 https://www.eff.org/
37 https://www.aclu.org/
38 Stampa, M., Sutorma, A., Jahn, U., Thiem, J., and Wolff, C. (2021). Maturity Levels of Public Safety Applications using Unmanned Aerial Systems: A Review. *Journal of Intelligent & Robotic Systems, 108*(3), 1-23. https://doi.org/10.1007/s10846-021-01462-7
39 City of Chula Vista. (2025). *Drone Program.* Retrieved from https://www.chulavistaca.gov/departments/police-department/programs/uas-drone-program.
40 City of Chula Vista. (2025). *Drone Program.* Retrieved from https://www.chulavistaca.gov/departments/police-department/programs/uas-drone-program.

41 Bratton, W., and Knobler, P. (1998). *The Turnaround: How America's Top Cop Reversed the Crime Epidemic*. Random House.
42 Afzal, M., and Panagiotopoulos, P. (2024). Data in Policing: An Integrated Review. *International Journal of Public Administration, 46*(2), 123-145. https://doi.org/10.1080/01900692.2024.2360586
43 Goldstein, H. (1979:236). Improving policing: A problem-oriented approach. *Crime & Delinquency, 25*(2), 236–258. https://doi.org/10.1177/00111287790 2500207
44 Goldstein, H. (1979:236). Improving policing: A problem-oriented approach. *Crime & Delinquency, 25*(2), 236–258. https://doi.org/10.1177/00111287790 2500207
45 Lexipol. (2022, January 19). Problems lying in wait: Why we should (but don't) conduct root cause analysis in public safety. https://www.lexipol.com/resources/blog/problems-lying-in-wait-why-we-should-but-dont-conduct-root-cause-analysis-in-public-safety/
46 Lexipol. (2022, January 19). Problems lying in wait: Why we should (but don't) conduct root cause analysis in public safety. https://www.lexipol.com/resources/blog/problems-lying-in-wait-why-we-should-but-dont-conduct-root-cause-analysis-in-public-safety/
47 Police Executive Research Forum. (2015:3). Constitutional policing as a cornerstone of community policing. Office of Community Oriented Policing Services. https://www.policeforum.org/assets/ConstitutionalPolicingCommunityPolicing.pdf
48 Legal Information Institute. (n.d.). Stare decisis. Wex, Cornell Law School. https://www.law.cornell.edu/wex/stare_decisis

REFERENCES

Afzal, M., and Panagiotopoulos, P. (2024). Data in policing: An integrated review. *International Journal of Public Administration, 46*(2), 123–145. https://doi.org/10.1080/01900692.2024.2360586

American Civil Liberties Union. (n.d.). https://www.aclu.org/

Bandura, A. (1986). *Social foundations of thought and action: A social cognitive theory.* Prentice Hall.

Bazerman, M. H., and Moore, D. A. (2012). *Judgment in managerial decision making* (8th ed.). Wiley.

Bratton, W., and Knobler, P. (1998). *The turnaround: How America's top cop reversed the crime epidemic*. Random House.

Cathcart, J. (1983). *The self-motivation handbook.* St. Martin's Press.

City of Chula Vista. (2025). Drone program. https://www.chulavistaca.gov/departments/police-department/programs/uas-drone-program

Clear, J. (2018). *Atomic habits: An easy & proven way to build good habits & break bad ones*. Avery.

DeGraff, J. (2026, January 20). Want deeper thinking? Let students wrestle with paradox first. Substack.

Duhigg, C. (2012). *The power of habit: Why we do what we do in life and business*. Random House.

Electronic Frontier Foundation. (n.d.). https://www.eff.org/

Ericsson, K. A., Krampe, R. T., and Tesch-Römer, C. (1993). The role of deliberate practice in the acquisition of expert performance. *Psychological Review, 100*(3), 363–406. https://doi.org/10.1037/0033-295X.100.3.363

Goldstein, H. (1979). Improving policing: A problem-oriented approach. *Crime & Delinquency, 25*(2), 236–258. https://doi.org/10.1177/001112877902500207

Graham, G. (2019, April). Performance evaluations: Worth the risk? 4 common mistakes. Police1. https://www.police1.com/chiefs-sheriffs/articles/making-performance-evaluations-worth-it-white-paper-4hplwXiZE1y9KmCs/

Hadeed, K. (2017). *Permission to screw up: How I learned to lead by doing (almost) everything wrong*. Greenleaf Book Group Press.

Harris, T. E., and Nelson, M. D. (2018). *Applied organizational communication: Theory and practice in a global environment* (4th ed.). Routledge.

Harvard Business School Online. (2022, April 13). Personal branding at work: Why it matters and how to build yours. Business Insights. https://online.hbs.edu/blog/post/personal-branding-at-work

Huberman, A. (2022). Dopamine and motivation: The science of progress and reinforcement [Video]. YouTube. https://www.youtube.com/watch?v=JZ9lBKg7KPA

Knight, R. (2023, August 25). How to become more visible at work. *Harvard Business Review*. https://hbr.org/2023/08/how-to-become-more-visible-at-work

Kolb, D. A. (1984). *Experiential learning: Experience as the source of learning and development*. Prentice Hall.

Lakoff, G., and Johnson, M. (1980). *Metaphors we live by*. University of Chicago Press.

Legal Information Institute. (n.d.). Stare decisis. *Wex*, Cornell Law School. https://www.law.cornell.edu/wex/stare_decisis

Lexipol. (2022, January 19). Problems lying in wait: Why we should (but don't) conduct root cause analysis in public safety. https://www.lexipol.com/resources/blog/problems-lying-in-wait-why-we-should-but-dont-conduct-root-cause-analysis-in-public-safety/

Police Executive Research Forum. (2015). *Constitutional policing as a cornerstone of community policing*. Office of Community Oriented Policing Services. https://www.policeforum.org/assets/ConstitutionalPolicingCommunityPolicing.pdf

Przeszlowski, K. (2021). How real-time crime centers can shorten response times and aid investigations. Police1. https://www.police1.com/tech-pulse/criminologist-how-real-time-crime-centers-can-shorten-response-times-aid-investigations

Redick, J. (2022, March 4). LEO supervisors, the results are in. It's all about YOU! Police1. https://www.police1.com/what-cops-want-2022/articles/leo-supervisors-the-results-are-in-its-all-about-you-9O9rSXdAYT5QhSpz/

Redick, J. (2024, July 10). Are you ready to lead cops? The interpersonal skills you need after you promote. Police1. https://www.police1.com/police-leader-playbook/are-you-ready-to-lead-cops-the-interpersonal-skills-you-need-after-you-promote

Redick, J. (2024, September 29). Leadership development series: Mastering the decision-making process. Police1. https://www.police1.com/police-leader-playbook/leadership-development-series-mastering-the-decision-making-process

Smith, M. (2024, October 10). Mark Cuban says his best employees share this soft skill: "You need to reduce stress, not create it." CNBC. https://www.cnbc.com/2024/10/10/mark-cuban-the-no-1-soft-skill-that-my-best-employees-share.html

Stampa, M., Sutorma, A., Jahn, U., Thiem, J., and Wolff, C. (2021). Maturity levels of public safety applications using unmanned aerial systems: A review. *Journal of Intelligent & Robotic Systems, 108*(3), 1–23. https://doi.org/10.1007/s10846-021-01462-7

Texas Privacy Protection Initiative. (2025). Surveillance ordinances in five U.S. cities. Texas Technology and Privacy Institute. https://texastipi.org/surveillance-ordinances-in-five-u-s-cities/

CHAPTER FOUR

Navigating Promotional Processes

Competitive Readiness

The journey toward promotion, law enforcement, and public safety is rarely linear. It is structured, competitive, and often opaque. Promotion is not simply an upward movement—it is the mechanism by which an organization select their stewards of culture, policy, and public trust. From this point forward, your success is not just about understanding the process but about how you strategically prepare to perform within it—because how you prepare is how you perform.

Many approach this process feeling overwhelmed by the complexity and high stakes involved, but understanding the rules of the game is the first step towards navigating it more masterfully.

This chapter will guide you through each phase of the promotional process, from deciphering eligibility criteria to mastering interview techniques, arming you with tools and insights to excel in this competitive journey. In addition, examine real-world narratives to gain valuable insights into the experience of law enforcement professionals who have navigated these rigorous pathways. Each story serves to illuminate specific challenges they faced, whether it be grappling with complex organizational rules, managing the expectations of their peers and superiors, or confronting overcoming biases within the system. These personal accounts highlight the struggles inherent in the promotional process and shed light on these individuals' innovative strategies to succeed, offering inspiration and guidance for others on a similar journey.

Across law enforcement agencies nationwide, the promotion success rates vary significantly. Mid-level promotional success often hovers around 30 percent, reinforcing that strategic preparation—not hope—determine outcomes.[1] Success often depends on meeting standardized performance

DOI: 10.4324/9781003728849-7

metrics, reinforcing that knowledge of the assessment process can be pivotal in achieving promotion. In addition, the absence of formal guidance and the limited availability of feedback further complicates the promotional journey, leaving candidates uncertain of their strengths and areas for improvement. According to the Bureau of Justice Statistics, over 50 percent of local law enforcement agencies lack structured preparation programs for promotion, creating a significant barrier for many candidates.[2] Promotion cycle timelines and waiting periods are also considered. Promotion timelines can differ significantly depending on the agency. On average, officers may experience a waiting period of three years between ranks, although some departments may extend this based on position availability or budget constraints.[3] Realistic timeline planning is essential for maintaining motivation throughout the process.

Many law enforcement agencies rely on merit-based promotional systems that incorporate written examinations, oral interviews, and assessment center exercises to evaluate leadership competencies.[4] In some jurisdictions, seniority or time-in-service may be incorporated into the final promotional score, either as a weighted tie-breaker or in ranking candidates. Understanding which path your department employs is essential for tailoring your preparation strategy.

For example, at the 2025 International Chiefs of Police (IACP) Conference, law enforcement leaders discussed the growing role of artificial intelligence in personnel processes such as hiring, promotional selection, and performance evaluations. Traditional systems—often based on written exams, oral boards, and supervisor evaluations—can be time-sensitive and may overlook important leadership traits.[5] New AI-supported 360-degree evaluation tools allow agencies to collect structured feedback from supervisors, peers, and subordinates and analyze it to identify leadership strengths, developmental needs, and patterns of performance. Early adopters report that these systems improve efficiency, increase evaluator participation, and provide comprehensive feedback that can inform both promotional decisions and leadership development plans.[6]

Fundamentally, as you tailor your approach to preparation, you want to think about the examination processes' inner workings, because promotional systems are not random. Whether written examinations, assessment centers, oral boards, or executive interviews, each mechanism evaluates core domains of professional readiness. Before candidates study for a specific format, they must understand what content, process, and leadership maturity the system is designed to assess in order to develop the proper study practices and response strategies for the best outcomes.

THE PROMOTIONAL PROCESS: FROM BULLETIN TO APPOINTMENT

Once an examination bulletin or notice is advertised, the clock begins and preparation becomes strategic.

A typical promotion example includes:

1. Examination Bulletin
2. Application submission for eligibility confirmation
3. Request for pre-examination materials (varies)
4. Written Examination
5. Assessment Center or qualification appraisal
6. Ranking and certification list
7. Command-level or executive hiring interviews
8. Final selection—promotional offer.

Promotion is competitive. Preparation must be deliberate.

Good practice is identifying your examination cycles to be well-prepared, avoiding being caught off guard, and minimizing the pressure to condense your study time. To assist with this, consider checking with your HR department for information well before your exam cycle begins, or as soon as you can. This will allow you to effectively plan your study schedule and reach out to leaders in your organization with any questions about key areas of focus or mentorship before confidentiality becomes an issue. Take time early to list at least two or three individuals you can contact for guidance to help shape your focus. Ask them about the organization's top priorities and the expectations related to your role or position.

UNDERSTANDING THE PROMOTIONAL PROCESS AND ORGANIZATIONAL CONTEXT

As you are preparing for promotion, begin with an honest assessment of readiness as discussed. By evaluating your experience and collaborating with trusted mentors, you can determine whether you meet the minimum requirements (MQs) required for the next rank or classification. Many agencies establish MQ thresholds—often tied to years of service, prior supervisory experience, or specialized training—to ensure candidates have the foundational experience necessary for the role.

For example, some departments may require a minimum number of years at the current rank or classification before eligibility for promotion. In one agency cited in national discussions on promotional practices, officers needed at least three years of experience before becoming eligible to test for sergeant, one year is a sergeant before testing for lieutenant, and additional supervisory experience before advancing to captain.[7] These MQs create a structured progression through leadership ranks, while ensuring candidates have time to develop operational and leadership competencies.

Once eligibility is confirmed, the promotional process typically begins with an application or qualification screening phase. In some agencies, the application simply verifies eligibility and is not scored and in other cases, the application itself becomes part of the evaluated package, particularly if it requires candidates to describe leadership experience, specialized assignments, or professional accomplishments. After eligibility is confirmed, candidates often move into the testing phase, which commonly begins with a written examination. Written exams assess a candidate's knowledge of policy, law, supervision/management principles, and operational procedures. These assessments may take the form of traditional proctored exams or written scenario prompts requiring candidates to analyze problems and propose solutions.

The candidates who successfully complete the written stage typically advance to assessment centers, oral interviews, and qualification appraisal interviews. These phases evaluate how candidates apply knowledge and practical situations, and participants may be asked to navigate complex leadership scenarios, respond to ethical dilemmas, conduct simulated briefings, manage personnel issues, and role-play exercises. These components are designed to measure core competencies such as decision-making, communication, judgment, and leadership presence.[8]

After all testing phases are complete, agencies establish a certification list (often called an eligibility list) ranking candidates who achieved a passing overall score. Placement on this list determines the order in which candidates may be considered for promotion. Civil Service rules and agency policies govern how these lists are created and how long they remain active, often weighing factors such as written exam scores, assessment center performance, since seniority points, or education.[9] Once the list is finalized, candidates may be required to express interest in open positions and participate in additional interviews with division commanders, unit leaders, or the chief executive officer of the department. In some cases, candidates higher on their certification list may have priority. When selecting assignments, however, specialized or administrative positions often require additional interviews to ensure the candidate skills align with the operational needs of the unit. Candidates who do not achieve a passing score should receive notification of their results. Rather than discarding this information, retain it and seek feedback whenever possible. Your score report can serve as a roadmap for improvement, helping you refine your preparation strategy for future promotional opportunities.

CIVIL SERVICE CONSTRAINTS AND LEADERSHIP CONSIDERATIONS

Generally, promotional systems are designed to promote fairness and reduce political influence; however, they can also create limitations. Some leaders argue that rigid civil service testing systems may overemphasize memorization of study materials rather than evaluating critical leadership attributes such as judgment, emotional intelligence, character, and resilience. Camden County Police Chief Scott Thompson described this tension, reflecting on a pilot program that temporarily allowed his department to promote supervisors through a more flexible merit-based process. During that period, leadership selections considered broader leadership qualities rather than relying solely on standardized testing. However, once the department returned to the statewide civil service system, promotions were again dependent primarily on written test rankings. Thompson noted that such systems can restrict leaders' ability to build a command staff that reflects community needs and organizational culture.[10]

The challenge for candidates is recognizing that promotional systems may not fully measure leadership potential, yet they remain the gateway to advancement. Therefore, preparation requires two parallel strategies:

- Mastering the formal testing process
- Developing leadership competencies that affect organizations that are ultimately required.

Understanding both the mechanics of the system and the broader leadership expectations will better position you for success, not only in achieving promotion but in thriving what you assume the role. The path to promotion is not easy and achieving anything worthwhile requires effort. It is important to remember why a promotion matters to you, as this will help you stay motivated and disciplined. Additionally, your promotion is beneficial to your personal growth and fostering a resilient and knowledgeable law enforcement community. Your leadership contributes to public service, supports officer retention, and addresses significant leadership gaps. In addition, do not let misconceptions about the promotional process discourage you or give you false hope. Common myths include "seniority guarantees promotion" or "you can only get promoted by knowing the right people." While there might be some truth to these statements in certain situations, it is essential to consider what happens if they are false and you have not prepared adequately.

WHAT PROMOTIONAL SYSTEMS ACTUALLY MEASURE

Preparation Insight: Promotional exams increasingly test how leaders think, not just what they know. Candidates who build knowledge across these domains are better prepared to stay agile and adaptable as they respond to complex scenarios, communicate clearly, and demonstrate leadership readiness.

CORE KNOWLEDGE DOMAINS FOR PROMOTIONAL PREPARATION

While the exact format of promotional processes may vary from one agency to another, most systems tend to evaluate candidates across similar set of leadership and operational competencies. These areas reflect the knowledge, judgment, and leadership capacity expected of supervisors, managers, and command staff. In many ways, promotion systems are designed to assess whether a candidate can move beyond performing the job themselves and begin guiding the work of others while supporting the broader mission of the organization.

Although agencies may use slightly different terminology, the following domains consistently appear across law enforcement and public safety promotional systems.[11]

1. **Leadership and Supervision**
   Candidates must demonstrate the ability to guide personnel, manage performance, address conflict, and support employee development. At the supervisory level, leadership shifts from individual to influencing others and creating conditions where teams can perform effectively. Key areas of focus include leadership theory and practical application, emotional intelligence and self-awareness, decision-making under pressure, conflict resolution and difficult conversations and counseling, crisis leadership and team building and stabilization, personnel development and coaching, employee wellness, and resilience awareness.
2. **Organizational Strategy and Governance**
   Supervisors, managers, and above are expected to understand how their decision support the agency's broader mission, policies, and strategic priorities. This is where effective leaders understand agency mission, vision, values, strategic planning, and performance goals. Labor relations and bargaining union considerations along with recruitment, retention, and succession planning, and budget.

3. **Policy, Law and Liability**
   A strong working knowledge of legal authority, departmental policy, and liability considerations is essential. Supervisors must be able to interpret policy, ensure compliance, and make sound decisions that reduce organizational risk and protect both employees and the public. It will be essential to know and understand constitutional law, progressive discipline, audits and inspections, and compliance requirements.
4. **Operational Command and Incident Management**
   Leaders will be evaluated on their ability to manage incidents, coordinate personnel, and maintain operational effectiveness during both routine operations and high-risk events. Sound judgment, situational awareness, and clear communication are critical in these moments. Key areas of focus include Incident Command System (ICS) and unified command, tactical and strategic decision-making, crisis communication, and situational awareness, along with multi-agency coordination and interoperability, emergency management principles, and disaster response.
5. **Fiscal Stewardship and Resource Management**
   Leaders are responsible for managing public resources responsibly. This includes personnel deployment, equipment oversight, and an understanding of how operational decisions impact budgets and organizational capacity. Key areas of focus include budget fundamentals, fiscal planning, resource allocation, staffing considerations, grant management and compliance, risk management, operational sustainability, financial accountability, and transparency.
6. **Ethics and Professional Standards**
   Promotion systems also assess a candidate's commitment to integrity, accountability, and professional conduct. Supervisors are expected to model ethical behavior, reinforce organizational values, and ensure standards are upheld consistently across all levels of the organization. Ethical leadership is not situational—it is demonstrated through daily decisions and the courage to act in alignment with policy and principle. Key areas of focus include professional conduct and discipline, supervisory responsibility in misconduct, organizational culture and ethical climate, and maintaining credibility and trust within the workforce and community.
7. **Community Engagement and Public Legitimacy**
   Modern public safety leadership increasingly emphasizes trust, transparency, and collaboration with the community. Leaders must understand that legitimacy is not granted by authority alone—it is earned through consistent, fair, and respectful interactions. Research and national policing frameworks continue to highlight the importance of legitimacy and community partnerships as core components of effective policing.[12] Good leaders

recognize that every contact, policy decision, and enforcement contact contributes to the public's perception of the organization. Key areas of focus include procedural justice and fairness, community partnership development, communication and transparency strategies, stakeholder engagement, policing practices, public perception management, collaborative-problem solving with community partners, and aligning enforcement strategies with community expectations and public safety outcomes.

A strategic Approach to Study Preparation

Candidates who study only for the format of the exam often struggle with when faced with scenario-based assessments, leadership exercises, or oral interviews. Promotional processes increasingly evaluate how candidates apply that knowledge, demonstrate their judgment, and leave through complex situations. developing a broad and well-structured range of study topics strengthens your ability and analyze problems, communicate decisions, and demonstrate leadership competencies during assessment exercises or oral panel boards. There are several effective strategies for expanding your study topics depending on the structure of your promotional exam, including reviewing leadership publication, agency strategic plans, policy manuals, and emerging trends in public safety leadership.

For example, the *Police1 Police Leadership Playbook: 26 on 2026* highlights several issues shaping modern policing, including staffing shortages, officer wellness, artificial intelligence governance, mental health crisis response, and preparedness for major critical incidents.[13] Reviewing materials like these can help candidates identify relevant study areas that align with current leadership expectations.

A simple framework for identifying study topics includes:

- *Review Current Leadership Publications*
  Look for emerging issues discussed by chiefs, command staff, and national organizations. Publications like Police1, PERF reports, IACP resources, and DOJ guidance frequently identify the topics that agencies expect supervisors to understand.
- *Identify Operational and Leadership Themes*
  Ask yourself what challenges your department currently faces. Topics often include use of force, supervision, recruitment and retention, crisis response, communication, officer wellness, technology, and community trust.
- *Convert Themes into Study Topics*
  Once you identify a theme, break it down into specific knowledge areas. These might include policies, tactical considerations, leadership decision-making, and interagency coordination.

EXAMPLE: ACTIVE SHOOTER RESPONSE AS A STUDY TOPIC

Active shooter response is a strong example of how a broad leadership issue can become a focused study topic. Leadership discussions increasingly emphasize that outcomes during these incidents are influenced not only by tactics, but also by command, coordination, and communication across responding agencies.[14]

A candidate studying this topic might break it down into the following areas, and of course depending on the rank or classification the details or expansion of these topics will evolve:

Active Shooter Study Topics

- First officer response principles
- Incident command and unified command structures
- Multi-agency coordination (police, fire, EMS)
- Communication and interoperability during critical incidents
- Rescue task force concepts and casualty care coordination
- Scene containment and threat neutralization
- Post-incident command decisions and investigation management

Training resources also emphasize that effective preparation requires multidisciplinary planning, realistic exercises, and post-incident debriefing to identify lessons learned and improve response capabilities.[15] By using professional leadership publications and operational guidance as a starting point, candidates can build a structured study list that reflects both exam expectations and real-world leadership challenges.

WRITTEN EXAMINATIONS: KNOWLEDGE AND APPLICATION

Written promotional examinations are designed to evaluate a candidate's knowledge, comprehension, and ability to apply professional standards related to policy, law, leadership, and organizational governance. In many promotional systems, the written examination serves as an initial screening tool allowing agencies to assess whether candidates possess the foundational knowledge necessary for supervisory, management or command responsibilities.[16] Again, while formats vary by jurisdiction, written examinations generally measure a candidate's ability to recall information, analyze complex situations, and interpret policy or legal standards within practical operational contexts.

COMMON QUESTION FORMAT

Promotional written examinations may include a variety of question types intended to assess different cognitive skills:

- Multiple choice questions—Evaluate factual knowledge, policy familiarity, and legal understanding
- True false questions—Test recognition of key concepts and regulatory standards
- Short answer questions—Require more detailed and concise explanations demonstrating comprehension and ability to apply knowledge in real-world situations and articulate their thoughts clearly
- Essay responses—Similar to short answer and assess analytical reasoning and written communication skill
- Scenario-based prompts—Present operational or leadership hypothetical situations (such as use of force incident, personnel issue, or community conflict) where candidates must choose the best course of action or solve a problem based on policies law, and judgment.

Scenario-based questions are increasingly incorporated into promotional examinations because they allow evaluators to assess how candidates apply knowledge in realistic situations rather than simply recalling memorized information.[17] These questions often require candidates to interpret policy, analyze risk, and articulate leadership response consistently with professional standards.[18]

CORE COMPETENCIES BEING ASSESSED

Although the structure of written examinations may differ as mentioned across agencies, most are designed to measure several key competencies:

- Knowledge retention which is understanding of policies, laws, procedures, and Professional Standards
- Analytical reasoning which is the ability to interpret information and evaluate complex problems
- Policy interpretation is the application of departmental policies and legal principles to specific situations
- Leadership judgment is demonstrating sound decision-making consistent with supervisory or management responsibilities.

These competencies form the foundation for later stages of the promotional process, such as assessment centers, oral boards, and leadership simulations, where candidates must demonstrate how they apply knowledge in practical situations.[19] Remember, candidates who prepare broadly across leadership, operational, and legal domains are typically better positioned to succeed in not only the written examination but also the more advanced evaluative stages of the promotional process.

NOTE: As a reminder, candidates still need to understand the technical and detailed underpinnings from these topics within the role and responsibilities of the rank, classification, or position for which they are testing.

SUBJECT MATTER COVERAGE (CONSIDERATIONS)

Written promotional examinations typically draw from several core knowledge areas relevant to supervisory leadership along with material specific to the knowledge, skill, and ability of the position in which you are testing. For example,

- *Agency Policies and Procedures*
  Questions assess knowledge of the department's general orders, standard operating procedures (SOPs), internal regulations, and protocols for daily operations within the department and emergency incident situations. Candidates may also be tested on familiarity with policies for internal investigations, communications and reporting protocols, crisis management and de-escalation techniques tailored to public safety settings, and media relations.
- *Laws and Legal Principles*
  Candidates are expected to understand local, state, and federal legal authorities relevant to their profession, including constitutional rights, use-of-force standards, civil liability, search and seizure principles, and arrest procedures. Additional topics may include familiarity with laws governing court procedures, sentencing, victim rights and legal considerations involving juveniles or vulnerable populations, depending on the profession.
- *Management and Leadership*
  This section tests knowledge of leadership and management principles, supervision or management, decision-making, conflict resolution, team management, time management, conflict resolution, employee counseling, personnel development, and employee wellness considerations. Candidates may also be expected to demonstrate familiarity with decision-making frameworks used in high-risk or high-pressure environments or situations.

- *Budgeting and Fiscal Accountability*
  High -level promotional examinations may include questions related to budget development, resource allocation, grant oversight, risk management and fiscal accountability, emphasizing responsible stewardship of public resources, understanding of budget implications within your governance systems (city, county, state, federal) depending on your rank.
- *Ethics and Professionalism*
  Candidates are expected to understand ethical decision-making, professional conduct expectations, accountability systems, internal investigations, early intervention systems, and the management of misconduct or conflicts of interest.
- *Community Engagement and Public Communication*
  Leaders must demonstrate awareness of community partnerships, workforce diversity considerations, community engagement best practices, media relations, and public communication strategies, for ongoing relationships and during critical incidents or high-profile events.

Specialized Knowledge Areas (Role-Dependent—example)

Depending the profession or assignment, additional subject areas may appear on promotional examinations, including:

NOTE: Corrections, Juvenile Justice, Courts and Victim Assistance

- Knowledge of corrections protocol, including inmate classifications, discipline, and rehabilitation programs.
- Legal considerations for managing incarcerated individuals, including constitutional rights and due process.
- Understanding of security measures and risk management within correctional facilities.
- Protocols for handling juveniles in detention, legal issues related to juvenile rights, sentencing, and treatment.
- Understanding of the juvenile court system and role of juvenile probation officers
- Understanding of criminal justice processes, including trial procedures, sentencing and appeals
- Knowledge of legal frameworks surrounding court proceedings, including evidence handling and witness testimony
- Role of public safety professionals in the court system, knowledge of victim rights and legal protections, services to victims of crime, including counseling, referrals, crisis intervention, restitution programs, and legal support.

EXAMINATION FORMAT

- Timed: Examinations, all phases, are typically timed and are to test not only knowledge but also how efficiently candidates can apply that knowledge under pressure.
- Length: The length of the exam varies but typically lasts between one to four hours, or longer, depending on the depth of the material covered, type of questions included and structure of your examination process.
- Administration: Written exams are often administered in a controlled environment, such as a testing facility or agency facility. In some cases, online exams may also be used.

PURPOSE OF A WRITTEN EXAMINATION

A written exam is a common part of the law enforcement promotion process. Its main purpose is to determine if candidates have the knowledge and judgment required for the next rank. Agencies use these exams to help ensure that those who earn a promotion are ready to take on new responsibilities and handle the challenges that come with a leadership role.

WHAT DOES THE EXAM TEST?

- *Knowledge Retention*: Can you recall and apply key information about department practices, policies, and applicable laws?
- *Analytical Thinking*: Are you able to interpret information and think through situations to make sound decisions?
- *Problem-Solving*: Can you tackle complex situations, whether they involve team members, legal issues, or operations, with critical thinking?
- *Leadership in Action*: Can you apply leadership principles when supervising a team, enforcing policies, or working on organizational goals?

WHY AGENCIES USE WRITTEN EXAMS

- *Fairness*: Written exams provide a consistent, objective way to evaluate everyone. This helps reduce personal bias and ensures everyone is held to the same standard.
- *Comprehensive Review*: These exams cover a wide range of topics, from tactical procedures to legal and leadership issues, to make sure candidates are well-rounded.

- *Transparency*: Candidates know what's being tested and can prepare accordingly, which helps make the process feel fair and open.

A strong written exam gives agencies confidence that those who are promoted have the knowledge, judgment, and readiness to lead effectively. Ultimately, written examinations serve as an important foundation in promotional assessment systems, helping ensure that candidates possess the necessary knowledge and expertise to assume greater leadership responsibilities within their organization.

So, how do you begin to structure your study practice for written examinations, assessment centers, and oral board interviews?

WRITTEN EXAMINATION: HOW TO STUDY

Stacking Your Study Plan

An effective technique for preparing for promotions is a technique known as stacking. But what exactly is stacking? At its core, stacking is the practice of organizing information by layering it systematically. While this concept may seem straightforward, it can significantly aid in managing large volumes of information, reducing overwhelming feelings, and enhancing the overall learning experience. Stacking enables learners to cultivate self-discipline by establishing a consistent study routine. As assignments are completed each week, students stack that week's work onto the previous week's material, allowing for a comprehensive review. This method of stacking information can be repeated throughout the designated study schedule, providing an effective strategy for sustained learning and retention.

When reviewing policy materials, ask yourself questions such as "What should the sergeant, lieutenant, or captain know?" and "What should the lieutenant know?" It is essential to understand the differences between "should," "may, " and "shall. " Please pay attention to the details, as they will be crucial. Focus on knowledge relevant to your current position and the position for which you are testing. As you move up in leadership, you must be competent in your current role, as you will be responsible for knowing what your subordinates are required to do. As you advance in rank, you will be expected to have a deeper understanding of administrative regulations and compliance policies that affect the organization, in addition to the knowledge you gained in your previous officer or supervisory roles. Additionally, identify policy manuals, articles, books, or materials that may contain relevant information, even if they are not essential. You never know what may appear on a test, so it is wise to prioritize these materials as well. You can obtain a list of your agency's policies from the publications unit or the HR department. Most exams will balance questions on field and administrative policies.

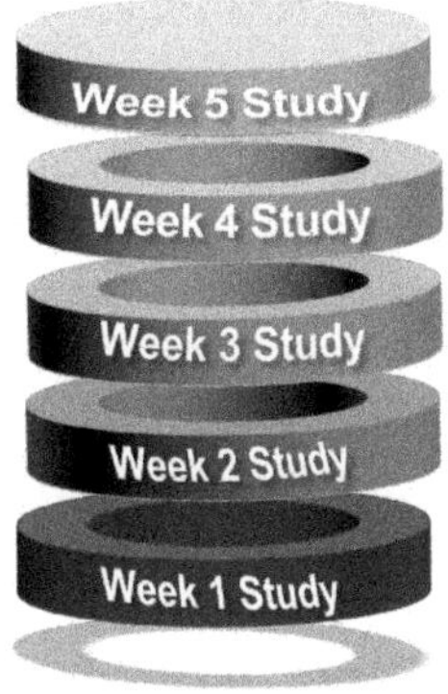

FIGURE 4.1 Study Stacking Model[a]

a Jonni Redick, *Survival Guide to Law Enforcement Promotional Preparation* (Curry Brothers Publishing, 2021)

Creating an effective study schedule is essential for optimal learning and retention. It is important to highlight and prioritize the agency's policy manuals, legal statutes, legislation, compliance regulations, compliance policies, required reading materials, and any other items you want to study first or group together. When preparing for exams for ranks such as sergeant, lieutenant, captain, or higher, consider which sections of each policy manual or general order you should focus on most, as this will vary by rank. It is advisable to dedicate at least three to five days a week to studying, each lasting one to two hours. Short study sessions may not provide enough time for meaningful engagement, while excessively long sessions can lead to burnout.

A suggestion is to use micro-learning techniques to break your study time into smaller segments to maximize your studying. Studying in short learning sessions can help with retention and create efficiency and timesaving if you are working long hours, finding time on breaks or in between the schedule of your daily activities. It is also important to identify your learning style: audio, visual, kinesthetic, or multi-sensory. Understanding this can significantly enhance your study methods. Depending on your preference, you might find it helpful to create flashcards, record audio summaries, gamification, or engage in verbal discussions with others to help with recall. With technology today, you can create a 'podcast' of your material using tools such as Notebook LM and others. Using this type of study tool creates an interesting way to learn, so leverage your resources and tools. As a note, it is up to you to keep confidential information protected from all forms of study tools. In addition, adjusting your study intensity based on the time frame leading up to your exam is also essential. Your study approach will vary significantly if the exam is far off compared to when it is approaching so adapting your study habits accordingly can ensure better preparation and information retention.

TABLE 4.1 Sample Study Stacking Plan Schedule

	Study Plan Details
Week 1	– Create a study session calendar with prioritized policies for studying weekly. – Select 2-3 policy manuals or segments to review. – Review materials relevant to the position (e.g., sergeant/supervisor, lieutenant/manager, captain/commander). – Create 20–25 questions and answers from the material. – Use questions for weekly quizzes and accumulate for mid-term and final exams.
Week 2	– Take the quiz from Week 1 and grade it. – Review the correct answers and discard the wrong ones. – Study the next 2–3 manuals or materials. – Continue creating 20-25 quiz questions and answers. – Create a new quiz for the week.
Week 3-4	– Repeat the Week 2 process each week until Week 5.
Week 5	– Administer a mid-term exam with 50-75 quiz questions from the first 5 weeks. – Score the exam, keeping only the correct answers. – Continue studying according to your schedule.
Week 6-8	– Continue the weekly study and quiz process, reviewing new materials and creating weekly questions and answers.
Week 9	– Administer a final exam with all correct quiz questions accumulated over the past 9 weeks (approximately 110 questions). – Score the exam and keep only the correct answers. – Create a final study document (40–50 pages) from all materials.
Week 10	– Review your final study document repeatedly throughout the week. – Relax the day before the exam. – Hydrate and relax on the morning of the exam. – Take the test confidently, knowing you have followed the process.

10-Week Study Plan: One weekly session for the written test if participating in a study group. This example can apply to all law enforcement and public safety professionals for written examinations—adjust accordingly.

TABLE 4.2A Example of Key Topics for Study Focus

Key Component	Study Topics
Agency Head Vision Statements	– Mission/Organizational Values/Professional Values – Employee Wellness – Equal Employment Opportunity (EEO)
Fiscal and Legal Knowledge	– Budget/Fiscal Accountability – Civil Liability – Audits and Inspections – Employee Misconduct/Progressive Discipline

TABLE 4.2A (Continued)

Key Component	Study Topics
Management and Policy	— Strategic Plan — Union Relations — Bargaining Unit/Associations
Current Trends and Issues	— Contemporary incidents (e.g., social unrest, legislative changes, use of force) — Community Engagement — Recruitment, Retention, and Succession Planning — Risk Management
Agency Policies and Procedures	— General Orders and Internal Regulations: Knowledge of department protocols and SOPs — Protocol for Managing Situations: Incident handling protocols, documentation, and crisis management techniques
Laws and Legal Principles	— Local, State, and Federal Laws: Criminal law, traffic laws, drug laws, juvenile justice, court procedures — Legal Issues: Use of Force, Civil Liability, Constitutional Rights, Search and Seizure, Arrest Protocols — Juvenile Justice Laws: Detention protocols, sentencing, and rehabilitation initiatives
Management and Leadership	— Leadership Principles: Leadership theories, team management, stress management — Supervision and Decision-Making: Supervisory techniques and decision-making frameworks — Leadership during crisis — Conflict Resolution and Personnel Issues: Resolving conflicts, addressing misconduct, promoting mental health and wellness
Budgeting and Fiscal Accountability	— Financial Management: Budgeting, resource allocation, and cost-effective planning, grant management, risk management — Resource Allocation: Prioritizing operations and initiatives
Ethics and Professionalism	— Ethical Standards Across Professions: Handling ethical dilemmas in public safety sectors — Professional Conduct: Adherence to codes of conduct, addressing misconduct — Managing Misconduct and Accountability: Internal reviews, accountability, and training on integrity
Community Relations	— Community Engagement: Community policing, partnerships for crime prevention, fire safety, and victim support — Diversity and Inclusion: Promoting inclusivity and cultural competency — Public Communication and Media Relations: Effective communication with the public and media

TABLE 4.2A (Continued)

Key Component	Study Topics
Fire Science, EMS, and Emergency Management	– Fire Science Principles: Fire suppression, safety protocols, and incident command systems – EMS Operations and Medical Protocols: Triage, first aid, patient transport, legal and ethical considerations in EMS – Disaster Response and Emergency Management: Incident command, multi-agency coordination, and managing large-scale emergencies
Corrections and Juvenile Justice	– Corrections Management: Inmate classification, discipline, rehabilitation programs, security measures – Juvenile Justice: Handling juveniles in detention, diversion programs, juvenile court system
Courts and Victim Assistance	– Court Procedures and Protocols: Trial procedures, sentencing, appeals, and evidence handling – Victim Assistance: Victim rights, counseling, legal support, crisis intervention, and restitution programs
Investigations (Detective)	Criminal Law and Legal Elements, Search and Seizure, Evidence Collection and Preservation, Interview and Interrogation, Case Documentation, Crime Scene and Incident Analysis, Investigative Resources and Technology, Victim Witness Considerations, Prosecution Preparation

Note: Study materials should include general orders, management memorandums, policy manuals, laws, codes, and other relevant materials specific to your position and agency. It is your responsibility to ensure that all materials are current and up to date and that you are selecting specialized material needed for your examination type—these are example areas.

ASSESSMENT CENTERS: DEMONSTRATING COMPETENCE IN ACTION

Most promotional processes eventually move beyond written exams and interviews. This is where assessment centers come in.

Assessment centers evaluate performance, not memorization.
Assessment centers are designed to evaluate how candidates perform, not simply what they know. Instead of testing memorized information, these exercises place candidates in realistic leadership scenarios, often sometimes those that can feel unfamiliar or uncomfortable, to see how they think, communicate, and make decisions under pressure. The approach enables evaluators to assess how effectively candidates demonstrate core competencies in realistic settings.[20] and observe whether they have the necessary skills and traits to succeed in their desired roles. Recognizing that the design of assessment center environments differs from real-world incidents.

Researchers and organizational psychology have consistently found that assessment centers are among the most reliable tools for evaluating leadership potential, particularly when multiple exercises and evaluators are used[21]. As a candidate, you may encounter simulations such as:

- Personnel counseling
- Internal investigations
- Critical incident management
- Budget or resource allocation decisions
- Strategic planning challenges
- Organizational culture or employee wellness issues.

Their goal is simple; observe how you lead.

WHAT ASSESSMENT CENTERS ACTUALLY MEASURE

While formats may vary by agency, most assessment centers focus on similar set of leadership competencies. Common competencies include:

- *Leadership and Supervision*: For example, this competency evaluates an individual's capability to effectively lead diverse teams toward common goals. It includes the ability to inspire and motivate employees, make strategic decisions, delegate tasks appropriately, and manage personnel dynamics to foster a productive work environment. Effective leaders not only guide their teams but also demonstrate adaptability and resilience in navigating challenges.[22]
- *Problem-solving and Critical Thinking:* This skill assesses one's capacity to thoroughly analyze complex situations and identify underlying issues. It involves systematic thinking to develop creative and effective solutions. Competence in this area includes gathering relevant information, evaluating alternatives, and implementing actionable plans while also considering potential consequences.[23]
- *Communication Skills:* This encompasses the effectiveness of both verbal and written communication. It is crucial for conveying ideas clearly and persuasively to various audiences, including subordinates, peers, stakeholders, and the public. Strong communicators also excel in active listening, ensuring that they understand and address the needs and concerns of others.
- *Interpersonal Effectiveness:* This competency focuses on the ability to build and maintain positive relationships within the workplace. It includes skills in collaboration, conflict resolution, and empathy.[24] Those who excel in this area create a supportive organizational culture that fosters teamwork and inclusivity, enhancing overall morale and productivity.

- *Organizational Knowledge:* Here, the emphasis is on the depth of understanding of the agency's policies, procedures, and strategic goals. Individuals demonstrating this knowledge can effectively navigate organizational structures and leverage resources for optimal outcomes. This competency also involves staying informed about changes within the organization and how they affect various stakeholders.[25]
- *Judgment and Decision-Making:* This skill pertains to the ability to weigh options and make informed, ethical decisions, especially under pressure. Competent individuals demonstrate sound judgment by considering both short-term and long-term implications, ethical standards, and the well-being of the organization and its members. They are adept at evaluating risks and benefits, ensuring their choices reflect integrity and accountability.[26]
- *Delegation and Prioritization:* One of the most revealing aspects of assessment center exercises is how candidates manage time, people and competing priorities. Leaders rarely have the capacity to handle every task themselves. Instead, they must determine what requires direct involvement and what should be delegated to others while identifying what's urgent and nonurgent, and what resources should be assigned. Research in leadership and organizational behavior consistently shows that effective delegation and prioritization are core supervisory competencies, directly influencing team performance, efficiency, and decision quality.[27]
  - NOTE: Finding a time management tool, or be able to identify your process for time management is integral to this part of the process. For example, if you use the Eisenhower Matrix for time management, or have an internal process or mechanism for project/priority tracking of tasks and to whom they were given with sequenced follow up measures—those are the hidden examination bonuses and in real-life situations, are very important.
- *Organizational Political Acumen: T*his is not often discussed as a competency—but should be. It is a competency that often appears—sometimes subtly—in assessment centers exercises is organizational awareness, or political acumen. This does not refer to partisan politics. Instead, it reflects a leader's ability to understand how decisions affect relationships, priorities, and stakeholders both inside and outside the organization. In real leadership roles, decision rarely occur in isolation. Supervisors and managers must consider how actions impact employees, command staff, community members, elected officials, and partner agencies. The best candidates demonstrate that they understand these dynamics and can balance operational needs with organizational and community expectations.

Leadership scholars describe organizations as operating through multiple lenses or frames. In the work of Lee Bolman and Terrence Deal in their book *Reframing Organizations*, they explain that effective leaders must learn to view decisions through structural, human resource, political, and symbolic perspectives.[28] Leaders who rely on only one perspective often miss the broader implications of their decision. Assessment centers scenarios test this type of thinking in the candidates depth of their responses. For example, a candidate may technically solve a problem but overlook how the decision affects employee morale, public perception, and relationships with other units. Candidates who score better show they can recognize competing interests, anticipate organizational ripple effects, and communicate decisions in a way that maintains trust and credibility. Remember, demonstrating political awareness does not need to be over-complicated; often it simply comes down to showing that you can:

- recognize who is affected by decisions
- consider organizational priorities and mission alignment
- balance employee concerns with operational demand
- be mindful of community impact in public
- communicate decisions in a way that maintains relationships.

When you can demonstrate this awareness, you are signaling that you are ready to operate at a broader organizational level rather than focusing on the immediate tasks.

WHAT THE EXERCISES OFTEN LOOK LIKE

1. *Simulated Scenarios*: In the examination process, candidates are presented with realistic situations they might encounter in their new role and include: responding to critical incidents, crisis management, managing personnel issues, counseling, conducting internal investigations, providing unified responses, executing tactical responses, demonstrating knowledge of departmental strategic plans, or handling community relations. Scenarios assess how candidates apply their leadership, decision-making, and problem-solving skills under pressure.[29] Candidates may be asked to review and respond to scenarios, analytical data, or information involving complex organizational or operational challenges to assess their strategic thinking, judgment, and ability to prioritize and solve problems effectively. A suggestion is to practice with real agency data and reports so you can become familiar with this information and be more specific in your responses.

2. *Role-Playing Exercises*: These dynamic exercises immerse candidates in realistic scenarios where they must role-play interactions with subordinates, colleagues, or members of the public. During these simulations, candidates may face various challenges, such as resolving conflicts, providing guidance, or addressing concerns. This hands-on approach allows evaluators to assess candidates not only on their communication skills but also on their ability to navigate complex interpersonal situations. By observing how candidates respond to unexpected developments and interact with different personalities, evaluators can gain valuable insights into their conflict resolution strategies and overall emotional intelligence, ultimately revealing their potential effectiveness in a real-world work environment which involves high-stress interactions.[30]
3. *Interview Panels*: In addition to the written or practical exercises, an assessment center typically features oral interviews conducted by a panel of evaluators. Also, interviews are designed to delve deeper into a candidate's qualifications and interpersonal skills. During this process, candidates are assessed on their ability to effectively communicate their thoughts and ideas, articulate their decision-making processes under pressure, and demonstrate their knowledge as it pertains to the specific role for which they're applying. The panel often poses complex scenarios or situational questions that require candidates to think critically and respond in a manner that reflects their judgment, demonstrates their leadership philosophy, adaptability, and problem-solving abilities.[31] This dynamic setting not only evaluates a candidate's technical expertise but also their soft skills, such as teamwork, leadership, and adaptability. Overall, the oral interviews play a crucial role in providing a comprehensive view of a candidate's capabilities and potential contributions to the team.
4. *Behavioral Exercises*: During the selection process, candidates may engage in dynamic exercises designed to evaluate essential leadership qualities. These activities are effective and real-world scenarios that test abilities such as motivating a team, delegating tasks effectively, and managing conflicts among team members. For instance, candidates might be placed in role-playing scenarios where they must lead a group through a challenging project, fostering collaboration and enthusiasm while navigating differing opinions and tensions. In-basket exercises may require candidates to prioritize tasks and make decisions about resource allocation, demonstrating their ability to delegate effectively and think strategically in high-pressure situations, and motivation under time constraints.[32] Additionally, interview panels may pose situational questions that challenge candidates to articulate their approach to resolving conflicts or nurturing team morale. These exercises are crafted to provide a comprehensive view of a candidate's potential to perform key leadership duties, showcasing their problem-solving

abilities, communication skills, and emotional intelligence in a realistic context.

5. *Evaluation by a Panel*: In the assessment center process, candidates are evaluated by a diverse panel of experts, which often includes executive officers, seasoned human resources professionals, and sometimes external subject matter experts who bring specialized knowledge to the assessment. The evaluators are to assess candidates holistically, offering a multi-dimensional view of leadership based on behavioral observations.[33] The panel is responsible for diligently evaluating candidates across a range of competencies, including leadership, problem-solving, communication skills, and teamwork. Throughout various exercises, including role-plays, group discussions, and individual presentations, the panel closely observes candidates to note their strengths and areas for improvement. Their collective insights and evaluations provide a comprehensive view of each candidate's capabilities and potential fit for the role, ensuring a fair and thorough assessment process.

Benefits of an Assessment Center

- *Objective Evaluation*: One of the advantages of using an assessment center is its ability to provide a more objective and unbiased evaluation of candidates. By integrating various assessment methods, such as situational judgment tests, role-playing exercises, and peer evaluations, this approach minimizes the impact of individual biases often present in traditional interviews or written exams. Research has consistently indicated that women and minorities face systemic barriers, leading to their promotion rates being lower than those of white male counterparts.[34] Human resource professionals are tasked with creating evaluation tools that not only recognize these disparities but actively foster a more equitable environment for all candidates.
- *Real-World Application*: Assessment centers assess candidates in scenarios that closely resemble the actual challenges faced in the work environment. By immersing candidates in realistic situations, evaluators can gauge their practical skills and decision-making abilities in action. This approach shifts the focus from merely theoretical knowledge to the candidate's ability to apply their skills effectively under pressure, providing insights into their potential performance in the job.
- *Comprehensive Insight*: Beyond evaluating technical skills, assessment centers delve deeper into a candidate's emotional intelligence, leadership qualities, and ability to manage stress. Evaluators can better capture a multifaceted view of each candidate, assessing not only their immediate responses but also their long-term suitability for the role. This comprehensive

evaluation can uncover hidden strengths and potential areas for development, ensuring that the selected candidates are well-rounded and capable of thriving in demanding positions.

Overall, an assessment center is purposefully designed to replicate the challenges and demands of the position, offering a more holistic and nuanced evaluation of a candidate's readiness for promotion in a complex field like law enforcement—not always perfectly—but with good intention.

PREPARATION INSIGHT FOR CANDIDATES

It is important to remember that assessment centers do not perfectly replicate real world incidents. However, they are structured environments designed to observe leadership behaviors within a limited time frame and they attempt to create realistic opportunities for you to demonstrate your readiness. The candidates who perform best typically will do these things well:

- Adopt the mindset of the role they are testing for. What that means is you want to think and respond as the supervisor, manager, or commander, not as your current position. How you do that is how you communicate verbally your responses as if you are actually doing them in that role. This takes practice.
- Explain your reasoning clearly. Evaluators are often as interested in how you think as they are in the final decision you make. So remember as you are working yourself through the different scenarios or questions, you are also taking time to verbally share some of your thought processes and consideration out loud, your reasoning, on how you are approaching your final decisions or outcomes.
- Demonstrate leadership presence. Communication, professionalism, and composure under pressure matter just as much as technical knowledge. This is where you are demonstrating your maturity, your experience, and your ability to regulate your emotions, emotional intelligence, as you navigate complex questions, scenarios, and your considerations for your responses.

Assessment centers are not about perfection. They are about showing that you can think, lead, and communicate as you need to for that next rank, position, or classification that you are seeking.

STRUCTURING YOUR WRITTEN RESPONSE TO SCENARIO PROMPTS

Most promotional processes can include some type of written prompt exercise that is a part of the examination process and can be before the assessment exercises, a part of the exercises, or the only exercise. The expectation is that candidates are to analyze an incident and produce a clear, organized response. These exercises generally evaluate a candidate's ability to demonstrate analytical reasoning, knowledge of law and policy, operational awareness, and the ability to communicate decisions clearly in writing.

Unlike oral interview panels, a written exercise allows evaluators to assess how well candidates organize their thinking and articulate their decision-making process on paper. Those candidates who perform well typically avoid unstructured responses and instead apply a disciplined analytical approach that demonstrates both reasoning and a more professional level of judgment. It is a very different style of writing than report writing, administrative writing or academic writing. It is a blend of that experience and composition, but it is more about understanding the limitations within the instructions, addressing the prompt specifically, and including key elements. It is helpful to keep the foundational writing framework of: have an opening, a middle and closing mindset when you develop your written response. A strategy you can consider is to organize written responses around four core elements:

1. **Identify the issue,** which is where you are going to define the incident or the problem that you are trying to solve clearly, which could be operational, or it could be investigative, or it could be your philosophy or approach on a particular topic, and this will depend on your rank, classification, and role that you are testing for.
2. Reference applicable law, policy, or procedure this is an opportunity for you to demonstrate awareness of the legal and organizational Frameworks guiding the response that you are creating for your particular written prompt.
3. Describe the response strategy in this element, you want to explain the actions that should be taken, including resource coordination, investigated or operational steps, and communication considerations.
4. Provide a clear conclusion as you summarize the course of action and how the situation will be documented or resolved. Include in follow up actions, training, or future implications—make your wrap up rich and robust, not fluff.

What you want to take into consideration is that you should treat the written response prompt with the same approach that you would for an oral interview panel question. That means that you want to consider the prompt exercise the same as you would if you were sitting in front of an interview panel. Stay structured and organized and be able to articulate important information like understanding how to identify the issue, are there any risks or additional concerns. Next, you want to look to see how you can show that your decisions are grounded in policy, legal standards, common organizational expectations by referencing any policy, law, or guidelines. And as you explain in your response, you want to walk through what you would do so think about any immediate actions, who needs to be involved, or notified, resources required, communication with supervisors, staff, or the public. Within the response, you also want to consider people, coordination, collaboration, and delegation when possible and why. For example, include any awareness of personnel or personnel issues, teamwork, and different types and forms of communication that may be needed. As you get ready to close out your response, identify a clear outcome or considerations for resolution. Was there documentation, and what follow-up is still needed, and are there any additional implications that you want to include? The bottom line is to keep it simple and structured, so when you are clearly walking a reader, or an outside evaluator, through the issue, your reasoning, and your actions, you make it easy for them to see your leadership thinking on paper.

NOTE: As you work through the Strategic Response Frameworks next, you can integrate those strategies into helping you formulate your approach and preparation for written exercises. For example, you might consider creating a simple checklist or drawing a quick mindmap and supporting it with your IRAC model, which can help keep your response focused and complete.

Key Takeaway: Have a process, step by step, to answer and show your ability to think clearly, follow procedure, and communicate like a leader. Stick to the facts, be concise, and demonstrate how you would handle the scenario in line with your agency standards and your role expectations, and apply a holistic response. Lastly, *practice, practice, practice.*

Strategic Response Frameworks

It is one thing to understand the structure of the assessment center, but that is only half the equation. The true differentiator is promotional process is not what you know, but how you put your ideas together under evaluation. The following is a strategic response framework that will help you organize your thinking, demonstrate your readiness and skills, and help you perform with better organizational clarity.

1. Think in Phases: PRE—DURING—POST

One of the most powerful tools for scenario-based responses is structured sequencing. Whenever you are presented with a case study, incident, conflict, or operational challenge, discipline your thinking into three phases:

PRE (Preventive)

- What systems, training, policies, or supervision could prevent this issue?
- What early warning signs could be recognized?
- What culture or communication practices reduce recurrences?

DURING (Mitigation and Management)

- What immediate actions are required?
- What legal, policy, and safety considerations apply?
- Who must be notified?
- What risks must be stabilized?

POST (Dispositions and Accountability)

- What follow-up investigation is required?
- Is this discipline, development, or both?
- What documentation and reporting must occur?
- What internal and external impacts must be addressed?
- What corrective systems or training adjustments are needed?

This sequencing demonstrates leadership thinking and the very things panels will be listening for evidence that you see beyond the moment and understand systemic implications.

2. THE PLLT-FIND Framework: Covering the Essentials

Strong responses consistently address foundational elements and you can create a practical mental checklist drawn from this acronym model:

PLLT—FIND

- P—Policy (process and procedures)
- L—Law (legal authority and compliance)
- L—Liability (risk exposure and public trust)
- T—Training (competency gaps and development needs)
- F—Follow-up/Controls
- I—Impacts (internal and external)
- N—Notifications (chain of command, HR, legal, stakeholders)
- D—Discipline vs. Development.

This model helps you ensure that you do not give narrow responses but instead, balance operational action with a well-rounded approach.

3. IRAC Model

AUTHOR NOTE

Using the IRAC Model for Investigative Analysis

During my career, I saw many promotional candidates struggle not because they lacked knowledge, but because they lacked a structured way to organize their thinking under pressure. Frameworks like IRAC help candidates slow down their reasoning and communicate their thought processes clearly. One of the most effective ways to organize your thinking during investigative or scenario-based questions is to use structured analytical frameworks. Legal professionals, investigators, and prosecutors often rely on models that help them systematically evaluate facts, apply relevant law or policy, and communicate conclusions clearly. One such framework is the IRAC model, which can be adapted for investigative analysis and promotional assessment responses. This analytical framework aligns closely with broader leadership competencies discussed throughout the book. Effective leaders learn to slow their thinking, identify the core issue, apply governing policy and legal statute, and communicate clear direction.

Detectives and investigators are frequently required to analyze complex incidents and articulate their reasoning clearly in reports, case presentations, and promotional assessment scenarios. One helpful framework for structuring responses for this type of analysis shared during a few dynamic study groups preparing for these exams is the IRAC model, which stands for Issue, Rule, Application, and Conclusion.

The IRAC framework originated in legal education during the development of the case-method approach at Harvard Law School in the late nineteenth century. Law students were trained to analyze court opinions by systematically identifying the legal issue, applying governing law, and explaining the outcome through structured reasoning. Over time, IRAC became a standard analytical tool used by attorneys, courts, and legal scholars to organize legal analysis.[35]

Although developed in the legal profession, the IRAC model has evolved into other professions and practices and is extremely useful for law enforcement investigators and those preparing for detective or supervisory promotional processes, particularly when responding to scenario-based questions that require disciplined problem-solving.

IRAC Investigative Thinking Model

Step	Investigative Focus	Key Questions to Consider
Issue	Identify the central investigative problem.	What crime may have occurred? What elements must be proven? What facts are currently known?
Rule	Identify governing law and policy.	What criminal statutes apply? What departmental procedures guide the investigation? What constitutional considerations are relevant?
Application	Apply law and policy to the facts of the case.	What evidence must be collected? What witnesses should be interviewed? What investigative tools or technology can assist?
Conclusion	Document findings and investigative direction.	How does the evidence support the elements of the offense? What additional investigative steps are needed?

Visual Flow of IRAC in an Investigation

Incident Occurs

↓

Identify the ISSUE

(What crime or problem exists?)

↓

Determine the RULE

(Law, policy, investigative standards)

↓

APPLY facts to the rule

(Evidence, witnesses, investigative strategy)

↓

Reach a CONCLUSION

(Document findings and investigative direction)

Why This Matters for Career Advancement

Structured reasoning models like IRAC help demonstrate:

- Analytical clarity when evaluating complex incidents
- Professional discipline in investigative decision-making
- Strong written communication in reports and case files
- Preparedness for promotional assessment scenarios.

Practicing structured frameworks like IRAC helps candidates move beyond simply recalling policies or statutes. Instead, it allows them to demonstrate analytical reasoning, investigative judgment, and clear communication: skills that promotional boards are often evaluating. The goal is not to memorize the framework verbatim, but to develop disciplined thinking that allows you to articulate your reasoning step by step, stay agile and adaptable in your responses.

4. Using Mind Mapping to Structure Your Promotional Response

Mind mapping is a simple but powerful technique that helps candidates organize complex information quickly during promotional examinations. In assessment centers, written prompts, and oral panels, evaluators are not only listening for the correct answer, they are also assessing how effectively you organize information, prioritize issue, and manage complexity under pressure. When candidates are presented with a challenging scenario, the brain often reacts emotionally first, especially when the situation involves conflict, risk, or potential liability. Also, I have found that, under stress, the body physiologically responds differently and can begin to cause you to blank out in your thoughts, give you a dry mouth, or start sweating profusely, and you forget what you said, so you begin repeating yourself. Mind mapping helps interrupt that reactive thinking, those stress responses, and replaces it with structured analysis and quickly outlining key elements of a problem. With this strategy, candidates can visualize the situation, identify priorities, and deliver a clear, organized response, and even recall your deliberate preparation practices. As you begin to focus on the information you are recalling, your body will become more at ease, feel more secure that you have some ideas developing and hopefully give momentum to the actual words you will write or say verbally.

A mindmap typically begins with the central issue or problem written in the center of a page and then create branches that represent the major areas that must be addressed, such as policy considerations, safety concerns, legal statutes, liability and risk, communication, training, EAP (Employee Assistance Program), resources, your role, notifications, and follow-up actions. Visualizing this mindmap allows candidates to mentally organize their response before speaking or writing. In addition, mind mapping can also be integrated with structured response frameworks, such as acronym-based strategies or the Pre–During–Post approach. These types of structured thinking strategies align with research on expertise development showing that high performers rely on deliberate, organized cognitive processes when responding to complex professional situations.[36]

For example, after briefly organizing the scenario using a mindmap, a candidate might articulate their response in a structured manner:

> There are several components I would consider in this situation. First, from a policy and legal standpoint, I would review the relevant department policies (specify them) and ensure our actions (specify them) comply with applicable law (specify). Second, I would address immediate safety and risk considerations to stabilize the situation. Third, I would ensure appropriate notifications are made to supervisors, investigative units, or partner agencies as needed (specify all). Finally, I would implement follow-up measures such as documentation (specify), supervisory review, and steps to prevent similar issues in the future.

Using a strategy like mind mapping allows candidates to slow down their thinking, organize complexity, and communicate clearly, which are key competencies promotional panels are also evaluating in leadership candidates. A good practice is to listen to radio calls or incidents that you are not involved in and take the issue, make it the center of your mind map, and then begin to create branches based on your role now, and then broaden it to the next level of promotion. Examine what you know currently and how it grows as you advance to begin to reinforce your awareness of role responsibilities, knowledge, and exposure to more experiences. Many agencies cannot afford to give you experiential exposure in the next rank you may be seeking in an interim or acting capacity, so create your own opportunities to grow your learning and professional readiness. Always be a continual learner in all aspects of your professional development.

An example of your mindmap can be found in figure 4.2 below:

5. The STAR-R[37] Method: Elevating Behavioral Responses

For competency-based and behavioral interviews, structured storytelling is essential. The STAR-R Method sharpens your responses so your story stays focused, intentional, and aligned with what evaluators are actually listening for—not just what happened, but how you think and lead through it.

- Situation—What was the context?
  Set the stage briefly. This isn't where you tell your whole career story—just enough to orient the panel to the environment, the stakes, and why the situation mattered.
- Task—What were you responsible for?
  Clarify your role. This is where you separate yourself from the team and demonstrate ownership. What were you expected to do, and what was at stake if it wasn't done well.
- Action—What specific steps did you take?
  This is your moment. Walk them through your decision-making, not just your actions, but why. What did you prioritize? Who did you communicate with? How did you lead and work through to a resolution?
- Result—What measurable outcome occurred?
  Close the loop with impact. Think in terms of outcomes—improved performance, reduced risk, strengthened relationships, or enhanced trust.

NOTE: The last R is for reflection—sometimes you can wrap a lesson learned into your response and show your leadership growth. It will depend on your process.

Strong leaders do not just have experiences—they extract lessons and apply them moving forward.

When used effectively, STAR-R keeps you from rambling or getting lost in details. It creates a disciplined way to communicate your leadership story while signaling to the evaluators that you are thoughtful, intentional, and continually developing your craft—because leadership isn't just about what you have done; it is about how you have grown from it and how you will show up next.

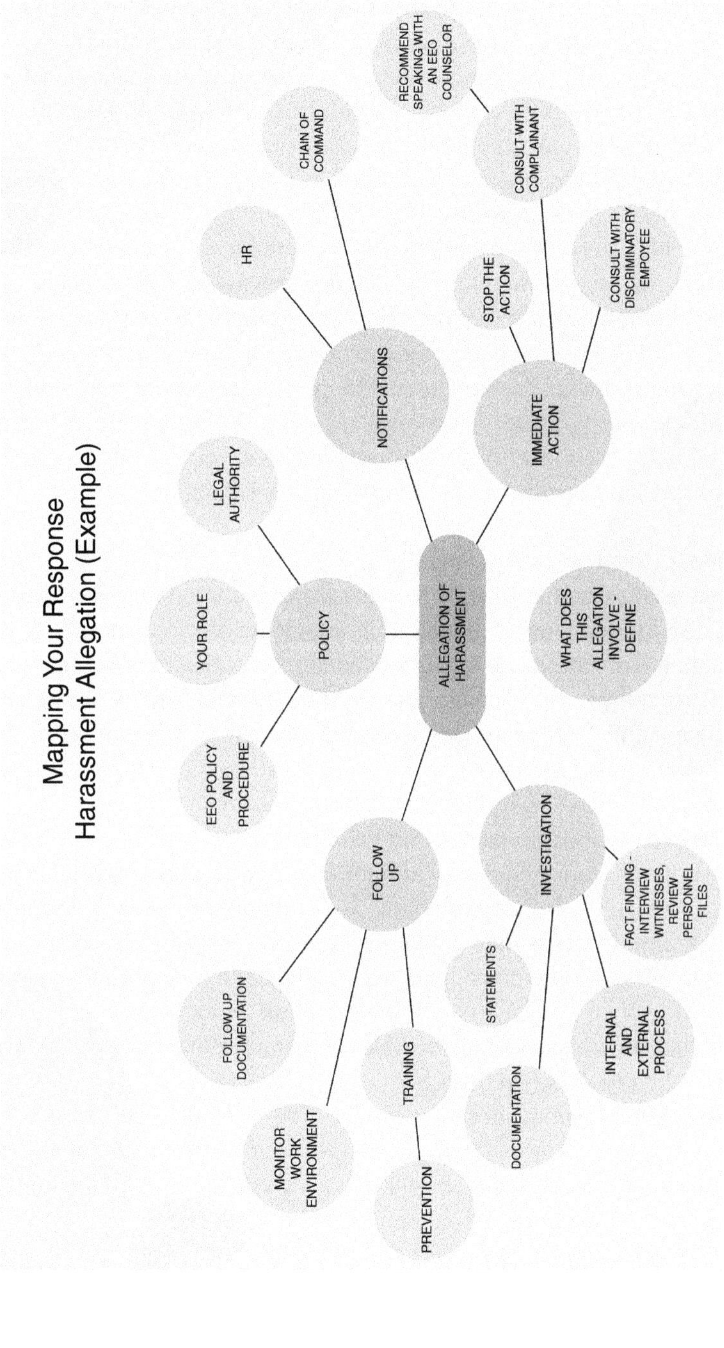

FIGURE 4.2 C.L.E.A.R. Leadership Decision Framework

6. Prioritization and Delegation

Many promotional assessment exercises are intentionally designed to evaluate a candidate's decision-making speed, judgment, and ability to prioritize competing demands. Scenarios may involve officer involved incident, employee misconduct allegations, staffing shortages, public safety emergencies, or community crises. In these moments, evaluators are watching how you organize your thinking, set priorities, and distribute responsibilities under pressure.

Depending on your personality style or the rank you are seeking, delegation may not come naturally—and that is okay. This is a skill that can be developed with intention. Take time to think about how you will prioritize and delegate ahead of the process so you are not trying to figure it out in the moment. In the exam setting, be clear about why you are delegating, what you are delegating, and who is best suited to handle it. An effective response should demonstrate that you quickly assess the situation and address several key leadership considerations:[38]

- Identify legal and safety urgency.
  Determine whether there is an immediate threat to life, public safety, or constitutional rights that requires urgent action. For example, when dealing with employee issues related to mental health or hostile work environments, ask yourself, what is discretionary time or nondiscretionary time? Are there immediate actions that need to be taken? What are they? What part is the natural cadence of the process? Say what the process is and what your concerns are.
- Mitigate organizational risk and liability.
  Ensure that your actions align with law, policy, and procedural justice principles. This is important, as you cannot operate in the grey. For example, what may appear to be a minor issue—like employee counseling—could reveal patterns of behavior that expose the agency to risk. When counseling employees, think about reviewing personnel files for a history of misconduct or pattern. What does progressive discipline look like in this case?
- Protect employee welfare.
  This is where your leadership becomes visible. Protecting employee welfare isn't a box to check—it is showing you understand the human side of the job while still accomplishing the mission.

  Start with employee safety—sound tactics, proper staffing, and awareness of fatigue and risk.

Then consider overall well-being. Public safety work carries cumulative stress for everyone, so strong leaders recognize burnout early and address it—sometimes with a simple check-in, or other times with adjustments to workloads or assignments.

Highlight support systems like EAP, peer support, or wellness programs. Effective leaders do not just know about these—they encourage their use and reduce stigma around them.

Practice supportive, positive, and accountable supervision. You can hold high standards and still lead with empathy. People perform better when they feel supported, seen, and valued.

In a promotional setting, what assessors are really looking for here is balance: can you protect your people and still get the job done? Because how you care about your people will shape how they serve the community.

- Maintain operational continuity.
  Ensure that the organization continues to function effectively while managing the incident or crisis. This may involve staffing adjustments, re-assignments, or establishing clear command oversight so nothing falls through the cracks. Large-scale or unexpected unplanned incidents can overwhelm a small agency, or a graveyard team if you do not know your contingency plans, MOUs with allied partners, and what authority and role you have when they do occur.
- Communicate and coordinate resources.
  Identify who needs to be notified and what resources should be activated, and in a testing environment, all resources are an option, even if in your reality of working day-to-day they are not. Don't wait for things to escalate; stay proactive and get the right people in the loop early.

Equally important is demonstrating strategic delegation. Leaders are not expected to perform every task during a critical event personally, and you should not do so. Instead, they must assign responsibilities in a way that ensures the work of completed efficiently while maintaining oversight and accountability.

The best way to effectively delegate is to consider:

- Assigning tasks to individuals with the appropriate expertise or authority. As a note, in assessment centers, you may be limited to who is available based on the instructions.

- Providing clear expectations and guidance along with follow-up. Do not assume that the assessors know that you will do this; you must speak it out loud.
- Delegation is a great development tool and helps maintain supervisory awareness of outcomes, using opportunities to develop and mentor subordinates, giving them experiential learning opportunities.

Delegation should never be confused with abdication; it is not. It is a strategic and intentional distribution of responsibility aligned with both competence and professional development goals when done properly. When candidates demonstrate this mindset in promotional scenarios, it signals that they understand how leaders build capable teams while maintaining responsibility for outcomes, and these competencies are essential for advancing into supervisory and command-level roles.

7. Aligning Responses with Organizational Strategy

Strong candidates show they understand how their decisions connect to the bigger picture. They do not answer in isolation—they align their responses with what the organization is trying to achieve. When discussing topics like community engagement, use of force, staffing, or morale, anchor your response to:

- Strategic plans and agency priorities
- Community survey data and stakeholder expectations
- Department pillars, mission, and values
- Public trust initiatives and legitimacy initiatives
- Crime trends, data analytics, performance metrics and operational realities.

This applies to both sworn and professional staff roles—whether you are in operations or a support function, your decision should reflect how your role contributes to the agency's overall mission and effectiveness. Always think about how you can demonstrate that you are not just thinking tactically, or one-dimensionally—you are thinking broader, like a leader who can connect day-to-day decisions to organizational direction and long-term impact.

8. Response Strategy for High-Risk Scenarios

For complex incidents—such as officer-involved shootings, use-of-force concerns, or allegations of misconduct—panels are evaluating how you think under pressure, how you lead through complexity, and how well you balance operational control with accountability and transparency. Strong responses should reflect the following:

- Incident command understanding—demonstrate clear knowledge of the command structure, ICS. Identify who is in command; this could involve knowing the authority legal for jurisdiction; establish control early, and ensure roles are defined. Show that you can bring order to chaos and maintain span of control.
- Understanding resource allocation and roles—assign the right people to the right tasks—scene security, medical aid, investigations, notifications, and documentation. Be intentional about using specialized units when appropriate and avoid over- or under- deploying resources.
- Monitoring the situation and adjusting as needed—incidents evolve. Good leaders do not just set a plan—they continuously reassess. Are conditions changing? Do you need additional resources? Consider how you minimize overtime due to budget constraints.
- Community and stakeholder transparency—acknowledge the importance of trust. Identify who needs to be informed—command staff, partner agencies, and community stakeholders—emphasize timely, accurate, and appropriate communication within legal and policy compliance.
- Media awareness is crucial during incidents that attract immediate media attention. It is important to coordinate information through the appropriate Public Information Officer (PIO) channels. Understand that the media landscape has evolved; it now includes social media and various styles of journalism that can amplify news coverage. To improve media relations, it is essential to know what information can be released and what should remain confidential, whether in a press release, on camera, or on social media.
- Situational awareness requires a broad perspective. Pay attention to what is occurring at the scene, with your personnel, among the involved parties, within the community, and regarding political dynamics. While it may seem repetitive, it is crucial to prioritize safety, preserve evidence, consider the emotional impact on staff, and assess potential implications that could create a ripple effect in the community.

Scenario Response Blueprint—Example

As you prepare, you can use any combination of response frameworks that work best for you and your learning, retention, and style. Here is an example of integrating IRAC reasoning, mind-mapping, and some of the response strategy concepts into a practical tool you can use for preparing for oral boards, written exercises, or assessment center scenarios.

A Structured Approach for Promotional Assessments

Promotional examinations in law enforcement and public safety frequently include scenario-based questions designed to evaluate a candidate's judgment, leadership reasoning, investigative logic, and communication skills. These scenarios may involve supervisory decision-making, investigative planning, personnel issues, ethical dilemmas, or operational incidents. Candidates who perform well typically demonstrate structured thinking rather than simply reacting to the situation. The blueprint below provides a disciplined approach that integrates three complementary thinking tools: mind-mapping, IRAC reasoning, and clear professional communication.

Step 1: Map the Situation (Mind-Mapping)

Before responding, mentally organize the scenario by identifying the major components of the problem. Remember what topic or issue for the: Center of the Scenario

*Incident, complaint, or operational challenge presented in the question.

Key Branches
PLLT—FIND

- P—Policy (process, procedures, evidence), and you could add people from the Five Ps.
- L—Law (legal authority and compliance)
- L—Liability (risk exposure and public trust)
- T—Training (competency gaps and development needs)
- F—Follow-up/Controls
- I—Impacts (internal and external)

- N—Notifications (chain of command, HR, legal, stakeholders)
- D—Discipline vs. Development

This quick mental map helps candidates avoid tunnel vision and consider the full scope of the situation.

Step 2: Structure Your Thinking (IRAC Model)

Once the scenario is understood, organize your response using the IRAC framework, a structured reasoning method commonly used in legal and investigative analysis.

IRAC Step	*Purpose*	*Example Thinking*
Issue	Identify the core problem or incident	What is the primary issue? What crime, policy violation, or leadership challenge exists?
Rule	Identify relevant law, policy, or procedure	What statutes, departmental policies, or ethical standards apply?
Application	Apply rules to the situation	What investigative steps, supervisory actions, or operational decisions are required?
Conclusion	Provide a clear outcome or direction	What is the appropriate resolution or next step for the organization?

The IRAC model originated in legal education as a method for analyzing legal problems and remains widely used in professional decision-making contexts (Neumann, 2018).

Step 3: Demonstrate Leadership Thinking

Promotional boards are not only evaluating technical knowledge; they are also assessing leadership judgment.

Strong responses typically include:

- Safety and stabilization first
- Respect for policy, law, and constitutional protections
- Clear communication with supervisors and stakeholders
- Professional documentation and accountability
- Consideration of organizational culture and community trust

Candidates should demonstrate an understanding that leadership decisions influence people, policy, processes, and the broader organizational environment.

Step 4: Communicate Clearly and Professionally

When delivering your response:

- Speak in a structured and organized manner
- Avoid rambling or speculation (STAR Method)
- Use professional terminology
- Clearly explain why you are taking specific actions

Evaluators and promotional boards often evaluate how effectively candidates can communicate decisions under pressure, not simply what decisions they make.

Visual Overview

• Scenario Presented

↓

Quick Mental Map

(Policy • Law • Liability • Training • Follow up • Impacts • notifications • documentation)

↓

IRAC Structure

Issue → Rule → Application → Conclusion

↓

Leadership Judgment

(Safety • Policy • Communication • Accountability)

↓

Clear Professional Response

Why This Blueprint Matters

When you can consistently apply structured thinking frameworks, as a candidate and leader, you demonstrate:

- Analytical discipline
- Operational awareness
- Leadership readiness
- Professional communication skills

These qualities are often the distinguishing factors between candidates who simply answer a question and those who demonstrate true promotional readiness.

Panel Interviews: Professional Presence and Judgment

Panel interviews assess readiness for responsibility.

Typical question formats:

- Behavioral (what you have done)
- Scenario-based (what you would do)
- Situational (how you would respond in context)
- Knowledge-based (what you know and how you apply it).

Core evaluation criteria:

- Leadership philosophy—Can you clearly articulate how you lead and why?
- Ethical reasoning—Do you demonstrate sound judgment, fairness, and integrity in complex situations?.
- Policy and legal fluency—Do your decisions align with law, policy, and organizational expectations?
- Communication clarity—Are your responses structured, confident, and easy to follow?
- Decision-making logic—Can you explain not just what you would do, but how you arrived there?
- Alignment with agency values—Do your answers reflect the mission, culture, and priorities of the organization?

A panel interview is where your preparation meets presence, in real-time.

Some Key Features of a Panel Interview

1. Diverse Panel Composition
   Oftentimes, a typical interview panel includes three to five members with varying areas of expertise, but also could have less. Internal participants may include sworn command staff (such as lieutenants or captains), while external participants might be civilian HR managers or community members.[39] The goal is to incorporate diverse insights and reduce bias by evaluating each candidate from multiple professional lenses, reducing subjectivity and increasing reliability of the evaluation.[40] Diversity in panel composition also sends a message about the department's commitment to equity and transparency in the promotion process.

2. Question Types
   Panel interviews are structured to elicit both past behavior and future-oriented thinking. The four common types of questions include:
   - *Behavioral Questions*: Designed to uncover how candidates have handled challenges in the past. These often start with "Tell me about a time when ..." and allow panelists to assess consistency in decision-making and leadership.[41]
   - *Scenario-Based Questions*: Present candidates with complex operational or ethical challenges reflective of the promoted role. For instance, candidates may be asked how they would respond to a use-of-force complaint or a breakdown in team morale. These assess problem-solving and crisis response.
   - *Situational Questions*: Focus on hypothetical, forward-looking situations. These help panelists assess a candidate's alignment with departmental values, judgment under pressure, and adaptability.
   - *Knowledge-Based Questions*: Test the candidate's grasp of current laws, department policies, labor agreements, and leadership protocols. For example, a candidate may be asked to explain steps they would take during an internal investigation.
3. Competency-Based Evaluation
   In most promotional interview processes, candidates are assessed using clearly defined leadership competencies. These competencies allow evaluators to measure performance consistently across candidates an focus on behaviors that are essential for effective leadership in public safety organizations.

   Common competencies evaluated during promotional interviews include:

   - *Leadership and Supervisory Skill*:
     How effectively does the candidate inspire trust, guide teams, and model departmental values and professional conduct.
   - *Decision-Making*:
     Can the candidate analyze information quickly, weigh risks and consequences, and respond decisively in high-stakes or time-sensitive situations?
   - *Communication*:
     Is the candidate clear, persuasive, and professional in their verbal and non-verbal communication? This includes the ability to articulate reasoning, provide direction, and communicate with internal personnel and the public.

- *Policy Knowledge*:
  Does the candidate demonstrate an understanding for departmental policies and procedures, and can they apply those policies accurately, and fairly when addressing operational and personnel issues?
- *Interpersonal Effectiveness*:
  How well does the candidate manage conflict, demonstrate emotional intelligence, and build rapport with personnel, supervisors, other members of the department and the community?

NOTE:
Depending on the classification being tested, there may be additional competencies or specialized evaluation categories. For example, detective promotional examinations may place greater emphasis on investigative logic, analytical reasoning, case management, and evidentiary decision-making.

These competencies are typically evaluated using a structured scoring system, which helps standardize the evaluation process and promote fairness and consistency across candidates.[42,43]

4. Interview Format
   A panel interview generally last 30–60 minutes and follow a semi-structured format and are timed. While the questions are often pre-determined to ensure consistency and reliability of testing, follow-up questions may be used to explore responses in more depth. Panelists typically take notes while you are responding to the questions and candidates may be scored in real-time or after the interview concludes. Structured evaluation forms guide panelists in rating each candidate across competency categories and when there is a variance in scoring, there are further protocols in place to narrow the scoring within a particular margin for a final score.

Benefits of Panel Interviews

1. *Fairness and Objectivity*: Candidates having multiple evaluators can help reduce individual bias and ensure decisions are balanced and evidence based.
2. *Comprehensive Evaluation*: A range of competencies are assessed: technical, relational, and cognitive, offering a holistic view of leadership readiness.

3. *Realistic Job Preview*: Candidates will be required to respond to issues they are likely to encounter if promoted, making the assessment more relevant and authentic, while under pressure.
4. *Consistency and Equity*: Structured interview formats help standardize the process across candidates, reinforcing procedural fairness.

Preparation Strategies for Candidates

- *Know Your Policies*: As referenced for the written examination and assessment center, be well-versed in organizational policies, disciplinary procedures, and state laws.
- *Practice Aloud*: Rehearse responses *out loud* to behavioral and situational questions with a trusted mentor or in a mock interview setting. Create a simi-stressful environment to understand how you will perform under pressure in a realistic setting.
- *Demonstrate Leadership Thinking*: When referencing leadership theories or frameworks, depending on what rank you are seeking, remember that they can show depth if you apply it to your contemporary leadership experience and actions. Using theories such as transformational leadership, servant leadership, or situational leadership models show depth, but they lack the context of application, they will be evaluated differently.
- *Stay Authentic and Professional*: Your demeanor, tone, and presence will be observed as closely as your responses. Remain calm, concise, and avoid preparation drift. If you feel nervous or anxious, take time to pause, take some quiet breaths to slow your heart rated and regulate your physiological response to the stress of the testing environment. Regain your composure and confidently continue.
- *Anticipate Follow-Ups*: On occasion, some panelists may have follow up questions to help them clarify some parts of your response. They may not be able to specifically ask you due to creating consistency in the process, but it is a signal to you that you may have left something out of your response and to do a quick inventory for that topic and situation, to make sure you give a more well-rounded response.
- *Use Strategic Response Frameworks for preparation.*

Study for Performance, Not Memorization

Promotion preparation should be structured, intentional, and focused on how you perform—not just what you remember. Experience alone does not elevate performance. Growth comes from deliberate practice—targeted repetition, meaningful feedback, and continuous refinement.

Study Structure Guidelines

- Study 3–5 days per week (based on your schedule and consistency)
- 1–2 hours per session or focused micro sessions when needed
- Prioritize agency policies and procedures—this is your foundation
- Build cumulative review cycles to reinforce retention over time
- Turn material into testable questions to stimulate real exam thinking.

The goal is not to memorize content only—it is to develop the ability to apply it under pressure, communicate it clearly, and demonstrate sound judgment when it matters most.

Study Stacking Method

Stacking is layered learning, similar to preparing for the written examination, but more narrowly focused for more effective retention, integrated into practice scenarios.

Now that you have a clear understanding of the requirements and expectations for your upcoming promotion in law enforcement, it is crucial to establish a systematic study routine that will pave your way to success. Crafting a personalized study schedule is not merely beneficial but essential for you to effectively absorb and retain the vast amount of information you will encounter. Begin by reflecting on your unique learning style. Whether you thrive through visual aids, auditory materials, or hands-on practice, tailoring your study methods to suit your preferences will enhance your learning experience. It is a good idea to design a weekly study plan that allocates specific time slots for each topic, ensuring that you balance your time between theory, practical skills, and real-life applications.

Organizing your study materials is equally important. Begin to collect relevant handbooks, case studies, and any reference materials that can aid your preparation. Finding a dedicated study space free from distractions will further bolster your focus and productivity. Thinking about how to incorporate practice scenarios that mirror real-world situations in law enforcement and public safety will not only deepen your understanding but also prepare you for the situational questions that may arise during the oral panel interview. It is highly recommended to engage in mock interviews or group study sessions where you can simulate these scenarios with peers, boosting your knowledge, confidence, and communication skills. The strategy is by adopting this structured approach to your preparation, you will maximize your readiness for the promotion process and significantly increase your chances of achieving your goals. Embrace the challenge and remember that organization and dedication will be your greatest allies on this journey.

Setting Up a Study Schedule

Preparing for your promotion examination begins with the critical step of creating a detailed and structured study schedule. Through numerous study group developments, this approach has not only organized time but also reinforced effective study habits that are essential for success. When you have a well-defined schedule, it allows you to focus on the key topics that will arise during your oral panel interview, ensuring that nothing is overlooked. The importance of structure cannot be overstated. A clear framework provides you with a roadmap, helping you allocate specific time slots for different subjects and practice sessions. By breaking down the material into manageable pieces, you can avoid feeling overwhelmed and track your progress systematically.

Developing consistent study habits is equally vital. By committing to a routine, you train your mind to absorb and retain information more effectively. These habits not only enhance your understanding of the topics but also build confidence as the examination date approaches. Remember, prioritizing the key areas and organizing your study time thoughtfully will significantly increase your preparation for the examination process. A structured approach, combined with disciplined habits, empowers you to tackle the challenges of both the written test and the oral panel interview with greater ease and assurance.

Study Plan Overview

- *Duration*: 8–10 weeks (or as recommended by your agency)
- *Weekly Breakdown*: Prioritize topics based on relevance and the time available.

TABLE 4.2B Example of a Weekly Schedule: Assessment Center and Oral Interview Panel Preparation

Week	Focus Area	Study and Preparation Activities	Additional Notes
Week 1	Agency Policies and Procedures	— Review department's general orders, protocols, policies, and SOPs — Understand internal regulations, communication protocols, and reporting procedures — Create summaries for key policies	Begin by prioritizing policies related to your role.
	Leadership and Management	— Study leadership principles (e.g., transformational, situational leadership) — Practice answering leadership-related questions using examples from personal experience	Focus on managing teams, motivation, job satisfaction, and conflict resolution.
Week 2	Laws and Legal Principles	— Review criminal law, constitutional rights, and relevant state/federal laws — Focus on search and seizure, use of force, civil liability, and arrest protocols — Study juvenile justice laws and procedures, or laws that pertain to your industry.	Prioritize scenarios where legal knowledge is critical.
	Oral Interview Skills	— Review common oral interview questions — Practice verbal responses to leadership and management questions — Record and critique yourself on video/audio	Focus on clear, concise responses. Practice timing yourself.
Week 3	Fiscal and Legal Knowledge	— Review budgeting and fiscal accountability — Understand resource allocation, financial management in public safety agencies, and cost-effective planning — Study civil liability, risk management, and audit procedures	Study financial management and accountability principles for your role.
	Scenario Practice	— Practice scenarios related to budget allocation or fiscal decision-making — Role-play decision-making under pressure with a study partner or mentor	Work on concise, structured decision-making.

(Continued)

TABLE 4.2B (Continued)

Week	Focus Area	Study and Preparation Activities	Additional Notes
Week 4	Community Relations	— Study community engagement strategies, including community policing and crisis communication — Review fair and inclusive principles in law enforcement	Focus on communication skills in community-based scenarios.
	Mock Oral Interview	— Participate in a mock interview with a mentor or study group — Receive feedback on your delivery and response strategies	Aim to simulate actual panel conditions.
Week 5	Employee Wellness and Ethics	— Study employee wellness programs, stress management, and mental health in public safety professions — Review the ethics policy in your agency	Consider ethical dilemmas and how to handle them. Consider the STAR method and apply policy.
	Scenario-Based Exercises	— Practice scenarios related to employee wellness, misconduct, and ethics violations — Focus on response strategies for handling conflicts and misconduct	Simulate handling both ethical and interpersonal challenges.
Week 6	Strategic Planning and Management	— Study agency's strategic plan and how leadership plays a role in its execution — Understand union relations, bargaining unit/association policies, and their impact on leadership decisions	Consider how strategic goals relate to daily operations.
	Mock Assessment Center Exercise	— Participate in a mock assessment center (problem-solving scenarios, leadership simulations) — Get feedback from peers or mentors	Practice handling multiple scenarios in a time-constrained environment.
Week 7	Incident Management and Crisis Communication	— Study protocols for handling critical incidents, public relations during crises, and media interactions — Review the agency's approach to crisis management, disaster response	Focus on how to manage a crisis while maintaining public trust.
	Scenario-Based Exercises	— Simulate a public relations or crisis communication scenario with a study partner or mentor — Focus on clear communication and decision-making	Review how to handle disruptive panel questions.

TABLE 4.2B (Continued)

Week	Focus Area	Study and Preparation Activities	Additional Notes
Week 8	Final Review and Practice	—Review all materials studied in previous weeks —Complete mock oral interviews and assessment center exercises —Focus on refining responses to common questions and scenarios	Final week for polishing responses and delivery.
	Final Mock Assessment and Oral Interview Panel	—Participate in a full mock assessment center, followed by an oral interview panel simulation —Receive feedback on strengths and areas for improvement	Treat this as a dress rehearsal for the real exam.

This study schedule is designed for candidates preparing for assessment centers and oral interview panels. It emphasizes a well-rounded approach that includes subject matter review, practical exercises, and mock interviews. The schedule spans 8 weeks and incorporates both individual study and group preparation activities.

- *Daily Sessions*: Aim for 1–2 hours per day of focused study. Adjust the time depending on your progress and comfort level.

Advice for Studying and Guidelines[44]

1. *Self-Assessment*: After each study session, take a reflective pause to evaluate your progress. Ask yourself which topics you feel most assured about and identify areas that may need additional focus. This self-awareness will help you allocate your study time more effectively and target areas for improvement.
2. *Peer and Mentor Feedback*: Actively seek out feedback by engaging with a mentor, colleague, or study group. Sharing your thoughts and experiences not only provides you with constructive insights but also exposes you to different perspectives. Participating in mock interviews or scenario-based exercises with peers can simulate real-world conditions and help you understand what to expect during the actual assessment process.
3. *Practice Under Pressure*: To truly prepare for the high-stakes environment of an assessment, practice your responses within a timed setting. Setting a timer during mock interviews helps mimic the pressure you will face, enabling you to refine your responses and maintain composure when it really counts.

4. *Video and Audio Recording*: Take advantage of technology by recording your oral responses. Watching or listening to your recordings allows you to critique your performance critically. Focus on key elements such as body language, tone of voice, and clarity of expression. Note any habits or idiosyncrasies that may detract from your overall presentation and work on improving them.
5. *Focus on Leadership*: Leadership is often a central theme in both assessment centers and oral interviews. Prepare thoroughly to discuss your approach to various leadership challenges and scenarios. Reflect on past experiences where you have demonstrated leadership, highlighting the skills and qualities that made you effective. Consider recruiting feedback on your leadership style to further refine your responses.

By adopting these detailed study tips and engaging actively in mock assessments, you will cultivate a strong sense of readiness and confidence, positioning yourself to excel in both the assessment center and oral interview panels.

Understanding Your Learning Style

Recognizing that everyone has a unique learning style is essential for effectively tailoring your study methods. By identifying and adapting to your preferred approach, you can significantly enhance your retention and understanding of the material. For instance, some individuals thrive in collaborative settings where discussing and sharing ideas can lead to greater insight, while others may find solitude to be more conducive to deep concentration and introspection.

Key Learning Style Considerations[45]

- *Visual Learners*: If you tend to learn best through visual stimuli, incorporating charts, diagrams, infographics, and instructional videos into your study routine can greatly improve your comprehension. Try creating mind maps to connect concepts visually or watch tutorial videos that illustrate the material. Recording your mock responses to interview questions can also be beneficial; when you review these recordings, you can better gauge your clarity and focus.
- *Auditory Learners*: For those who absorb information more effectively through listening, engaging with the material in a verbal format can be key. Consider reading your notes out loud, discussing the concepts with a study partner, or even recording yourself as you explain the material.

Listening to relevant podcasts or lectures will allow you to hear different perspectives and enhance your overall understanding of the subject.

- *Kinesthetic Learners*: If you are a kinesthetic learner, you thrive on hands-on experiences and active participation. Engaging in role-playing scenarios or conducting mock interviews can help mimic real-life situations, making the learning process more engaging and tactile. You might also benefit from moving around while studying or utilizing tools like flashcards, where you can physically manipulate the material as you learn.

Side Note: In preparing for oral interviews, many individuals discover the immense value of self-recording. Whether through audio or video, capturing your practice sessions allows for effective self-review. Watching or listening to these recordings can reveal critical areas for improvement, such as the overuse of filler words like "um" or "like," which can detract from your overall presentation. Additionally, self-evaluation of body language and facial expressions in these recordings can provide insights into how you might be perceived by an audience, enabling you to approach your interviews with greater confidence and poise.

Creating a Study Group

While the concept of study groups may initially appear to be exclusive or daunting, it is essential for individuals to proactively embrace the opportunity to join or create one. Forming a study group provides a collaborative environment where members can share insights, receive valuable feedback, and gain access to diverse perspectives. By connecting with mentors and peers who are eager to engage in constructive discussions, participants can significantly enhance their learning experience. In essence, you are creating a community of practice, and when you become a part of a structured study group, you tap into the powerful benefits of networking. This experience can inspire you to organize similar open study workshops for other staff members, thereby fostering a culture of continuous learning and support within your professional community.

Benefits of a Study Group

- *Diverse Perspectives*: One of the greatest advantages of being in a study group is the wealth of knowledge that comes from collaborating with individuals in higher positions or diverse roles. These members typically have firsthand experience with the promotion process and can provide invaluable insights, strategies, and tips that can guide you through your own journey.

- *Motivation*: A study group creates a sense of shared commitment among its members. Collective enthusiasm and ambition within the group can be incredibly motivating, helping everyone to stay engaged and focused on their goals. As you witness your peers working diligently, it often inspires you to maintain your own momentum, encouraging a positive cycle of motivation and accountability.
- *Accountability*: One of the substantial benefits of having study partners is the accountability it fosters. Group members can support one another in staying on track with their study schedules, project deadlines, and preparation timelines. Knowing that others are counting on you can serve as a powerful motivator to follow through on your commitments and push yourself to achieve your objectives.

By harnessing the synergy of a study group, individuals can not only enhance their personal development but also contribute to a thriving, supportive community that fosters the success of everyone involved.

Study Topics—What to Focus On?

Grasping the variety of topics that may come up during your oral panel interview is essential for effective preparation. To enhance your readiness, I suggest taking the time to compile a detailed list of key subjects, similar to the ones for the written examination. However, for this list, you are going to refine your study to 10-15 areas of focus. These will be areas that align with the specific examination requirements outlined in the bulletin scope, knowledge, and abilities sections. It will also take into consideration current agency priorities. This targeted approach will not only help you anticipate potential questions but also enable you to demonstrate your knowledge and relevance to the role for which you are applying. Additionally, consider revisiting recent agency initiatives, challenges, and goals, as these can provide valuable context and show your commitment to understanding the broader organizational landscape. Also, what is trending in the national landscape for your specific line of work? What's in the headlines for law enforcement and public safety—because often scenarios are literally ripped from the headlines—what are yours?

Oral Board and Scenario Preparation

- **High-Impact Topic Areas**

1. **Use of Force and Public Transparency**
   - Agency use of force policy
   - Constitutional standards
   - Documentation requirements
   - Supervisory/Management review responsibilities

   Situational Example:
   Body-worn camera footage of a controversial arrest is circulating on social media before your agency releases a statement.

   Why it strengthens preparation
   - Public messaging
   - Policy requirements
   - Officer wellness
   - Community trust
   - Media response
   - Internal morale

   Note: Modern oral boards evaluate judgment in a digital environment, not just tactical legality.

2. **Employee Misconduct and Internal Accountability**
   - Study Focus
   - Progressive discipline
   - Internal Investigations
   - EEO policy
   - Due process

   Situational example:
   A respected senior employee is accused of harassment by a new employee, and the complaint is being discussed informally across the unit.

   Why it strengthens preparation
   - Forces you to balance:
   - Procedural justice
   - Organizational politics

- Reinforce policy and expectations
- Psychological safety

3. **Community Trust and Social Climate Sensitivity**

- Study Focus
- Community engagement strategies
- Cultural competency
- De-escalation
- Public legitimacy

Situational example:
A community group is organizing a protest after a high-profile arrest involving a juvenile.

Why it strengthens preparation
Requires articulation of:

- Community listening and active engagement
- Transparency
- Restorative practices
- Youth justice awareness

4. **Crisis Leadership and Incident Command**
Study Focus

- Incident Command System (ICS)
- Role clarity
- Unified Command
- Resource deployment

Situational example:
Simultaneous protest activity and a natural disaster strain staffing resources.

Why it strengthens preparation
Tests:

- Prioritization
- Resource allocation strategies
- Interagency coordination
- Leadership under competing demands
- Role clarity

The following are additional dynamic topics you can develop for yourself, and there will more specialized policy, procedure, practices and statutes depending on your examination so tailor as you see fit:

5. Wellness and Burnout
6. Recruitment and Retention Challenges
7. Ethical Decision-Making Under Pressure
8. Labor Relations and Union Dynamics
9. Budget and Fiscal Accountability
10. Media Relations and Information Management
11. Technology and AI Integration
12. Diversity and Belonging
13. Juvenile Justice and Vulnerable Populations
14. Conflict Resolution and Team Dynamics
15. Strategic Vision and Organizational Direction

Performance Simulation and Scenario Practice

Create structured scenarios aligned with your study areas of focus.

Preparing for promotional examinations, I have found to effectively prepare for an oral panel interview, one of the most beneficial strategies is to develop hypothetical scenarios that simulate real-life challenges relevant to the position. These scenarios should be thoughtfully designed to test your ability to think critically and respond in a clear, concise, and policy-driven manner. Imagine facing a situation where you need to navigate a complex issue that requires not only your technical knowledge but also your experience and leadership skills. For example, consider a scenario where a significant policy change is met with resistance from team members. How would you address their concerns while ensuring that the implementation aligns with organizational objectives?

Such exercises compel you to draw upon your understanding of pertinent laws, regulations, and best practices, while also tapping into your prior experiences to provide a well-rounded resolution. Preparing for these types of challenges not only sharpens your problem-solving abilities but also boosts your confidence in articulating your thoughts during the interview. By doing so, you will be better equipped to demonstrate your qualifications and decision-making prowess in a high-pressure environment.

Scenario Example:

Question: "How would you handle a situation where there is an allegation of discrimination in the workplace?"

Response Strategy (again, use any combination of response strategy frameworks that work best for you: PLLT FIND, IRAC, Mindmap, STAR):

1. *Policy*: Review and apply your agency's Equal Employment Opportunity (EEO) policy.
2. *Role*: Understand your role and responsibilities as a supervisor or manager.
3. *Action*: What immediate actions will you take? Consider all options while staying within the confines of policy.
4. *Documentation*: Ensure all necessary reports and documentation are filed in accordance with policy.
5. *Follow-Up*: Outline the steps for follow-up, including training and any required interventions, such as Employee Assistance Programs (EAP).

Creating similar scenarios for all potential topics allows you to respond thoughtfully and confidently during the oral panel interview.

Mock Interviews and Feedback Loop

Conducting mock interviews midway through your study period is an invaluable strategy for assessing your readiness and identifying areas that need further development. These practice sessions serve not only as a way to simulate the actual interview environment but also as a means to gauge your progress against your goals. During these mock interviews, it is crucial to seek honest feedback from mentors and colleagues who can provide diverse perspectives on your performance. Their insights can highlight strengths you may not have recognized and pinpoint weaknesses that require further attention. The value of this immediate feedback is immense; it allows you to make quick adjustments and improvements before the real interviews take place.

Creating a feedback loop is just as important. After obtaining feedback, take the time to reflect on what was shared and how you can implement the suggestions. Then, schedule follow-up mock interviews to practice those specific areas of improvement. This iterative process fosters a continuous cycle of growth, ensuring that you not only prepare effectively but also evolve your skills and confidence with each round of feedback. Embracing this proactive approach can significantly enhance your overall readiness and performance in the actual interview setting.

1. Schedule Mock Interviews
    - Identify colleagues or mentors, ideally those who are familiar with the industry you are targeting and can provide valuable insights.

- Aim to conduct these interviews in a realistic setting, such as a conference room or a video call platform, to mimic the actual interview environment.
- Consider scheduling multiple mock interviews to cover various types of interviews (e.g., behavioral, technical, case studies) to gain broad experience.

2. Record Your Performance
   - Use a video or audio recording device to capture the entire mock interview. This will allow you to review your performance and become aware of aspects you might not notice in real-time.
   - Pay close attention to body language: assess whether you maintain good eye contact, sit up straight, and use gestures appropriately.
   - Analyze your speech patterns: note your tone of voice, pace, and clarity of expression. Be aware of filler words (like "um" and "uh") that can detract from your professionalism.
   - Focus on the clarity of your responses: ensure you are answering questions succinctly and directly.
3. Incorporate Feedback
   - After each mock interview, seek constructive feedback from your interviewer. Ask specific questions about your strengths and areas for improvement.
   - Reflect on your self-assessment and compare it with the feedback received to identify consistent themes or discrepancies.
   - Use the feedback to refine your answers. Modify your responses for better clarity and practice them to enhance delivery.
   - Consider preparing a list of common questions related to your industry and formulating your answers based on the feedback to further enhance your responses.
   - Repeat the mock interview process multiple times, integrating new insights and continuously improving with each session.

FINAL PREPARATION: GAME DAY STRATEGY

As the date of the oral panel interview draws near, the final weeks should be dedicated to honing your responses and perfecting your overall presentation. Begin by revisiting the key topics and subjects you have studied, ensuring you have a deep understanding of the material. It is important to not only memorize facts but also to be able to discuss them with insight and clarity.

Set aside time each day for practice. This might include rehearsing answers to common interview questions, as well as formulating responses to potential follow-up inquiries. Speaking clearly and confidently is essential, so consider practicing in front of a mirror or recording yourself to review your body language and vocal tone. You may also want to ask a friend or mentor to conduct a mock interview, which can provide valuable feedback and help ease any nerves.

In addition to your verbal preparation, pay attention to your presentation. Choose professional attire that makes you feel confident and comfortable, and ensure that you present yourself well overall. A polished appearance can enhance your self-assurance and make a positive impression on the panel. Lastly, take care of your mental and physical well-being in these final days. Get plenty of rest, stay hydrated, and engage in activities that help you relax and focus. By investing this time in preparation, you will be setting yourself up for success in the interview ahead.

Final Tips for the Oral Panel Interview:

- Know Your Audience: Before your panel presentation, take the time to research the individuals who will be joining you. Familiarize yourself with their backgrounds, roles, and perspectives within the relevant industry or topic. Understanding these elements will not only enhance your credibility but also allow you to tailor your responses in a way that resonates with their interests and concerns.
- Engage with All Panelists: Interaction is key during a panel discussion. Make a conscious effort to establish eye contact with each panelist, regardless of whether they appear engaged or reserved. This practice helps to create a connection and makes each member feel acknowledged. By addressing the entire panel, you promote a more inclusive atmosphere and encourage dialogue among all participants.
- Stay Concise and Clear: When responding to questions, aim for clarity and brevity. Ensure that your answers provide thorough insights while avoiding unnecessary jargon and filler content. Focus on delivering the most relevant points that directly address the question. This not only keeps your responses impactful but also respects the time and attention of your audience and fellow panelists.

Applied Leadership and Critical Thinking Questions

1. How does your current understanding of your agency's promotional process influence the way you prepare, and where any gaps in that understanding create risk for your performance or outcomes?
2. Many candidates study hard but not strategically. Based on your current approach, how are you ensuring your preparation aligns with what is actually being evaluated (decision-making, communication, leadership judgment) rather than just content recall?
3. When faced with a complex scenario in an assessment center or oral board, how do you ensure your response demonstrates not only knowledge, but structured leadership thinking; for example policy, risk, people, and organizational impact?
4. In what ways are you engaging in deliberate practice such as timed scenarios, mock interviews, or feedback loops to improve performance, rather than relying solely on experience or repetition?
5. Think about a recent policy or leadership topic you studied. How would you translate that knowledge into a real-time decision during a high-pressure incident or personnel issue?
6. How well do your responses and preparation reflect your organization's mission, priorities, and current challenges, and how might misalignment impact your credibility during the promotional process?
7. After practicing a scenario or mock interview, how do you evaluate your performance, identify gaps, adjust your strategy to improve? What specific feedback mechanisms are you using?

KEY TAKEAWAYS

- Promotion isn't about chance: it is about strategy. The candidates who succeed are the ones who understand how the system works and prepare accordingly and intentionally, not just those who work the hardest.
- The process is designed to evaluate how you think as a leader, not just what you know. If your preparation does not include applying knowledge with a working practitioner mindset under pressure, you are leaving a critical gap.

- Experience alone will not carry you through the this process, but growth comes from intentional, structured practice, especially when you are pushing yourself beyond your comfort zone and outside of what you are familiar with.
- Every phase of the exam, written, assessment center, or board is connected and strong, candidates prepare in a way that builds consistency across all three, not in isolation.
- The most competitive candidates do not just prepare for the test, they prepare for the role and demonstrate awareness of people, policy, organizational priorities, and the broader impact of their decisions. As a note: depending on what rank or classification in which you are promoting into, for example, frontline positions into supervisory or middle management positions, will require you to be more technical and explain detailed policy steps, processes and procedures.

CONCLUSION

Establishing a structured study routine, focusing on critical topics, rehearsing various scenarios, and effectively framing your responses will comprehensively prepare you for the oral panel interview process. By investing time in focused study, actively seeking constructive feedback, and developing strategies to manage the inevitable pressures of the interview setting, you can significantly elevate your chances of success. Remember, preparation is about more than rote memorization; it is about applying your knowledge and experiences in ways that not only reflect your leadership abilities but also resonate with the core values and goals of your agency. Embrace this opportunity to demonstrate your readiness for promotion and the transformative impact you can bring to your future role.

KEY TERMS

Promotional Architecture—a competitive system through which law enforcement agencies evaluate, rank, and select candidates for advancement, encompassing formal testing, evaluation phases, and organizational expectations.

Examination Bulletin—an official agency announcement outlining the promotional process, including eligibility requirements, timelines, testing components, and evaluation criteria.

Certification List (Eligibility List)—a ranked list of candidates who have successfully completed the promotional process and are eligible for selection based on scoring and civil service rules.

PLLT-FIND Framework—a response model emphasizing Policy, Law, Liability, Training, Follow-up, Impacts, Notifications, and Discipline/Development in decision-making.

IRAC Model (Issue, Rule, Application, Conclusion)—an analytical framework used to structure responses to investigative or scenario-based questions, demonstrating logical reasoning and clarity.

STAR-R Method (Situation, Task, Action, Result, Reflection)—a structured approach for answering behavioral interview questions, emphasizing experience, decision-making, outcomes, and leadership growth.

Pre-During-Post Framework—a phased approach to decision-making that addresses prevention, real-time management, and post-incident accountability and improvement.

Study Stacking—a learning method that layers study material over time, reinforcing retention through cumulative review and repeated practice.

Voices from the Field Installment Four: The Transition to Mid-Management

This *Voices from the Field* installment builds on the mindset, preparation suggestions, and pitfalls-to-avoid themes, to offer advice specific to those seeking middle-management positions. Arguably, the professional shift to a mid-management role like Lieutenant may be the most substantial in one's career trajectory. In this capacity, a mid-manager serves as a critical conduit between command staff and frontline supervisors and personnel. Our respondents consistently highlighted that this change requires a recalibration in mindset and approach, as well as a recalibration of how one prepares for such a promotion.

The Mid-Management Conduit

Our respondents confirmed that successful mid-managers are able to translate the vision of the command staff to the frontline teams who actually execute that vision. This skillful translation requires a genuine investment in the success of others.

A Sergeant from a small municipal Police Department in California spotlighted this investment in others, emphasizing the importance of empowering others without being overbearing. "I had to shift my mindset from "How do I solve this?" to "How do I help others succeed?" Mid-management is where you learn to guide people without micromanaging them. I prepared by talking to mentors, reading leadership material, and being honest with myself about where I needed to mature. Ultimately, know your strengths and weaknesses, it will mold you to be a better and effective leader."

Risk management is a prominent topic in both the leadership literature[46] and public safety industry[47]. A Chief of Police from a small municipal Police Department in California emphasized the role of mid-managers as risk managers. "Mid-management is a challenging transition because your responsibilities extend beyond yourself and your team members. You are now responsible for your agency. It is essential to adopt a risk management perspective and seek opportunities to prevent issues, rather than a reactive approach."

The Professional Development Marathon

Mirroring our previous discussion of best practices for those seeking frontline leadership promotions, preparing yourself for a mid-management role requires a longstanding investment in your own professional development. While technical and role-specific expertise is a good start, successful candidates are often those who proactively seek out training, education, and mentoring on a diverse array of substantive topics and skill sets. Undeniably, these investments in yourself should take place long before a promotional vacancy.

A lieutenant from a large municipal police department in California described their self-investment for promotional readiness:

> I volunteered for other assignments within the department (Hostage Negotiation member, academy instructor, etc.), applied for trainings (especially those involved leadership and development aspects), and achieved my masters with the LEPSL program.[48]

A captain from a very large county sheriff's department in Florida emphasized the key competencies that demonstrated they were ready to serve their organization at the next level in the hierarchy:

> The most effective actions in demonstrating my readiness for the next level were consistently taking ownership, seeking out responsibilities beyond my current role, and focusing on developing the people around me. I made it a point to solve problems instead of simply elevating them, and I regularly provided thoughtful recommendations supported by data and policy. I also worked to model calm, steady leadership in high-pressure situations and maintain strong communication with both supervisors and peers. By demonstrating reliability, initiative, and the ability to think strategically, I showed organizational leadership that I was already functioning at the next level before ever holding the title.

A Human-Centric Skill Set

Respondents consistently highlighted that mid-managers must possess advanced human-centric skills. Sometimes referred to as "soft skills," and including empirically proven concepts like emotional intelligence,[49] these communication, interpersonal, and self-regulation skills are essential to execute the conduit role inherent in mid-management.

A sergeant from a small municipal police department in California described the value of several human-centric skills:

> Understanding people, how they think, react, communicate, and struggle was more important than any textbook skill. Technical knowledge matters, but being able to stay calm under pressure, talk to anyone with respect, and show good judgment in tough moments is what truly moved me forward.

A tribal chief of police in Texas links successful leadership with the ability to recognize and tailor one's leadership approach to the individual situation, often referred to as adaptive leadership.[50] This adaptation requires the ability to understand others' needs and the broader context, which are arguably high-level interpersonal and human-centric skills:

> The most crucial skill I developed was understanding when to lead with a servant mindset and when to step forward with a warrior mindset. Preparing for promotion required learning how to balance humility, service, and support for my officers with the ability to act firmly and assertively when the situation demanded it. Building this balance sharpened my judgment, strengthened my leadership

presence, and ensured I could lead effectively in both day to day and high-risk environments.

An undersheriff from a large county sheriff's department in California added an important nuance to the development of human-centric skills, not letting one's own ego and public safety demeanor detract from collaborative relationships, "Education! I tried to learn as much as I could, not only about law enforcement but about everything the county is responsible for… I could engage without the 'cop ego' in a collaborative meeting. It is one path to promotion, but an entirely different path to being successful once the promotion occurs."

The Challenge of the "Balcony Perspective"

Public safety is disproportionately comprised of assertive, goal-oriented individuals.[51] Several respondents candidly shared the challenges posed by a mid-management role that requires a more detached and delegation-based approach to problem-solving.

A captain from a medium-sized municipal police department in California candidly reflected on the personal cost of the mid-management transition:

> I was unprepared for the feeling of not really being a cop anymore. It was almost depressing and I contemplated whether I really wanted the job. For someone who is a get things done type of person it was a difficult transition to move toward more delegation . I find that setting deadlines for subordinates has been really helpful for me and helps with accountability.

A lieutenant from a very large municipal police department in California described this transition as the "balcony perspective":

> I had to make the mental shift from being focused on the task at hand to a balcony perspective. Trying to always see how an issue relates on a global perspective rather than what was in front of me. Then upon my promotion, I no longer focused on a problem affecting one patrol squad but how might that one issue affect all 8 of my patrol squads, which in turn affects both service areas, which then affected the entire division.

This *Voices from the Field* section on the middle-management role in a hierarchical organization reaffirmed some major themes from the book, while also injecting several new critical points into the analysis. Respondents highlighted that mid-management promotional preparation is a marathon, not a sprint, and the importance of human-centric skills, not just technical, role-specific knowledge. But respondents also candidly shared the challenges and opportunities inherent in the broader perspective and approach required at this level.

Concept Bootcamp: Emotional Readiness for Promotion

Many experts argue that a significant part of the promotional process is introspective. Successful promotion is in part about mastering skills and functions associated with your current rank and role. However, to truly demonstrate your holistic readiness for both promotion and the associated leadership responsibilities, you have to be emotionally ready for promotion. The below concepts related, directly and indirectly, with this key pillar of promotional readiness.

- *Imposter Syndrome*: Evidence suggests that imposter syndrome is a commonplace reflective feeling experienced by high-level leadership in the private sector, public safety, and many arenas associated with high-performing individuals.[52] [53] According to psychology experts, *imposter syndrome* is a more casual term for the well-studied dynamic called impostor phenomenon.[54] Moreover, this self-feeling might disproportionately impact individuals from traditionally marginalized groups historically underrepresented in high level leadership roles.[55]

  Downing et al (2020) define this concept as follows:

  The impostor phenomenon (IP) is a psychological cycle experienced by individuals who, despite successes, are plagued by self-doubt and a concern of being identified as fraudulent.[56]

  In the public safety professions, some level of imposter syndrome is likely ubiquitous. However, if allowed to persist and expand, extreme feelings of imposter syndrome can contribute negatively to mental health, stress, and decrease job performance. As a result, leaders should take proactive steps to recognize their self-worth and intentionally combat the mental gymnastics inherent in the experience of impostor syndrome. In *Tackling Imposter Syndrome,* Cordico recommends five tangible strategies:[57]

- "Build a network of peers"
- "Recognize and remember your strengths"
- "Change the way you talk to yourself"
- "Continue to educate yourself"
- "Accept that perfection isn't realistic."

This is sage advice that all leadership should follow to recognize, reflect on, and mitigate the harms of imposter syndrome.

- *Emotional Intelligence (EI)*: Modern organizations are increasingly expected to nurture and expect employees at all levels to develop emotional intelligence skills. According to recognized emotional intelligence firms, EI involves enhanced ability to recognize and manage one own's emotions, empathize with others, and effectively navigate relationships[58].

  Proponents of emotional intelligence in public safety argue that it improves communication skills both in the field and with colleagues, increases empathy, facilitates effective decision-making, and aids in deescalation in tense encounters in the field. A workplace culture that expects advanced EI skills has a multitude of advantages for an organization, including recruitment, retention, and succession planning advantages. Like all core leadership competencies, evidence shows that EI can be actively taught and learned at the individual and organizational levels[59].
- *Active Listening*: Many experts argue that active listening is a core leadership competency relevant to every role and rank within public safety organizations. Listening is not only about communicating information or resolving the issue at hand; listening can be an opportunity to build relationships, nurture trust, and foster collective buy-in from both a leadership and management perspective. Gordon Graham offers the following actionable recommendations for becoming a better active listener:

First, make eye contact and stay in the moment. Nodding your head and using simple gestures or verbal affirmations keeps the person speaking engaged. Don't forget to identify important or supporting elements of the conversation. Then, summarize or reframe what the person is telling you. Try not to interrupt the speaker. And wait for a pause to ask questions. It is also important to pay attention to non-verbal cues. Limit judgments and ask clarifying questions as the opportunities arise.[60]

Graham's advice dovetails well with research in the field of communications, which consistently finds that the vast majority of communication is nonverbal, with body language and tone of voice prominent in the interaction.[61]

- *Feedback Fluency*: A mission-critical element of the leadership skill dossier is the ability to provide quality, actionable feedback to those you lead. Leaders at all levels of an organization must be intentional in how they deliver both praise and constructive criticism to help grow those within the organization to maximize their potential, as well as organizational efficacy.

Feedback does not exist in a vacuum; rather, it dovetails with a broader organizational context and lived history. As Deputy Chief Ben Murphy of the East Windsor Police Department in Connecticut puts it: "If the criticism comes from a trusted colleague, mentor, or friend, it's likely rooted in concern and thoughtfulness."[62] Like many leadership responsibilities, successful feedback, regardless of its substance, is predicated on the leader establishing themselves as trustworthy, honest, and as a servant to the organization. Regardless of how well the micro-moment providing feedback is executed, it depends on that leader having firmly established themselves as someone who leads others with integrity and with the goals, mission, and long-term health of the organization at the forefront.

Providing positive feedback to those you lead is likely easier and more natural compared to providing constructive criticism. However, that positive feedback still needs to be delivered with intention and specificity. Hollow praise filled with soaring verbiage, even when done publicly, may boost morale but lacks the precision necessary to recognize and encourage continued excellent performance. Praise that is coupled with specific, tangible examples can serve the person being praised, as well as others who now have an actionable playbook that can be applied to other similar situations, both in the field and within the organization.

Similarly, constructive criticism must be delivered with forethought and precision. Holding others accountable and providing constructive criticism is a key skill that many leaders struggle with. In *Harvard Business Review*, Patrick Thean (2023) offers some tangible best practices in "How to Give (and Receive) Critical Feedback".[63] Thean argues that creating a long-standing coaching approach to leadership is not only a best practice, but helps new leaders in particular create an environment in which feedback of all types of normalized. Thus, constructive criticism and holding others accountable becomes a regular part of the dialogue between the leader and those being lead. More specifically, he recommends holding regular individual meetings, held in private, that provide an environment for feedback and related discussion and dialogue. While challenging for many leaders at all levels, the Calibre Press Training Network reaffirms the centrality of constructive criticism to professional development: "[c]riticism helps us self-reflect, set goals for development and continue our personal and professional growth."[64]

NOTES

1 Jones, T., and Peters, L. (2022). *Promotion Patterns in Law Enforcement: A Statistical Analysis*. Journal of Police Leadership, *10*(3), 45-62.
2 Bureau of Justice Statistics. (2023). *Promotional Pathways in Local Law Enforcement: Challenges and Opportunities*. Bureau of Justice.
3 Smith, A. (2021). *Career Development and Promotions in U.S. Law Enforcement Agencies*. Law Enforcement Research Journal, *15*(4), 102-117.
4 International Association of Chiefs of Police. (n.d.). *Testing and assessment centers*. https://www.theiacp.org/testing-assessment-centers
5 Nancy Perry, "IACP 2025 Quick Take: Using AI in Candidate Selection, Promotions and Annual Reviews," *Police1*, October 22, 2025, hleadership-fromttps://www.police1.com/artificial-intelligence/iacp-2025-quick-take-using-ai-in-candidate-selection-promotions-and-annual-reviews
6 Nancy Perry, "IACP 2025 Quick Take: Using AI in Candidate Selection, Promotions and Annual Reviews," *Police1*, October 22, 2025, https://www.police1.com/artificial-intelligence/iacp-2025-quick-take-using-ai-in-candid ate-selection-promotions-and-annual-reviews
7 Police Executive Research Forum. (2018). *Testing and Selection of New First-Line Supervisors*. Washington, DC: Police Executive Research Forum.
8 Police Executive Research Forum. (2018). *Testing and Selection of New First-Line Supervisors*. Washington, DC: Police Executive Research Forum.
9 Police Executive Research Forum. (2018). *Testing and Selection of New First-Line Supervisors*. Washington, DC: Police Executive Research Forum.
10 Police Executive Research Forum. (2018). *Testing and Selection of New First-Line Supervisors*. Washington, DC: Police Executive Research Forum.

11 International Task Force on Assessment Center Guidelines, *Guidelines and Ethical Considerations for Assessment Center Operations*, Journal of Management, 2015.
12 President's Task Force on 21st Century Policing, *Final Report of the President's Task Force on 21st Century Policing* (Washington, DC: Office of Community Oriented Policing Services, 2015).
13 Nancy Perry, *26 on 2026: A Police Leadership Playbook*, Police1, December 29, 2025, discussing emerging leadership priorities such as active shooter preparedness, technology governance, staffing challenges, and crisis response coordination.
14 Nancy Perry, *26 on 2026: A Police Leadership Playbook*, Police1, December 29, 2025, discussing emerging leadership priorities such as active shooter preparedness, technology governance, staffing challenges, and crisis response coordination.
15 Jim Morrissey, "How to Design an Effective Active Shooter Exercise," *Police1*, emphasizing multi-disciplinary planning, coordination, and debriefing in active threat training.
16 Police Executive Research Forum. (2018). *Testing and Selection of New First-Line Supervisors*. Washington, DC: Police Executive Research Forum.
17 International Association of Chiefs of Police. (2019). *Police Officer Promotional Testing and Assessment Centers*. Alexandria, VA: IACP.
18 International Association of Chiefs of Police. (2019). *Police Promotional Testing and Assessment Centers*. Alexandria, VA: IACP.
19 Police Executive Research Forum. (2018). *Testing and Selection of New First-Line Supervisors*. Washington, DC: Police Executive Research Forum.
20 Cascio, W. F., and Aguinis, H. (2019). *Applied Psychology in Talent Management* (8th ed.). Thousand Oaks, CA: Sage.
21 Thornton, G. C., and Rupp, D. E. (2006). *Assessment Centers in Human Resource Management.* Lawrence Erlbaum Associates.
22 Peter G. Northouse, *Leadership: Theory and Practice* (Thousand Oaks, CA: Sage Publications, 2018).
23 Peter A. Facione, *Critical Thinking: What It Is and Why It Counts* (Millbrae, CA: Insight Assessment, 2015).
24 Daniel Goleman, *Working with Emotional Intelligence* (New York: Bantam Books, 1998).
25 Bolman, L. G., and Deal, T. E. (2017). *Reframing organizations: Artistry, choice, and leadership* (6th ed.). Jossey-Bass.
26 Max H. Bazerman and Don A. Moore, *Judgment in Managerial Decision Making* (Hoboken, NJ: Wiley, 2012).
27 Yukl, G. (2013). *Leadership in Organizations.* Pearson.
28 Lee G. Bolman and Terrence E. Deal, *Reframing Organizations: Artistry, Choice, and Leadership*, 6th ed. (San Francisco: Jossey-Bass, 2017).

29 Thornton, G. C., and Rupp, D. E. (2006). *Assessment Centers in Human Resource Management: Strategies for Prediction, Diagnosis, and Development.* Mahwah, NJ: Lawrence Erlbaum Associates.
30 Joiner, L. M. (2019). Emotional intelligence in assessment centers: Predicting performance in simulated law enforcement scenarios. *Police Practice and Research*, *20*(2), 101–114.
31 Collins, P. D., and Schmidt, F. L. (1993). Personality, integrity, and assessment center performance of law enforcement personnel. *Personnel Psychology*, *46*(2), 295–312.
32 Schmidt, F. L., and Hunter, J. E. (1998). The validity and utility of selection methods in personnel psychology. *Psychological Bulletin*, *124*(2), 262–274.
33 Silzer, R., and Church, A. H. (2009). The pearls and perils of identifying potential. *Industrial and Organizational Psychology*, *2*(4), 377–412.
34 30x30 Initiative, "Women in Policing: What the Data Reveal About Representation," Police1, March 14, 2026, https://www.police1.com/women-in-law-enforcement/where-are-the-women-in-policing-what-the-data-reveal
35 Neumann, R. K. (2018). Legal reasoning and legal writing: Structure, strategy, and style (8th ed.). Wolters Kluwer.
36 K. Anders Ericsson (2008). "Deliberate Practice and the Acquisition of Expert Performance: A General Overview," *Academic Emergency Medicine, 15*(11), 988–994.
37 Lyons, M. (2025, February 27). *Use the STAR Interview Method to Land Your Next Job*. Harvard Business Review. https://hbr.org/2025/02/use-the-star-interview-method-to-land-your-next-job
38 Redick, J. (2022). *Survival Guide to Law Enforcement Promotional Preparation.* Curry Brothers Publishing
39 William G. Cunningham, *The Interviewer's Handbook* (New York: McGraw-Hill Education, 2020).
40 George C. Thornton III and Deborah E. Rupp, *Assessment Centers in Human Resource Management: Strategies for Prediction, Diagnosis, and Development* (Mahwah, NJ: Lawrence Erlbaum Associates, 2006).
41 Michael A. Campion, David K. Palmer, and James E. Campion, "A Review of Structure in the Selection Interview," *Personnel Psychology*, *47*(3) (1194): 655-702.
42 Peter G. Northouse, *Leadership: Theory and Practice*, 8th ed. (Thousand Oaks, CA: Sage Publications, 2018).
43 Daniel Goleman, *Working with Emotional Intelligence* (New York: Bantam Books, 1998).
44 Redick, J. (2022). *Survival Guide to Law Enforcement Promotional Preparation.* Curry Brothers Publishing
45 Redick, J. (2022). *Survival Guide to Law Enforcement Promotional Preparation.* Curry Brothers Publishing

46 Kaplan, R. S., and Mikes, A. (2012, June). Managing risks: A new framework. Harvard Business Review. https://hbr.org/2012/06/managing-risks-a-new-framework

47 Graham, G. (2021, November 17). Identifiable risks are manageable risks. Lexipol. https://www.lexipol.com/resources/blog/identifiable-risks-are-manageable-risks/

48 University of San Diego. (n.d.). Master of Science in Law Enforcement & Public Safety Leadership. https://onlinedegrees.sandiego.edu/masters-law-enforcement-leadership/

49 See emotional intelligence section of the Concept Bootcamp for a full discussion

50 See adaptive leadership section of the Concept Bootcamp for a full discussion

51 Beshears, M. L. (2021, November 1). The impact of personality on performance. Police1. https://www.police1.com/police-leader-playbook/articles/the-impact-of-personality-on-performance-2e1hbVAsk5t0yEFW/

52 Cordico Staff. (2022, July 29). *Tackling imposter syndrome mentality.* Police1. https://www.police1.com/health-wellness/articles/tackling-imposter-syndrome-mentality-Lx6qpUOrvMjbNVIE/

53 Dorsey, K. D. (2023, June 2). *You're not powerless in the face of imposter syndrome.* Harvard Business Review. https://hbr.org/2023/06/youre-not-powerless-in-the-face-of-imposter-syndrome

54 Garba, R., Coleman, C., and Kelley, T. (2024). *The impostor phenomenon and mental health.* In K. Cokley (Ed.), *The impostor phenomenon: Psychological research, theory, and interventions* (pp. 61–79). American Psychological Association. https://doi.org/10.1037/0000397-004

55 Dorsey, K. D. (2023, June 2). *You're not powerless in the face of imposter syndrome.* Harvard Business Review. https://hbr.org/2023/06/youre-not-powerless-in-the-face-of-imposter-syndrome

56 Downing, M. S., Arthur-Mensah, N., and Zimmerman, J. (2020). *Impostor phenomenon: Considerations for leadership practice. International Journal of Organization Theory & Behavior, 23*(2), 173–187. https://doi.org/10.1108/IJOTB-05-2019-0065

57 Cordico Staff. (2022, July 29). *Tackling imposter syndrome mentality.* Police1. https://www.police1.com/health-wellness/articles/tackling-imposter-syndrome-mentality-Lx6qpUOrvMjbNVIE/

58 TalentSmartEQ. (2025). *Emotional Intelligence Programs & EQ Skills Training.* Retrieved from https://www.talentsmarteq.com/

59 Police1. (2025). *Emotional Intelligence: The Hidden Skill Every Police Officer Needs.* Retrieved from https://www.police1.com/police-training/emotional-intelligence-the-hidden-skill-every-police-officer-needs.

60 Graham, G (2021). Active Listening in Public Safety: A Critical Skill. Lexipol. https://www.lexipol.com/resources/todays-tips/active-listening-in-public-safety-a-critical-skill/

61 Mehrabian, A., and Wiener, M. (1967). Decoding of inconsistent communications. *Journal of Personality and Social Psychology, 6*(1), 109–114. https://doi.org/10.1037/h0024532

62 Murphy, B. (2024, October 11). *Criticism got you down? Here's how smart officers turn it into a superpower.* Police1. https://www.police1.com/patrol-issues/criticism-got-you-down-heres-how-smart-officers-turn-it-into-a-superpower[1](https://www.police1.com/patrol-issues/criticism-got-you-down-heres-how-smart-officers-turn-it-into-a-superpower)

63 Thean, P. (2023, June 30). *How to give (and receive) critical feedback.* Harvard Business Review. https://hbr.org/2023/06/how-to-give-and-receive-critical-feedback (https://hbr.org/2023/06/how-to-give-and-receive-critical-feedback)

64 Gilmartin, K. (2018, September 18). *Making criticism constructive.* Calibre Press. https://calibrepress.com/2018/09/making-criticism-constructive/[1](https://www.mybib.com/tools/apa-citation-generator)

REFERENCES

30x30 Initiative. (2026, March 14). Women in policing: What the data reveal about representation. Police1. https://www.police1.com/women-in-law-enforcement/where-are-the-women-in-policing-what-the-data-reveal

Bazerman, M. H., and Moore, D. A. (2012). *Judgment in managerial decision-making*. Wiley.

Beshears, M. L. (2021, November 1). The impact of personality on performance. Police1. https://www.police1.com/police-leader-playbook/articles/the-impact-of-personality-on-performance-2e1hbVAsk5t0yEFW/

Bolman, L. G., and Deal, T. E. (2017). *Reframing organizations: Artistry, choice, and leadership* (6th ed.). Jossey-Bass.

Bureau of Justice Statistics. (2023). *Promotional pathways in local law enforcement: Challenges and opportunities*.

Campion, M. A., Palmer, D. K., and Campion, J. E. (1994). A review of structure in the selection interview. *Personnel Psychology, 47*(3), 655–702.

Cascio, W. F., and Aguinis, H. (2019). *Applied psychology in talent management* (8th ed.). Sage.

Collins, P. D., and Schmidt, F. L. (1993). Personality, integrity, and assessment center performance of law enforcement personnel. *Personnel Psychology, 46*(2), 295–312.

Cordico Staff. (2022, July 29). Tackling imposter syndrome mentality. Police1. https://www.police1.com/health-wellness/articles/tackling-imposter-syndrome-mentality-Lx6qpUOrvMjbNVlE/

Cunningham, W. G. (2020). *The interviewer's handbook*. McGraw-Hill Education.

Dorsey, K. D. (2023, June 2). You're not powerless in the face of imposter syndrome. *Harvard Business Review*. https://hbr.org/2023/06/youre-not-powerless-in-the-face-of-imposter-syndrome

Downing, M. S., Arthur-Mensah, N., and Zimmerman, J. (2020). Impostor phenomenon: Considerations for leadership practice. *International Journal of Organization Theory & Behavior, 23*(2), 173–187. https://doi.org/10.1108/IJOTB-05-2019-0065

Ericsson, K. A. (2008). Deliberate practice and the acquisition of expert performance: A general overview. *Academic Emergency Medicine, 15*(11), 988–994.

Facione, P. A. (2015). *Critical thinking: What it is and why it counts*. Insight Assessment.

Garba, R., Coleman, C., and Kelley, T. (2024). The impostor phenomenon and mental health. In K. Cokley (Ed.), *The impostor phenomenon: Psychological research, theory, and interventions* (pp. 61–79). American Psychological Association. https://doi.org/10.1037/0000397-004

Gilmartin, K. (2018, September 18). Making criticism constructive. Calibre Press. https://calibrepress.com/2018/09/making-criticism-constructive/

Goleman, D. (1998). *Working with emotional intelligence*. Bantam Books.

Graham, G. (2021). Active listening in public safety: A critical skill. Lexipol. https://www.lexipol.com/resources/todays-tips/active-listening-in-public-safety-a-critical-skill/

Graham, G. (2021, November 17). Identifiable risks are manageable risks. Lexipol. https://www.lexipol.com/resources/blog/identifiable-risks-are-manageable-risks/

International Association of Chiefs of Police. (n.d.). Testing and assessment centers. https://www.theiacp.org/testing-assessment-centers

International Association of Chiefs of Police. (2019). *Police promotional testing and assessment centers*.

International Task Force on Assessment Center Guidelines. (2015). Guidelines and ethical considerations for assessment center operations. *Journal of Management*.

Joiner, L. M. (2019). Emotional intelligence in assessment centers: Predicting performance in simulated law enforcement scenarios. *Police Practice and Research, 20*(2), 101–114.

Jones, T., and Peters, L. (2022). Promotion patterns in law enforcement: A statistical analysis. *Journal of Police Leadership, 10*(3), 45–62.

Kaplan, R. S., and Mikes, A. (2012, June). Managing risks: A new framework. *Harvard Business Review*. https://hbr.org/2012/06/managing-risks-a-new-framework

Mehrabian, A., and Wiener, M. (1967). Decoding of inconsistent communications. *Journal of Personality and Social Psychology, 6*(1), 109–114. https://doi.org/10.1037/h0024532

Morrissey, J. (n.d.). How to design an effective active shooter exercise. Police1.

Murphy, B. (2024, October 11). Criticism got you down? Here's how smart officers turn it into a superpower. Police1. https://www.police1.com/patrol-issues/criticism-got-you-down-heres-how-smart-officers-turn-it-into-a-superpower

Neumann, R. K. (2018). *Legal reasoning and legal writing: Structure, strategy, and style* (8th ed.). Wolters Kluwer.

Northouse, P. G. (2018). *Leadership: Theory and practice* (8th ed.). Sage Publications.

Perry, N. (2025, October 22). IACP 2025 quick take: Using AI in candidate selection, promotions and annual reviews. Police1. https://www.police1.com/artificial-intelligence/iacp-2025-quick-take-using-ai-in-candidate-selection-promotions-and-annual-reviews

Perry, N. (2025, December 29). 26 on 2026: A police leadership playbook. Police1.

Police1. (2025). Emotional intelligence: The hidden skill every police officer needs. https://www.police1.com/police-training/emotional-intelligence-the-hidden-skill-every-police-officer-needs

Police Executive Research Forum. (2018). *Testing and selection of new first-line supervisors.*

President's Task Force on 21st Century Policing. (2015). *Final report of the President's Task Force on 21st Century Policing.* Office of Community Oriented Policing Services.

Redick, J. (2022). *Survival guide to law enforcement promotional preparation.* Curry Brothers Publishing.

Schmidt, F. L., and Hunter, J. E. (1998). The validity and utility of selection methods in personnel psychology. *Psychological Bulletin, 124*(2), 262–274.

Silzer, R., and Church, A. H. (2009). The pearls and perils of identifying potential. *Industrial and Organizational Psychology, 2*(4), 377–412.

Smith, A. (2021). Career development and promotions in U.S. law enforcement agencies. *Law Enforcement Research Journal, 15*(4), 102–117.

TalentSmartEQ. (2025). Emotional intelligence programs & EQ skills training. https://www.talentsmarteq.com/

Thean, P. (2023, June 30). How to give (and receive) critical feedback. *Harvard Business Review.* https://hbr.org/2023/06/how-to-give-and-receive-critical-feedback

Thornton, G. C., and Rupp, D. E. (2006). *Assessment centers in human resource management: Strategies for prediction, diagnosis, and development.* Lawrence Erlbaum Associates.

University of San Diego. (n.d.). Master of Science in law enforcement & public safety leadership. https://onlinedegrees.sandiego.edu/masters-law-enforcement-leadership/

Yukl, G. (2013). *Leadership in organizations.* Pearson.

CHAPTER FIVE

Crossing the Promotion Threshold

Leading in the Position

Often, promotion is experienced as a finish line of preparation. In reality, it is a transfer of accountability. The very moment you step into that new role, the metrics change. In that transition, the organization transfers not just authority but risk, people's trust, and consequences into your care, and that can be exciting, or it can make you shake in your new shoes. Performance is no longer measured primarily by your individual competence, technical mastery, or output. Instead, your effectiveness is judged—yes judged—by decisions made through how you lead others, the health of systems you oversee or are connected to, and the trust built across people, as well as the broader organizational ecosystem. Research on leadership transitions shows that the shift from individual contributor to supervisory and, above all, responsibility requires a cognitive and relational framing, as performance becomes collective rather than personal. Leaders who fail to recalibrate this transition often struggle with over-reliance on technical competence rather than developing the broader systems perspective required of leadership roles.[1]

Many leaders discover quickly that, while the promotion validated their competence and their ability to earn the next step, it did not automatically prepare them for the pace, complexity, and emotional weight of leadership at the next level—whatever that next level looks like for you. Promotion in a sense confirms you can perform but does not give you the full extent of your expanded responsibility. This chapter speaks to one of the most consequential—and least—formally taught—transitions in public safety leadership with consistent timeliness, moving from being evaluated to being responsible … for more. That is, more people, more decisions, more scrutiny, more consequences. And here is why that matters. Most leadership failures do not stem from lack of intelligence, or even from good intent. They stem from unclear expectations,

DOI: 10.4324/9781003728849-8

inconsistent follow-through, neglected relationships, and avoidance of discomfort. If those are left unaddressed, those small gaps compound into credibility problems that follow your career and your opportunity for future advancement. Behavioral decision research demonstrates that leadership failures often unfold incrementally through small boundary shifts and ethical fading rather than dramatic misconduct.[2] Over time, minor inconsistencies in follow-through or fairness accumulate into legitimacy erosion.

Drawing on concepts around the assumption of new leadership roles, leader strategy playbooks, and evidence-based research, Chapter 5 reframes promotion as a systems transition rather than as a personal achievement alone. The goal is not simply to survive the first year; rather, it is to stabilize, align, and lead with intention, without burning yourself out or your people, or feeling like you want to give up or give in.

I think most of us know that a promotion changes more than your title. When people choose to promote, many shifts can occur simultaneously. Let us talk about three of them. The first is that your scope expands from tasks to systems, from processes to people. Second, visibility increases both internally and externally, almost like you are under a microscope all the time, and that pressure can be intense if you are not prepared. And third, your risk focuses on operational, personnel, ethical, and reputational risks. If you ignore any one of these, it can create blind spots that surface later and could be considered morale problems, discipline issues, or perhaps credibility loss. Consistent research shows that managers, not policies, are the strongest drivers of employee engagement, retention, trust, and job satisfaction. In public safety, which has high-stakes environments, this influence becomes even more pronounced. Empirical studies within policing organizations demonstrate that officers' perceptions of supervisory fairness and internal procedural justice significantly predict morale, job satisfaction, and organizational commitment.[3,4]

Looking at the first year as a leadership system, not as a timeline, what will help is not treating it as a checklist of events. Instead, create a structure that is a repeatable operating cadence.

THE FIVE PS: PEOPLE, POLICY, PROCESSES, PRACTICES, AND POSSIBILITIES

To start, here are five integrated domains that can help you organize your leadership responsibilities within this framework. The Five Ps framework includes:

- People: trust, morale, wellness, relationships, performance
- Policy: standards, risk management, compliance requirements, fairness and equity

- Processes: workflows, decision paths, documentation
- Practices: daily habits, communication norms
- Possibilities: development, culture change, succession effectiveness

Newly promoted leaders often default to what feels safest: policy mastery and task execution. While necessary, this narrow focus can unintentionally erode trust and stall organizational momentum. Effective leaders learn quickly that leadership at the next level requires balancing five interdependent domains.

People remain the most critical variable. It is not uncommon to come from a role where you did not naturally have to deal with many of your peers, co-workers, or other stakeholders that are outside your daily duties. Perhaps you had some social interactions, but you may find them less comfortable, especially if there was any disagreement or conflict. Oh, and personalities play a significant part in how we want to open up and engage with others. But here is the deal: when you choose to promote into a leadership role, you have to be the one who leans in, not digs in. Research on trust in organizations consistently demonstrates that employees' perceptions of fairness, voice, and relational respect directly influence morale, performance, and retention. When you prioritize people, you begin to foster a more positive culture where they feel valued and empowered to contribute their best work, making the organization and them more resilient. In practical terms, leaders who take time to really understand their team, both as individuals and as a group, create a sense of legitimacy and trust that cannot just be created later on. Procedural justice theory consistently finds that perception of voice, neutrality, and respectful treatment shape voluntary compliance and trust—even when outcomes are unfavorable.[5] Within public safety and law enforcement, internal fairness predicts both well-being and endorsement of ethical practices.[6]

Policy provides guardrails and a roadmap for daily operations. Yet policy without context becomes rigid. Helping your people understand that policy provides structure and guidelines for decision-making streamlines internal processes and identifies issues so they can be addressed quickly. In addition, the policy provides protection for those who follow it, reduces liability risks, and your people can feel safer. And as you put on your risk management hat, your role is to interpret policy through the lens of purpose, equity, and situational nuance. And yes, you will face cognitive overload, time pressure, and organizational norms that will unintentionally create blind spots. Decision science shows that leaders frequently narrow the framing of policy decisions under time pressure, leading to predictable blind spots and unintended ethical drift.[7] Without deliberate scrutiny, compliance can replace discernment. Therefore, leaders who do not critically examine the implications of their policies and their application risk making decisions that comply with standards but lack genuine discernment and wisdom.

Processes translate intent into action. If policy tells us what must be done, processes determine whether it actually happens, consistently, fairly, and without unnecessary friction, if possible. When you are newly promoted, or advance in a role, you often inherit workflows that you did not even design. Sometimes you will find that reports get routed different ways that make no sense to you and you are being trained on this new process. As you will find, decisions can also stall in those process chains, and accountability is implied but not explicit. Over time, these invisible inefficiencies do not just slow work down; they quietly erode morale, douse your enthusiasm for your new role, and possibly impact your credibility. Because here is the truth: confusion can feel like incompetence to the people experiencing it.

If we think about processes as an organization's nervous system, and when they are unclear or overly complicated, the entire body feels it. And your role as a new leader or as you advance in your career is to be someone who treats process clarity as a form of care. When workflows are transparent, expectations are predictable, decisions are faster, errors decrease, and psychological safety can increase[8,9]—it is a form of structure, instead of silent chaos. Research and organizational design show that role clarity and decision rights are among the strongest predictors of both performance and trust. Studies in organizational psychological identify role clarity and decision transparency as strong predictors of psychological safety and performance outcomes. When decision pathways are ambiguous, employees shift toward self-protection rather than performance.

When people know who decides, how decisions are made, and what happens next, they stop operating defensively and start operating effectively. In your first months after promotion, your job is not immediately to fix everything; oftentimes, there is a period of observation and maybe a consideration and rephrasing to map before you move. A couple of strategies to consider for leadership alignment that moves processes are to think about how you can audit the top five recurring workflows, and that could include scheduling, reporting, personnel processes, or incident response. Another good area is to examine how you can eliminate unnecessary handoffs and duplications of work by building in good feedback loops so your frontline employees can help you flag friction points and solutions to improve efficiency. Remember, you might have been one of those frontline employees with ideas to create change, so do not forget to reach back and tap into that resource of your people. When processes are clean, people conserve energy for the mission, rather than navigation.

If processes are the structure, *practices* are the daily behaviors that bring the structure to life. Oftentimes, policies sit in binders, and some still sit on shelves, but today most reside in electronic files. Processes live in flowcharts, in software systems. But practices show up in how you act on any given day. This is where many leaders underestimate their influence. Because when you think about it, culture is not shaped by speeches or memos: it is really shaped by what leaders repeatedly do, tolerate, reward, and ignore. Every small behavior sends some type of signal. For example, do you return calls promptly or provide responses back to your teams in a timely manner? Are you someone who prepares for meetings and follows through when you say you will? And what about this one? Do you address issues directly or avoid discomfort? Your team is watching, not critically, but calibrating. They are asking: "What really matters here?"[10] Reminding us that credibility is the foundation of leadership, and credibility is built through behavioral consistency—those things that you do daily. Consistent alignment between words and actions creates room for trust. Research suggests that when employees perceive fairness and procedural justice within their own organizations, they are more likely to demonstrate legitimacy-building behaviors in their interactions internally and with the public.[11]

As a note, misalignment destroys it faster than any policy violation ever could. So, in this sense, leadership practices are your reputation in motion. Think of practices as micro-investments, individually small, but collectively transformational. And when you are considering your leadership alignment moves and practices, consider establishing non-negotiable personal standards. As mentioned above, think about your personal timeliness, how you prepare, and your responsiveness. It is really important that you understand that you model the communication norms you expect. And it is a good practice to address those small issues early before they compound, giving you an opportunity to reinforce desired behaviors, and to balance the ones you need to do in private with the ones you should do in public. In addition, build in a practice of holding regular one on ones, listening sessions, and have those brief after-action reflections to normalize learning and to continue to reinforce expectations and desired behavior. Over time, consistency becomes credibility, and credibility becomes influence.

Possibilities. Many leaders get promoted and immediately enter survival mode. The swirl of emails, meetings, staffing challenges, internal and external complaints, and the metrics, before you know it, weeks pass, and then months. And before you realize it, you have become excellent firefighters, but absent architects. When you think about possibilities, it is what pulls leaders out of reaction and into intention. Possibilities include growth, development, creativity, and future-readiness, which includes succession planning, talent development, innovation, and culture shaping. Without this lens, your leadership and your teams stagnate, but with it you both expand. When we think about vision in this space of possibility it is not motivational fluff; it is truly a strategic filter. When people understand where their team, their unit, their division, their organization, is going and why it matters and how they contribute, the engagement increases exponentially, that discretionary effort increases, and resilience overflows. Research on motivation and engagement shows that individuals perform more effectively when they experience some autonomy, competence, and meaningful connection in their work environments.[12] These factors also contribute to higher levels of work engagement and improved performance outcomes.[13] As mentioned above, leaders who invest here will multiply their impact when they stop being the center of all solutions and start building capability in others. And this is the shift from the previous role you were in to becoming and being the leader that your people will need.

To align your leadership for possibilities, think about the following:

How you identify and mentor emerging leaders intentionally as you build succession depth, so the system does not depend solely on you.

Identify and delegate stretch assignments, not just tasks; this helps to celebrate learning and innovation, not just outcomes.

Do not forget to schedule quarterly strategic time to think, not just reactions. This is where you can also think about how you create a six, twelve, or eighteen-month vision with some of your priorities; they do not have to be top priorities, they could be lower ones too.

What is important in the ultimate measure of leadership is not how indispensable you become; it is how well the system performs when you are not in the room.

Together, the Five Ps, when aligned, transform leadership from reactive supervision into intentional stewardship. Remember, promotion is not about doing more work yourself; it is about designing systems where good work happens reliably, even when you are not present. That is the threshold, and crossing it means shifting from operator to architect.

The Five Ps provide the architecture of leadership responsibility and introduces these concepts to newly promoted leaders and reminds leaders who are looking to advance their careers at different levels in the organization. This leadership responsibility helps you see the system and reminds you that architecture alone is not enough. As we know, systems only work when leaders consistently animate them through their judgment, dialogue, trust, and integrity. In other words, the Five Ps define what you steward and the next step defines how you show up while stewarding it. Because when we think about promotion, it is not just structural—it is behavioral, cognitive, relational, and ethical. And what really follows are the leadership capabilities that bring the framework to life.

EVOLVING THE DECISION-MAKING PROCESS

Promotion fundamentally alters decision velocity and sequence and has consequences because leaders are no longer deciding only for themselves; they are deciding on behalf of others, the organization in a greater way, with often limited information and competing priorities. This was touched on briefly under the Five Ps in policy. In this new expansion of your responsibilities, the stakes expand, the timeline compresses, the margin for error narrows, and the consequences of those errors become greater. Decisions that were once routine may now carry operational, ethical, and human implications. Research on decision-making demonstrates that experience alone does not improve judgment. There is work by Anders Ericsson[14] on deliberate practice which underscores that expertise develops through structured reflection, feedback, and intentional learning, not just tenure. Deliberate practice research further indicates that experience without structured reflection does not reliably improve judgment quality. Expertise requires feedback loops, performance evaluation, and intentional correction.[15]

Therefore, time and rank does not equal wisdom and action and we can get caught up in that if we do not intentionally think about how we want to evolve our leadership decision-making process. Behavioral decision research identifies systematic vulnerabilities such as escalation of commitment, overconfidence bias, and ethical fading that distort leadership judgment under pressure.[16] Without safeguards, even well-intentioned leaders drift into avoidable mistakes but you do not have to be one of those leaders. So, the implication for new leaders is clear: decision quality must be treated as a leadership discipline, not an instinct. That means that effective leaders adopt a disciplined decision rhythm, distinguishing between decisions that require speed, those that require consultation, and those that demand more scrutiny—whether that is ethical scrutiny, procedural scrutiny, legal scrutiny, or policy scrutiny. The best way to approach that is to create feedback loops that allow course correction without loss of credibility because effective leaders do not simply make decisions faster—they make decisions smarter and, when decisions improve, outcomes are better.

Equally important, leaders must develop the discipline to manage their time in alignment with their decisions, as well as other priorities. Not every demand requires immediate action and not every urgent issue is truly important. Some of the best leaders find ways to prioritize intentionally—that means allocating their attention to high-impact decisions rather than being consumed by constant reactivity. There are some great tools such as structured prioritization frameworks like the Eisenhower Matrix—widely attributed to Dwight D. Eisenhower—who categorized decisions and tasks based on urgency and importance. The framework was later formalized by Stephen Covey as the Time Management Matrix.[17,18] The Leadership Decision-Making Matrix builds on the prioritization framework, enabling leaders to categorize decisions and tasks based on urgency and importance. By distinguishing between immediate operational demands and long-term strategic responsibilities, the model reinforces disciplined decision-making, intentional leadership, and effective delegation. Because ultimately, how you as a leader manage your time directly shapes the quality of your decisions, interactions, and effectiveness of your leadership.

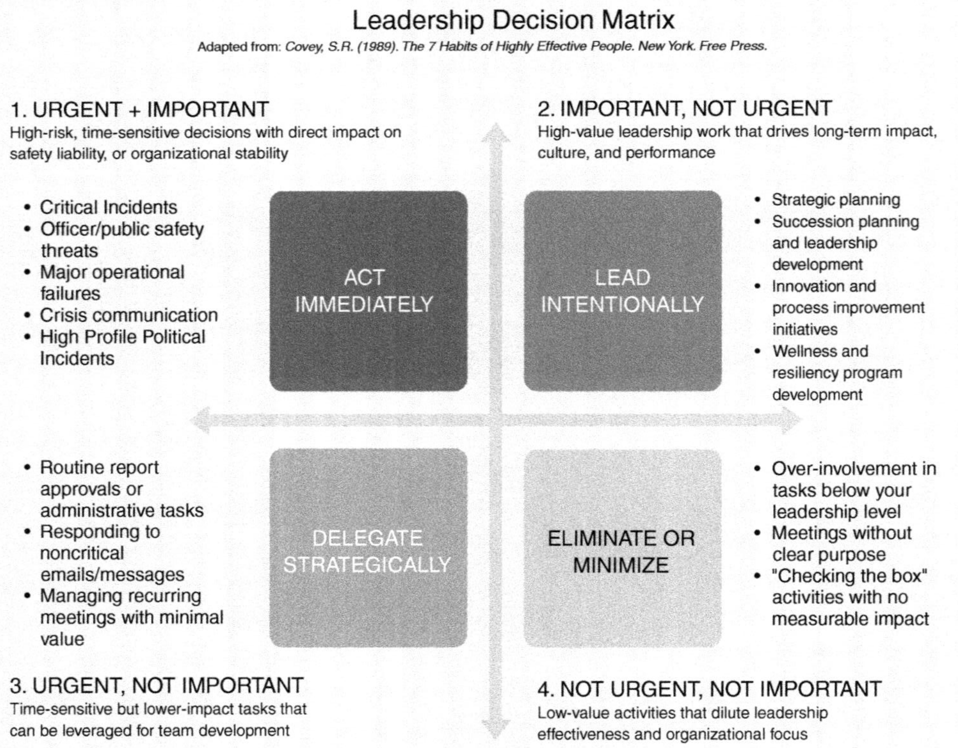

FIGURE 5.1 Leadership Decision-Making Matrix

CREATING A CULTURE OF CONSTRUCTIVE DIALOGUE

If decision-making is the internal discipline of leadership, then communication is its external expression because even the right decision fails when people do not understand it, or do not trust the intent behind it. From experience—and research—communication shifts after promotion and messages are interpreted not just as information, but as signals of intent, alignment, and safety by the person who is doing the communication. Therefore, every word now carries weight and silence can carry even more weight. When we think about psychologically safe workplaces, research consistently shows that environments where employees feel heard outperform those where silence and fear dominates[19] and this can be a great way to think about creating a culture of constructive dialogue. Constructive dialogue is not the absence of conflict; it is literally the presence of trust strong enough to hold disagreement without fracture. This is the opportunity for re-defining how conflict is perceived and addressed, not as a disruption but as a catalyst for growth, clarity, and connection. Effective leaders understand that conflict is inevitable in a high-performance environment, but how it is managed can either strengthen or splinter the organization. Instead of reacting defensively, you have to consider how to design systems that invite dialogue, surface unspoken tensions, and bridge divides through intentional conversation and relational trust. There is a great opportunity to embed conflict resolution into training, performance expectations, and leadership development initiatives, making it a skill, not a personality trait. It allows you in your new leadership to help your team members move from reaction to resolution, and accountability is delivered without harm, teams are empowered to disagree constructively, hold one another accountable with integrity, and move forward with shared understanding.[20,21]

How much time you invest and how intentional you are will create the result of the strength of that constructive dialogue. But when you think about how you can build that trust, leaders who foster open communication through regular check-ins, transparent expectations, and active listening help to reduce rumor cycles and resistance and build more space for relations. In research, for example, women and underrepresented leaders consistently identified lack of transparent communication and informal power dynamics as barriers to leadership effectiveness.[22] This is where dialogue becomes not just a tool but also an equity strategy; when leaders intentionally create space for diverse voices, they can redistribute influence and credibility grows. It is often argued that people do not necessarily resist change: they resist feeling excluded from it in some manner.

BUILDING CIRCLES, NOT SILOS

Dialogue can open the door and connection is what sustains it, because communication without relationship still leaves people working in parallel rather than together, and this is where we need to work on intentionally creating systems for connection versus separation that becomes the default. Silos rarely form because people do not care; they emerge when leaders are uncomfortable—or too busy—to slow down and connect people, functions, and perspectives. So teams retreat to what feels safe: their lane, their unit, their checklist. But collaboration is not a personality trait—it is a structural outcome. Harris and Nelson remind us that communication in organizations is not just the exchange of information. It is the process through which relationships, meaning, and culture are created.[23] In other words, how we talk to each other is how we build the organizational DNA itself. When you walk the floors, go out in the field, show up at meetings, and take time to greet your team, ride-along with your patrol officers, or start your day with five minutes of human connection—which can be called the golden hour—these are not "soft skills" or symbolic gestures; they are infrastructure, leadership systems. These opportunities apply to how you create cross-building collaboration with other peers, teams, and stakeholders in how you escape the administrative desk chains and go talk to people, meet with them, share ideas, and stay engaged.

It is easy to see how leaders who invest in these practices early can build something invaluable: relational capital. Relational capital is what carries you through crisis, allows you to implement change without, or at least less, resistance, and makes people lean in instead of lean away when the pressure hits. Simon Sinek's work reinforces this idea. He argues that people do not commit to organizations because of policies or incentives alone; they commit because they feel a sense of belonging and shared purpose, and see their contribution as part of something larger than themselves. When leaders create what he calls a "circle of safety," trust grows, collaboration increases, and discretionary effort follows.[24] People show up fully when they feel safe and seen—not managed, but seen. And just as important is supportive environments that help build better wellness outcomes and reduce leadership behaviors that are some of the primary indicators of burnout, engagement, and retention around organizational stress. Supportive environments begin to normalize check-ins, model boundaries, and actually acknowledge human impact and foster resilience because leadership in those silos affects your people, and burnout and disengagement can become real when they are unsupported, not included, unheard, and do not feel appreciated. To give context, people do not give discretionary effort to systems; they give it to leaders they trust. But even with trust and alignment, one reality remains: that leadership does not occur in a vacuum; it occurs inside systems of power, influence, and competing interests and it requires a level of maturity beyond technical skill in your evolution.

NAVIGATING THE MORAL MAZE OF ORGANIZATIONAL POLITICS

Yes, politics are going to be unavoidable in most circumstances, but they definitely are in a complex organization. However, the danger lies not in politics by themselves but in unexamined participation. What does that mean? If we are talking about ethical leadership, behavioral ethics research demonstrates that silence, inaction, avoidance, and disengagement are themselves potentially political acts and neutrality is often interpreted as complicity through gradual moral disengagement.[25] So as a new leader you must learn to read power dynamics without being consumed by them or swayed by them. This requires moral clarity, self-awareness, and the most important, courage. When leaders reflect on their values, they should anchor their decisions in fairness, transparency, and service as they navigate political landscapes with integrity rather than fear, doubt, or uncertainty. More importantly, political skill does not mean compromise of ethics: it means understanding stakeholders, anticipating impact, and communicating decisions with respect and clarity. It is an opportunity for influence without manipulation, advocacy without favoritism, and strategy without sacrificing your character. The challenge here is leaders who fail to engage this dimension risk isolation and diminished influence, but those who engage in it thoughtfully, intentionally, can earn something more powerful than authority: legitimacy.

Crossing the promotion threshold is not about proving worth; it is about stewarding this new responsibility. That first year is not about perfection; it is about pattern setting for your style of leadership and how decisions made early shape trust trajectories, cultural norms, and your leadership credibility for not just that first year but for years to come. Remember leadership is not built in dramatic moments: it is truly built in daily repetitions, so make sure to get your reps in. Develop the discipline and habit of repeated, reflective practice rather than isolated moments of crisis.[26] What does that look like? It is in the small decisions, consistent behaviors, intentional conversations, and the values anchored choices that you make. What you will see, over time, is that those repetitions compound into your reputation. So try to keep the perspective that the promotion is not the reward: it is the responsibility, the stewardship, and the practice. And the leaders who embrace that mindset do not simply survive the threshold: they thrive and they bring others with them.

Voices from the Field Installment Five: Command Staff Insights

This *Voices from the Field* installment explores the shift from mid-management to the command staff and executive level. The last section argued that the transition to mid-management is about becoming a conduit for organizational vision. The command staff, executive level, and top-of-the-pyramid positions are about creating that vision. At this level, the breadth of responsibility expands beyond a team, beyond an initiative, and beyond the walls of your organization. The command staff is now tasked with multi-agency collaboration, navigating legislative dynamics, and community relationships that foster trust. Respondents were actually aware of this breadth of responsibility and emphasized the importance of balancing competing political interests, and fostering a functional and healthy organizational culture.

Embracing a Big Picture Mindset: The Wider and Higher Balcony

At the command level, the privilege of focusing on a single outcome, single task, or single initiative is largely non-existent. Rather, public safety leaders in these roles must oversee daily operations, but in many ways detach from them. Previous respondents coined the phrase "the balcony perspective"; at this level, the balcony is even higher and wider, encompassing the entire organization, as well as the larger social, political, and economic contexts.

A chief of police from a small municipal police department in California clearly embraced the broader relationships necessary for executive-level success:

> For me, one of the most essential skills for the command and executive positions was the ability to build professional relationships outside of my agency. As the scope of responsibility grows, it becomes more necessary to collaborate with other agencies, government entities, community members, business owners, and other stakeholders.

A captain from a medium municipal police department in California reaffirmed the mix of operational skills and big-picture mindset in their role:

> Command staff must be able to view the operations of the department from a broader lens. Strategic planning, balancing the budget, making personnel decisions, overseeing policy and legislative changes are all key concepts. Those is command positions need to have earned the trust of their personnel before they assume these roles.

Like the California captain above, a captain from a very large municipal police department in Colorado similarly emphasized the mix of broad skills and a broad mindset necessary to lead by example:

> Dovetailing off the above, "know thyself." It was important to know how I would handle all sorts of situations whether I had experienced them before or not. As I matured in my roles, I understood the importance of communication, adult learning, and emotional intelligence in knowing how to lead my followers. As a result, I have taught aspiring leaders to learn as much as possible in these areas.

Lastly, a lieutenant from a large municipal police department in California once again spotlighted communication as a core leadership competency, especially at the command staff level:

> "Organizational culture, trends and political awareness are critical in understanding how to navigate the complexity of executive leadership. Being a great communicator on all levels is essential for the success of our executive leaders. Far too often, our executive leaders fail to recognize the impact of their words and the precipitating effect their words and actions have on organizational culture. Many lack organizational credibility, therefore, they are occupying leadership positions yet deliberately being avoided by their subordinates."

Be Others-Centric

While the command staff level may inherently pose the risk of inflating one's ego and self-centeredness,[27] our respondents consistently highlight that executive-level leadership is truly about serving others. Moreover, interpersonal skills are once again present in this group's advice as pivotal to developing and nurturing relationships both within, and beyond, the walls of your department.

A chief of police in a medium-sized municipal police department in California clearly embraces a servant-leadership philosophy: "Focus on continuous improvement and be intentional about helping those around you be better too! Demonstrating influence [equals sign] leadership."

A deputy chief from a small municipal police department explicitly continues this theme of service. "You have to come to the realization that you are only ready for leadership when you realize that your job is to care and support others, not just taking care of yourself." Serving others can also be about modeling the behavior that you want to see in your organization.

This point was emphasized by a captain from a very large municipal police department in California: "Every day you should be an example that the department looks at in a positive manner. This is a lifelong process, you cannot 'push the button' and morph into a leader because you now aspire to be a leader."

Politics: A Skill and an Obstacle

The opportunities and challenges posed by intra-agency and external political dynamics were recurring and prominent themes among our respondents. The undersheriff of a large California Sheriff's Department framed political dynamics in the context of organizational change and agility. "Command staff are often the first to feel the pressure of the 'doom loop'—the tendency of stagnant organizations to repeat past mistakes. Leaders must manage this by being comfortable with calculated risks and maintaining integrity when facing political headwinds."

Similar to skillfully navigating the "political headwinds," a captain from a very large County Sheriff's Department in California also emphasized that true leadership is about making the right decision for your people and your organization, despite any formal or informal political pressure, within or beyond your organization. As the captain put it: "Doing what is right, ethical, and best for the department, even when it was unpopular."

Unfortunately, quite a few respondents discussed intra-agency politics as a confounding factor in the promotional process. This book has argued throughout that modern public safety organizations should have transparent, systematic, ethical, merit-based promotional systems in place. Regrettably, this is not always the case.

A major from a very large municipal police department in Tennessee candidly shares that their organization is more about informal relationships that formal qualifications: "I'm the Executive Major for my station; however, everything here is politics or who you know to move up."

A special agent in charge (SAC) from a state policing agency in California expressed a similar sentiment, emphasizing the disheartening reality of cronyism:

> There are so many leadership skills you need, but let me look at this question from a different angle. Many times, it's who you know and if you're liked. I recommend making strong relationships with your bosses. Go to department events and extracurricular activities. It's a sad but true fact that cronyism plays a significant role in promotion and it needs to be understood and prepared for.

The primary purpose of this book is to empower public safety personnel in agencies that do not yet have systematic, transparent, and ethical promotional processes on several fronts: first, to have access to tools, techniques, and strategies to stack your advantages to be successful in the promotional process, even when that process is confounded by internal politics and cronyism; second, to empower public safety professionals to be ready for opportunities outside their current agency when and if that is the prudent choice.

In sum, these *Voices from the Field* further substantiated that leadership at the command staff level is once again about focusing on the betterment of others and the betterment of the organization as a whole, often embracing that servant leadership philosophy. Moreover, the "balcony view" introduced at the mid-management level is now wider and higher, expecting skilled command staff personnel to embrace a mindset of culture and relationship building within and outside the organization. Lastly, this section delved into both the opportunities and challenges posed by some very challenging internal political dynamics described by several respondents. We hope that this book is another tool in your toolkit to transcend confounding organizational politics that may hamper those meritoriously ready for promotion, and put you in a position to lead future change and improve these processes for the future health of your organization.

Concept Bootcamp: The Five Ps in Action

People is the first of the five Ps, and intentionally so. Contemporary law enforcement is in essence about people; people in your organization, people in your community, and yourself as a whole human. Effective law enforcement leaders, before, during, and after promotion must prioritize the health and wellness of those within their sphere of influence. A progressive law enforcement professional must have a working and applicable understanding of cutting-edge best practices related to wellness at all phases of the career cycle. Below is a non-exhaustive sampling of empirically proven health and wellness initiatives for public safety.

- *Organizational Wellness*: The evidence regarding the cumulative impact of stress and trauma on the public safety community is devastating. Progressive, human-centric law enforcement leaders arguably have a moral and ethical obligation to themselves, their peers, and their organization to advance organizational wellness. The average law enforcement professional will be involved with 178 critical incidents—incidents that involve significant trauma and tragedy—in the course of their career. This is nearly ninety times the amount of trauma experienced by the average person in society.[28]

  Trauma has an inherent and cumulative impact on all people, even resilient first responders. Research shows that cumulative stress can impact physical health, mental well-being, sleep, and the performance of one's job duties, as well as social and community impacts.[29] Cumulative trauma is a significant contributor to the tragic commonality of suicide among public safety professionals, resulting in deaths by suicide being more common than line-of-duty deaths.[30]

  Thankfully, research has shown that leaders and organizations can put in place evidence-proven strategies to help promote health broadly construed among their personnel and mitigate the negative impacts of cumulative trauma and stress.
- *Peer-Support Programs*: A staple of a holistic organizational wellness program, peer-support programs have a comparatively long history in the field. Peer-support programs typically involve a network of peers within a public safety organization, or in the region, that provide emotional and psychological support, and intervene during potential times of crisis. Since by definition this is a peer-to-peer model within the public safety space, trust and rapport are more easily achieved compared to other wellness modalities. Experts recommend that

effective peer-support programs must have intentional implementation, policy guidelines, and oversight. In addition, ongoing high-quality training is essential for both those serving on the peer-support team and those tasked with overseeing it.[31]

- *Mental Health Check-Ins*: Regular mental health check-ins are a mainstay of modern, comprehensive organizational wellness programs. The research clearly shows that the trauma and stressors of the law enforcement profession are cumulative.[32] Mental health check-ins are just one component of a diverse and encompassing organizational wellness program to address this cumulative stress.

  The typical model for mental health check-ins requires that every sworn and professional staff member of an organization regularly attends a required individual therapy session. Generally done annually, bi-annually, or even quarterly, these check-ins are designed to provide individually tailored tools to mitigate the impacts of the inherent stress and trauma in the profession. These session can also be a gateway to more regular therapy and services if desired.[33]

  While generally an emerging strategy, a series of best practices have been established that maximize the efficacy and utility of mental health check ins. Best practices suggest that the therapy sessions themselves should be conducted by vetted, culturally component therapists who possess a meaningful understanding of the culture and demands of public safety. Mental health check-ins must be totally confidential, and employees must feel confident in that confidentiality to facilitate meaningful and candid sessions. Some recommend that, after establishing any wellness program, top leaders in an organization should reinforce its importance by visibly participating in the process early on. Lastly, as noted, this must not be an isolated self-standing practice, but rather one pillar of a diverse and career-long investment in officer and organizational wellness.[34]

- *Therapy Dogs*: Another component of a comprehensive, contemporary, and evidence-driven wellness program are therapy dogs. According to the International Association of Chiefs of Police (IACP): "Interactions with dogs have been shown to lower an individual's heart rate and blood pressure levels. Studies also show that interactions between humans and dogs help alleviate Post Traumatic Stress Disorder (PTSD) symptoms."[35]

  Dogs have various uses in modern therapeutic approaches, but the roles most germane to public safety are likely what IACP describes as a facility dog and a therapy dog. As the name implies, a facility dog spends the majority of its day in a public safety agency facility to provide comfort, relief, and a mental reset from the stressors of the profession. Relatedly, a therapy dog has been specifically trained and certified to assist and comfort public safety personnel and potential victims of crime who are actively managing trauma.[36] Like any wellness program, therapy dogs cannot be short-term or symbolic; rather, they should exist within a long-standing culture of organizational wellness.

- *Mindful Badge*: The Mindful Badge Initiative is another pioneering wellness program in contemporary public safety that can be incorporated into a wide-ranging investment in officer and organizational wellness. Spearheaded by Richard Goerling, a retired lieutenant from Oregon, this mindfulness program aims to nurture resilience among law enforcement officers. Utilizing evidence-driven strategies like meditation, interpersonal skills development, and stress management techniques, public safety professionals learn new ways to manage trauma, regulate their emotions, and enhance performance both personally and professionally. Proponents argue that incorporating mindfulness into policing not only promotes health and resilience among law enforcement professionals, but also creates more empathetic and human-centered police officers.[37]

APPLIED LEADERSHIP AND CRITICAL THINKING QUESTIONS

- You've just been promoted and notice yourself defaulting to task execution instead of leading people in systems.
  - How would you intentionally shift your approach from Individual contributor to systems level leader? What specific behaviors would signal that shift to your team?
- Your unit is experiencing low morale, policy confusion, and efficient workflows simultaneously.
  - How would you prioritize action across the Five Ps (people, policy, processes, practice, possibilities)?
  - What would you address first and why?
- You are under pressure to make a quick decision that is technically compliant but may feel unfair to your team.
  - How would you apply clarity, legitimacy, and ethics before acting?
  - What risks emerge when you prioritize speed over discipline decision-making?

- Two employees are involved in a conflict, and one perceives favoritism and leadership decisions.
    - How would you ensure your response builds trust even if the outcome is not favorable to one party?
    - What leadership behaviors reinforce internal procedural justice?
- Your team has started missing deadlines and communication has become inconsistent.
    - What daily leadership practices would you adjust immediately?
    - How do small behaviors compound into either credibility or erosion over time?
- As you prepare for promotional process, you recognize that performance alone may not be enough.
    - How can you strategically increase your professional visibility while maintaining authenticity?
    - What role do relationships, reputation, and organizational awareness play in promotional success?
- You have been in your role for a couple of years but feel your decision-making has plateaued.
    - How would you apply deliberate practice principles (feedback, repetition, reflection) to improve your leadership performance?
    - Which structures would you build to avoid stagnation in continually evolving?

KEY TAKEAWAYS

- Promotion is a transfer of responsibility, not a reward.
- The moment you step into leadership, success is measured by how well you lead people, systems, and trust, not just how well you perform individually.
- Leadership effectiveness is system-based.
- The Five Ps framework reinforces that strong leadership requires balance over focusing on policy or task alone which will create blind spots that impact culture and performance.
- Decision-making must become a discipline practice.
- Experience alone does not improve judgment; leaders must intentionally build reflection, feedback loops, and structure thinking into how they make decisions and execute them.
- Culture is shaped through daily behaviors, not formal authority.
- What leaders consistently do, tolerate, and reinforce become the organization's operating reality—credibility is built in small, repeated actions.

- Visibility, trust, and relationships drive advancement and influence.
- Leadership impact and promotional success is not just about competence; it is about how that competence is communicated, perceived, and aligned with organizational needs.

KEY TERMS

The Five Ps Framework—an integrated leadership model consisting of: people, policy, processes, practices, and possibilities, used to guide leadership priorities and organizational effectiveness.

Leadership Decision-making Matrix—a prioritization framework that categorizes decisions based on urgency and importance to support strategic and operational effectiveness.

Psychological Safety—a work environment where individuals feel safe to speak up, share ideas, and engage without fear of retaliation or embarrassment.

Balcony Perspective—a strategic leadership viewpoint that allows leaders to see the broader organizational landscape, including systems, relationships, and external influences.

Tools and Templates

Closing the Promotion Threshold: From Title to Trusted Leadership

These tools are designed to help newly promoted leaders move from role assumption to leadership effectiveness by creating clarity, discipline, and alignment during the most formative period of their transition.

Tool 5.1: The Five Ps Leadership Audit

People | Policy | Processes | Practices | Possibilities

Purpose:
The Five Ps Leadership Audit provides a structured way for newly promoted leaders to assess their command, team, or unit holistically, beyond tasks and titles. And it is also an audit that can be used periodically at any time through your career to realign your leadership priorities and effectiveness. When you complete the audit, it helps to surface blind spots, prioritize

attention, and align leadership behavior with organizational impact, which helps give you focus during your leadership role transition.

Leadership insight: What you assess intentionally, you lead proactively.

Instructions:

Within the first thirty to sixty days, complete your self-audit honestly. Revisit it quarterly during your first year to create a disciplined practice for self-awareness and reflection.

Use the scale below:

1 = Needs Immediate Attention
2 = Adequate but Inconsistent
3 = Strong and Sustainable

P1: PEOPLE

Reflection Questions	Rating (1–5)	Notes/Action
Do I understand the strengths, stressors, and aspirations of my team?		
Have I established trust through visibility, consistency, and follow-through?		
Are morale, workload, and wellness being proactively monitored?		
Do employees feel heard—even when outcomes do not favor them?		

P2: POLICY

Reflection Questions	Rating (1–5)	Notes/Action
Do I clearly understand the policies governing my authority and discretion?		
Am I applying policy consistently and fairly? Do I explain the why behind the policy decisions?		
Have I identified policy gaps or unintended consequences?		

P3: PROCESSES

Reflection Questions	Rating (1–5)	Notes/Action
Are key workflows clear, efficient, and understood by staff?		
Do decision-making and approval pathways cause delays or confusion?		
Are accountability and documentation processes working as intended?		
Where does process friction create frustration or risk?		

P4: PRACTICES

Reflection Questions	Rating (1–5)	Notes/Action
Do my daily behaviors align with stated values?		
Am I reinforcing standards through action, not just messaging?		
Are feedback and recognition loop timely and meaningful?		
What behaviors am I unintentionally tolerating?		

P5: POSSIBILITIES

Reflection Questions	Rating (1–5)	Notes/Action
Have I articulated a clear vision for the first 90–180 days, or year?		
Do my decisions align with long-term goals, not just short-term fixes?		

Am I developing people for future leadership roles?

Where can innovation or improvement realistically occur?

Audit Outcome
Top 3 priority areas for the next 90 days:

1.
2.
3.

Tool 5.2: Leadership Decision Frameworks

Improving Judgment Under Pressure

Purpose:
As discussed, career advancement and promotion change the scale of consequences. The CLEAR Framework is adapted from interdisciplinary research in decision science, ethics, and organizational leadership to help leaders slow down just enough to improve judgment and without sacrificing effectiveness.[38] The framework also helps to identify your own cognitive bias, application of procedural justice, ethical blind spots, and deliberate practice into a usable leadership model to build a foundation for decision-making as you apply your organizational policy, procedures, and processes (see Figure 5.2 below).[39,40]

Decision Principle: Not every decision deserves the same speed, audience, or authority.

The C.L.E.A.R. Leadership Decision Framework
Clarity, Legitimacy, Ethics, Alignment, Review

C—Clarity
Many leadership failures begin with poorly framed problems.
Before acting, ask yourself:

- What is the real issue?
- Is this a symptom or root cause?
- What facts to I have? What assumptions am I making?

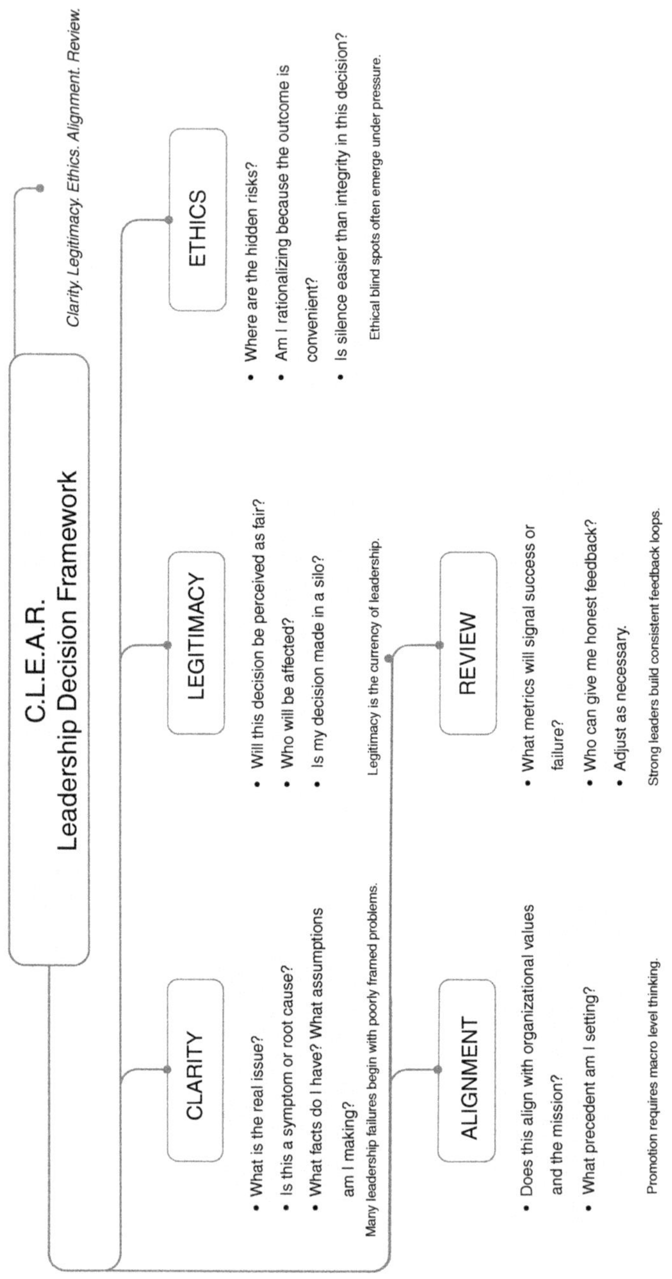

FIGURE 5.2 C.L.E.A.R. Leadership Decision Framework

Additional questions:

- What time horizon matters most (immediate vs long-term)?
- Who will be impacted by the decision?

Leadership Discipline:

⇒ Separate facts from interpretations.
⇒ Name constraints explicitly (policy, staffing, political, legal).

Research note: Decision science shows that leaders often frame problems too narrowly, leading to predictable errors and judgment.[41]

L—Legitimacy

Legitimacy is the currency of leadership.
Before acting, ask:

- Will this decision be perceived as fair?
- Who will be affected?
- Is my decision made in a silo?

Additional questions:

- Have relevant stakeholders had voice or is was this made in a silo?
- Am I applying standards consistently and equitably?
- If I were on the receiving end, would this feel fair? If not, do I have an explanation for why?

Research note: Procedural justice research consistently shows that fairness perceptions drive compliance, morale, and trust, even when outcomes are unfavorable.[42]

Leadership discipline:

⇒ Do not just ask is this allowed?
⇒ Ask is this just?

E—Ethics

Ethical blind spots often emerge under:

- Time pressure
- Organizational politics
- Loyalty conflicts

- Outcome pressures
- Personal ego and pride

Before acting, ask:

- Where are the hidden risks?
- Am I rationalizing because the outcome is convenient?
- Is silence easier than integrity here?

Additional questions:

- What unintended harm could result?
- Would I be comfortable explaining this internally or publicly?

Research Note: Research on bounded ethicality demonstrates that most ethical failures emerge gradually through narrow framing, ethical fading, and incremental boundary shifts rather than dramatic, intentional misconduct.[43]

A—Alignment
Promotion requires macro level thinking.
Before acting, ask:

- Does this align with organizational values and the mission?
- What precedent am I setting?

Additional questions:

- Does this build or erode team, unit, organizational culture?
- Is this consistent with my leadership vision?

This is where transaction thinking shifts to transformational leadership.

Leadership discipline:

⇒ Short-term fixes must not undermine long-term credibility.

R—Review
Strong leaders build consistent feedback loops.
Before acting, ask:

- What metrics will signal success or failure?
- Who can give me honest feedback?
- Adjust as necessary.

Additional questions:

- What would make me change course?
- When will I reassess?

Research Note: Ericsson's deliberate practice model shows that improvement requires structured reflection—not just experience.[44]

Leadership Discipline:

⇒ Every major decision should include a review point.

Applied Leadership Decision-Making Scenarios

These following scenarios go beyond test preparation—they are about learning how to lead. While they can absolutely support promotional study and structured practice, their real value is in helping leaders think critically, make sound decisions under pressure, and understand the broader implications of their choices.

Employee Misconduct—Scenario 1:

A respected employee with tenure is accused of harassment by a newer employee. Morale is divided. Informal loyalty networks are forming, and you are newly promoted into your leadership role.

C—Clarity

- What is alleged?
- What evidence exists?
- What policies guide and govern this issue?
- What is my role and responsibility?

Separate rumor from documented behavior.

L—Legitimacy

- Is the process consistent with prior cases? Should it be?
- Are investigative steps transparent? Or should they be?
- Does the complainant feel safe?
- Does the employee with the allegations against them feel protected in the process?

Procedural justice determines cultural outcomes.

E—Ethics

- Am I influenced by personal loyalty?
- Is there pressure to minimize the issue?
- Would I make the same decision if roles were reversed?

Bounded ethicality is common in internal investigations.

A—Alignment

- Does the response reinforce professional standards?
- What message does this send throughout the organization?
- Does this build or erode trust?

Leadership precedent is being set.

R—Review

- Monitor team morale.
- Assess if additional training is needed.
- Evaluate communication gaps.
- Ensure no retaliation occurs.
- Be approachable and available.

Misconduct decisions reverberate long after closure.

Media Crisis—Scenario 2
Body-worn camera footage of a controversial arrest is circulating online. Political pressure is mounting.

C—Clarity

- What actually occurred?
- What does the footage show in context?
- What policies apply?

Avoid reacting to public narrative before confirming facts. Have a clear and timely statement.

L—Legitimacy

- Are we transparent without compromising investigation?
- Are community leaders being briefed?
- Is messaging consistent internally and externally?

Trust erosion happens quickly in information vacuums.

E—Ethics

- Are we minimizing language?
- Are we defensive instead of accountable?
- Are we protecting the organization at the expense of integrity?

Ethical leadership may require uncomfortable transparency.

A—Alignment

- Does our communication reflect our values?
- Are we reinforcing commitment to fairness?
- Are we modeling accountability?

Mission alignment stabilizes reputation.

R—Review

- Conduct communication audit.
- Evaluate media response timing and consistency.
- Identify improvement areas.
- Reassess social media strategy.

Reputation recovery depends on reflection.

Tool 5.3: Frontline to Supervisor Transition Map

First-Year Leadership Alignment Tool
The transition is not a role change, it is a leadership identify shift. The first year sets the tone for credibility, trust, and long-term influence. This tool is designed to help newly promoted professionals balance leadership with their new positions, help leaders pace themselves, avoid burnout, and move from survival to strategy—without losing relational capital.

Phase 1: Orientation, Trust, and Credibility (0–60 Days)
Leadership Focus: Learn, align, and establish presence

- Clarify expectations with your supervisor and role scope
- Build relationships with team members (individually and collectively) and key partners
- Attend all briefings and operational touchpoints
- Understand unit functions, workflows, and priorities

- Understand role and relationship with employee unions and stewards
- Review policies, procedures, and compliance expectations (create your go bag/binder)
- Establish communication norms and availability
- Reinforce expectations, timeliness, and quality standards
- Review reports for accuracy, liability, and completeness
- Establish boundaries between supervision and prior peer relationships
- Build your decision-making frameworks (ethical, legal, organizational)
- Seek good mentorship from senior leaders, internally and externally

Watchouts: Over-promising, performative proving, making premature change

Phase 2: Stabilization and Structure (2–4 Months)
Leadership Focus: Create consistency and accountability

- Assess team strengths, gaps, morale, and workload distribution
- Address early performance or conduct issues appropriately
- Understand grievance and disciplinary frameworks (keep internal procedural justice in mind)
- Balance accountability with development
- Understand leave protocols (vacation, OT, sick leave, parental leave, military leave)
- Analyze recent incidents, crime patterns, and patrol trends (or data analytics for your position)
- Assess staffing levels, deployment, and equipment readiness
- Review personnel files and performance histories
- Assess team dynamics, informal leaders, and influence networks
- Identify high performers and those needing development
- Begin coaching conversations and performance alignment
- Develop stress management and resilience strategies
- Build the habit of recognition and affirmation of employees to build a supportive work environment

Watchouts: Avoiding hard conversations because you are uncomfortable, decision fatigue, and poor time management

Phase 3: Integration and Influence (3–6 Months)
Leadership Focus: Lead people and systems

- Strengthen collaboration across units, roles, and disciplines
- Establish consistent communication rhythm with leadership, peers, and employees
- Stay connected to frontline realities and service impact
- Understand timekeeping, scheduling, and staffing systems
- Practice clear, concise, and timely reporting or messaging
- Understand formal vs informal communication pathways
- Manage information flow with accuracy and professionalism
- Develop supervisors, managers, and emerging leaders
- Normalize feedback and accountability

Watchouts: Complacency, disengagement from frontline realities, ego

Phase 4: Momentum and Sustainability (6–12 Months)
Leadership Focus: Vision, succession, culture

- Continue to build leadership bench strength
- Reinforce wellness, balance, and resilience
- Find opportunities to attend advanced leadership training
- Reflect on emotional intelligence and conflict management style
- Articulate the team/unit's forward direction
- Build leadership bench strength
- Evaluate what to sustain, stop, or re-design
- Reinforce, wellness, balance, and resilience

Watch Outs: Draft back into operational overload, complacency

Tool 5.4: Command Level First-Year Leadership Map

30–60–90 Days to 12 Months: From Operational Oversight to Strategic Leadership
Having a structured pacing model for middle management and command staff transitioning into broader leadership responsibilities is helpful. This framework is designed to help leaders sequence priorities, protect relational capital, and scale their impact—moving from reactive oversight

to intentional, system-level leadership without burning out or losing their connection to their people.

Phase1: Orientation and Trust (0–30 Days)
Leadership Focus: Listening, Visibility, Strategic Awareness

Core Actions:

- Conduct structured listening sessions with direct reports and key stakeholders
- Clarify expectations, priorities, and decision-making latitude with executive leadership
- Identify formal and informal influence networks across the organization
- Establish communication rhythms
- Observe operational flow before initiating change
- Build strong relationships with union executives for more effective employee relations management
- Understand your role and relationship expectations in key contact partnerships (Local elected officials, legislators)
- Understand budgeting, leveraging limited resources, grant management, purchasing

Strategic Intent: Build credibility through presence and restraint. Signal that your leadership is informed, not reactive.

Watch Outs:

- Over-promising outcomes or changes without full system awareness
- Leading to prove capability vs leading to understand context
- Premature restructuring or policy shifts
- Forgetting to acknowledge and affirm your employees consistently

Phase 2: Stabilization and Clarity (31–90 Days)
Leadership Focus: Alignment, Consistency, Organizational Discipline

Core Actions:

- Address early personnel and performance issues with transparency and fairness
- Align expectations across teams, units, commands, and divisions
- Conduct command audits for operational efficiency, compliance, and accountability

- Identify risk and liability areas and address accordingly
- Conduct climate assessment of health of the command, or team, and morale
- Evaluate your occupational safety goals and policy
- Build a culture of recognition and affirmation of employees to build a supportive work environment
- Develop supervisory leadership to support and nurture a climate of learning for those they lead

Strategic Intent: Create clarity where there is confusion, frustration, or ambiguity. Establish that your leadership brings structure, fairness, follow through, and accountability.

Watch Outs:

- Avoiding necessary but crucial conversations
- Decision fatigue from over-involvement in lower-level issues
- Attempting to solve everything simultaneously

Phase 3: Integration and Influence (3–6 Months)
Leadership Focus: Systems Thinking, Leader Development, Cross-Functional Influence

Core Actions:

- Refine processes to improve efficiency, accountability, and alignment
- Develop your supervisors/managers—shift from directing to coaching and empowering
- Strengthen cross-training collaboration and reduce silos
- Normalize feedback loops, performance conversations, and accountability standards with consistency
- Begin aligning unit-level efforts with broader organizational strategy (strategic planning goals)

Strategic Intent: Transition from managing functions to leading systems and people who lead others.

Watch Outs:

- Gradual drift away from frontline realities
- Over-reliance on high performers without developing others
- Complacency once initial stability is achieved

Phase 4: Momentum and Sustainability (6–12 Months)
Leadership Focus: Vision, Culture, Succession, Long-Term Impact

Core Actions:

- Stay futures forecasting focused by using social, technological, economic, environmental, and political (STEEP) factors
- Build bench strength through intentional succession planning
- Evaluate what to sustain, stop, or re-design across operations and culture
- Institutionalize leadership development and accountability structures
- Reinforce wellness, balance, and resilience at both leader and team levels

Strategic Intent:
Shift from short-term performance to long-term organizational health and leadership continuity.

Watch Outs:

- Being pulled back into constant operational firefighting
- Losing strategic focus due to competing demands
- Neglecting leader development in favor of immediate outputs
- Complacency around trends that might impact your organization

Remember, your leadership is not just a one-time effort; it is a continuous journey that you nurture, refine, and put into practice at every stage of your career. As you grow and advance, the leaders who thoughtfully reflect, make purposeful choices, and set a sustainable pace do not just weather the challenges of promotion; they thrive. By doing so, you will build trust, create stability, and foster a culture where people feel empowered to lead confidently.

NOTES

1 T. J. Maurer and M. London, "From Individual Contributor to Leader: A Role Identity Shift Framework for Leader Development Within Innovative Organizations," *Journal of Management* 44, no. 8 (2018): 3159–3187.

2 Max H. Bazerman and Don A. Moore, *Judgment in Managerial Decision Making* (8th ed.) (Hoboken, NJ: Wiley, 2016).
3 Rick Trinkner, Tom R. Tyler, and Phillip A. Goff, "Justice from Within: The Relations Between a Procedurally Just Organizational Climate and Police Organizational Efficiency, Endorsement of Democratic Policing, and Officer Well-Being," *Psychology, Public Policy, and Law* 22, no. 2 (2016): 158–172.
4 Justice Tankebe, "Organizational Justice and Police Legitimacy," in *The Oxford Handbook of Police and Policing*, edited by Michael D. Reisig and Robert J. Kane (Oxford: Oxford University Press, 2019).
5 Rick Trinkner, Tom R. Tyler, and Phillip A. Goff, "Justice from Within: The Relations Between a Procedurally Just Organizational Climate and Police Organizational Efficiency, Endorsement of Democratic Policing, and Officer Well-Being," *Psychology, Public Policy, and Law* 22, no. 2 (2016): 158–172.
6 Rick Trinkner, Tom R. Tyler, and Phillip A. Goff, "Justice from Within: The Relations Between a Procedurally Just Organizational Climate and Police Organizational Efficiency, Endorsement of Democratic Policing, and Officer Well-Being," *Psychology, Public Policy, and Law* 22, no. 2 (2016): 158–172.
7 Max H. Bazerman and Don A. Moore, *Judgment in Managerial Decision Making* (8th ed.) (Hoboken, NJ: Wiley, 2016).
8 Amy C. Edmondson and Zhike Lei, "Psychological Safety: The History, Renaissance, and Future of an Interpersonal Construct," *Annual Review of Organizational Psychology and Organizational Behavior* 1 (2014): 23–43.
9 Alexander Newman, Ross Donohue, and Nathan Eva, "Psychological Safety: A Systematic Review of the Literature," *Human Resource Management Review* 27, no. 3 (2017): 521–535.
10 Kouzes, J. M., & Posner, B. Z. (2017). *The leadership challenge: How to make extraordinary things happen in organizations* (6th ed.). Wiley.
11 Nicole E. Haas, Justice Tankebe, and Paul A. M. L. van der Wal, "Building Legitimacy in Policing: The Role of Internal Procedural Justice and Leadership," *Policing: A Journal of Policy and Practice* 9, no. 4 (2015): 358–369.
12 Edward L. Deci, Anja H. Olafsen, and Richard M. Ryan, "Self-Determination Theory in Work Organizations: The State of a Science," *Annual Review of Organizational Psychology and Organizational BehMichael S. Christian, Adam S. Garza, and Jerel E. Slaughter, "Work Engagement: A Quantitative Review and Test of Its Relations with Task and Contextual Performance," Personnel Psychology 64, no. 1 (2011): 89–136.avior* 4 (2017): 19–43.
13 Redick, J. (2024). *The factors that influence and nurture women law enforcement officers to promote into leadership roles within law enforcement.*

California Baptist University. Proquest. https://www.proquest.com/docview/3065843306?sourcetype=Dissertations%20&%20Theses

14 Ericsson, K. A. (2008). Deliberate practice and acquisition of expert performance: A general overview. *Academic Emergency Medicine, 15*(11), 988–994.

15 Ericsson, K. A. (2008). Deliberate practice and acquisition of expert performance: A general overview. *Academic Emergency Medicine, 15*(11), 988–994.

16 Bazerman, M. H., & Moore, D. A. (2016). *Judgment in Managerial Decision Making* (8th ed.). Wiley.

17 Covey, S. R. (1989). *The 7 habits of highly effective people: Powerful lessons in personal change*. Free Press.

18 The Eisenhower Matrix is widely attributed to Dwight D. Eisenhower, who articulated the distinction between urgent and important tasks in a 1954 speech. The framework was later formalized and popularized by Stephen R. Covey in *The 7 Habits of Highly Effective People* (1989) as the "Time Management Matrix." Related concepts have also been associated with David Allen in *Getting Things Done* (2001), referencing similar prioritization principles.

19 Amy C. Edmondson and Zhike Lei, "Psychological Safety: The History, Renaissance, and Future of an Interpersonal Construct," *Annual Review of Organizational Psychology and Organizational Behavior* 1 (2014): 23–43.

20 Kenneth Cloke and Joan Goldsmith, *The End of Management and the Rise of Organizational Democracy* (San Francisco, CA: Jossey-Bass, 2002).

21 Thomas E. Harris and Mark D. Nelson, *Applied Organizational Communication: Theory and Practice in a Global Environment* (3rd ed.) (New York, NY: Routledge, 2018).

22 Redick, J. (2024). The factors that influence and nurture women law enforcement officers to promote into leadership roles within law enforcement. California Baptist University. Proquest. https://www.proquest.com/docview/3065843306?sourcetype=Dissertations%20&%20Theses

23 Thomas E. Harris and Mark D. Nelson, *Applied Organizational Communication: Theory and Practice in a Global Environment* (3rd ed.) (New York, NY: Routledge, 2018).

24 Simon Sinek, *Start with Why: How Great Leaders Inspire Everyone to Take Action* (New York, NY: Portfolio, 2009).

25 Max H. Bazerman and Don A. Moore, *Judgment in Managerial Decision Making* (8th ed.) (Hoboken, NJ: Wiley, 2016).

26 Ericsson, K. A. (2008). Deliberate practice and acquisition of expert performance: A general overview. *Academic Emergency Medicine*, 15(11), 988–994.

27 Hougaard, R., & Carter, J. (2018, February 21). Ego is the enemy of good leadership. Harvard Business Review. https://hbr.org/2018/02/ego-is-the-enemy-of-good-leadership

28 FBI Law Enforcement Bulletin. (2021). *Perspective: The Impact of Life Experiences on Police Officers*. Retrieved from https://leb.fbi.gov/articles/perspective/perspective-the-impact-of-life-experiences-on-police-officers.

29 Illinois Criminal Justice Information Authority. (2022). *Understanding Police Officer Stress: A Review of the Literature*. Retrieved from https://icjia.illinois.gov/researchhub/articles/understanding-police-officer-stress-a-review-of-the-literature/

30 CNA Corporation. (2024). *Suicide Data for Public Safety Officers*. Retrieved from https://www.cna.org/our-media/indepth/2024/04/suicide-data-for-public-safety-officers.

31 Lexipol (2025) 3 key considerations when developing a police officer peer support program. https://www.police1.com/health-wellness/articles/3-key-considerations-when-developing-a-peer-support-program-Wj4FeWexMXeXkSyG/

32 Jetelina, K. K., Beauchamp, A. M., Reingle Gonzalez, J. M., Molsberry, R. J., Bishopp, S. A., and Lee, S. C. (2020). Cumulative, high-stress calls impacting adverse events among law enforcement and the public. *BMC Public Health, 20*, 1137. https://doi.org/10.1186/s12889-020-09219-x

33 Fritsvold, E. (n.d.) Police Wellness Programs: Resources & Tools For Supporting Your Officers. University of San Diego https://onlinedegrees.sandiego.edu/police-officer-wellness-programs/

34 Ridgeway, M. (2022) Mental Wellness Check-ins: What They Are and How They Help. Lexipol. https://www.lexipol.com/resources/blog/mental-wellness-check-ins-what-they-are-how-they-help/

35 Internal Association of Chiefs of Police (n.d.) The Impact of Dogs on Resilience: Facility and Therapy Dog Programs to Enhance Officer Wellness https://www.theiacp.org/sites/default/files/278439_IACP_TherapyDogs_508c%5B1%5D_0.pdf

36 Internal Association of Chiefs of Police (n.d.) The Impact of Dogs on Resilience: Facility and Therapy Dog Programs to Enhance Officer Wellness https://www.theiacp.org/sites/default/files/278439_IACP_TherapyDogs_508c%5B1%5D_0.pdf

37 Mindful Badge Initiative. (n.d.). *Mindful Badge*. https://www.mindfulbadge.com/

38 Bazerman, M. H., & Moore, D. A. (2016). *Judgment in managerial decision making* (8th ed.). Wiley.

39 Ericsson, K. A. (2008). Deliberate practice and acquisition of expert performance: A general overview. *Academic Emergency Medicine, 15*(11), 988–994. https://doi.org/10.1111/j.1553-2712.2008.00227.x

40 Tenbrunsel, A. E., & Messick, D. M. (2004). Ethical fading: The role of self-deception in unethical behavior. *Social Justice Research, 17*(2), 223–236. https://doi.org/10.1023/B:SORE.0000027411.35832.53

41 Max H. Bazerman and Don A. Moore, *Judgment in Managerial Decision Making* (8th ed.) (Hoboken, NJ: Wiley, 2016).

42 Rick Trinkner, Tom R. Tyler, and Phillip Atiba Goff, "Justice from Within: The Relations Between a Procedurally Just Organizational Climate and Police Organizational Efficiency, Endorsement of Democratic Policing, and Officer Well-Being," *Psychology, Public Policy, and Law* 22, no. 2 (2016): 158–172.

43 Max H. Bazerman and Don A. Moore, *Judgment in Managerial Decision Making* (8th ed.) (Hoboken, NJ: Wiley, 2016).

44 K. Anders Ericsson, "Deliberate Practice and Acquisition of Expert Performance: A General Overview," *Academic Emergency Medicine* 15, no. 11 (2008): 988–994.

REFERENCES

Allen, D. (2001). *Getting things done: The art of stress-free productivity*. Viking.

Bazerman, M. H., and Moore, D. A. (2016). *Judgment in managerial decision making* (8th ed.). Wiley.

Christian, M. S., Garza, A. S., and Slaughter, J. E. (2011). Work engagement: A quantitative review and test of its relations with task and contextual performance. *Personnel Psychology, 64*(1), 89–136.

Cloke, K., and Goldsmith, J. (2002). *The end of management and the rise of organizational democracy*. Jossey-Bass.

CNA Corporation. (2024, April). Suicide data for public safety officers. https://www.cna.org/our-media/indepth/2024/04/suicide-data-for-public-safety-officers

Covey, S. R. (1989). *The 7 habits of highly effective people: Powerful lessons in personal change*. Free Press.

Deci, E. L., Olafsen, A. H., and Richard, M. R. (2017). Self-determination theory in work organizations: The state of a science. *Annual Review of Organizational Psychology and Organizational Behavior, 4*, 19–43.

Edmondson, A. C., and Lei, Z. (2014). Psychological safety: The history, renaissance, and future of an interpersonal construct. *Annual Review of Organizational Psychology and Organizational Behavior, 1*, 23–43.

Ericsson, K. A. (2008). Deliberate practice and acquisition of expert performance: A general overview. *Academic Emergency Medicine, 15*(11), 988–994.

FBI Law Enforcement Bulletin. (2021). Perspective: The impact of life experiences on police officers. https://leb.fbi.gov/articles/perspective/perspective-the-impact-of-life-experiences-on-police-officers

Fritsvold, E. (n.d.). Police wellness programs: Resources and tools for supporting your officers. University of San Diego. https://onlinedegrees.sandiego.edu/police-officer-wellness-programs/

Haas, N. E., Tankebe, J., and van der Wal, P. A. M. L. (2015). Building legitimacy in policing: The role of internal procedural justice and leadership. *I, 9*(4), 358–369.

Harris, T. E., and Nelson, M. D. (2018). *Applied organizational communication: Theory and practice in a global environment* (3rd ed.). Routledge.

Hougaard, R., and Carter, J. (2018, February 21). Ego is the enemy of good leadership. *Harvard Business Review.* https://hbr.org/2018/02/ego-is-the-enemy-of-good-leadership

Illinois Criminal Justice Information Authority. (2022). Understanding police officer stress: A review of the literature. https://icjia.illinois.gov/researchhub/articles/understanding-police-officer-stress-a-review-of-the-literature/

International Association of Chiefs of Police. (n.d.). The impact of dogs on resilience: Facility and therapy dog programs to enhance officer wellness. https://www.theiacp.org/sites/default/files/278439_IACP_TherapyDogs_508c%5B1%5D_0.pdf

Jetelina, K. K., Beauchamp, A. M., Reingle Gonzalez, J. M., Molsberry, R. J., Bishopp, S. A., and Lee, S. C. (2020). Cumulative, high-stress calls impacting adverse events among law enforcement and the public. *BMC Public Health, 20*, 1137. https://doi.org/10.1186/s12889-020-09219-x

Kouzes, J. M., and Posner, B. Z. (2017). *The leadership challenge: How to make extraordinary things happen in organizations* (6th ed.). Wiley.

Lexipol. (2025). 3 key considerations when developing a police officer peer support program. Police1. https://www.police1.com/health-wellness/articles/3-key-considerations-when-developing-a-peer-support-program-Wj4FeWexMXeXkSyG/

Maurer, T. J., and London, M. (2018). From individual contributor to leader: A role identity shift framework for leader development within innovative organizations. *Journal of Management, 44*(8), 3159–3187.

Mindful Badge Initiative. (n.d.). Mindful badge. https://www.mindfulbadge.com/

Newman, A., Donohue, R., and Eva, N. (2017). Psychological safety: A systematic review of the literature. *Human Resource Management Review, 27*(3), 521–535.

Redick, J. (2024). *The factors that influence and nurture women law enforcement officers to promote into leadership roles within law enforcement* [Doctoral dissertation, California Baptist University]. ProQuest Dissertations and Theses Global.

Ridgeway, M. (2022). Mental wellness check-ins: What they are and how they help. Lexipol. https://www.lexipol.com/resources/blog/mental-wellness-check-ins-what-they-are-how-they-help/

Sinek, S. (2009). *Start with why: How great leaders inspire everyone to take action*. Portfolio.

Tankebe, J. (2019). “Organizational justice and police legitimacy,” in *The Oxford Handbook of Police and Policing*, edited by Michael D. Reisig and Robert J. Kane (Oxford: Oxford University Press, 2019).

Trinkner, R., Tyler, T. R., and Goff, P. A., Justice from Within: The Relations Between a Procedurally Just Organizational Climate and Police Organizational Efficiency, Endorsement of Democratic Policing, and Officer Well-Being. *Psychology, Public Policy, and Law* 22 no. 2 (2016): 158–172.

CHAPTER SIX

The Leadership Ripple

Relational Leadership and Culture Influence

Promotion changes the scope of your authority, but leadership changes the scope of your impact. Earlier in this book, we explored professional readiness as preparation through examining identity, mastery, strategic positioning, and promotional intelligence. But readiness does not end at promotion; it expands, or at least it should. As you advance in rank and position, your responsibilities go well beyond tactical decisions, operational efficiency, and performance metrics. In fact, you begin influencing something less visible but far more enduring and meaningful. What you will quickly realize is that your influence no longer operates at the level of tasks—it operates at the level of systems: trust, norms, psychological safety, decision-making patterns, and ethical climate. All of these could be considered your leadership ripple; through every interaction, every decision, every correction, every silence, it sends waves outward. What you do and do not tolerate becomes the climate and culture. And the higher your rank, the further those waves will travel.

As a newly promoted captain, I thought I was doing what I was supposed to do—be decisive, move things along, keep control of costs, keep people safe, and repeat. During my tenure, there was a moment when we had a deployment change to the way things had always been done: they may sound familiar. There was tension around the issue and I was addressing the staff in a briefing when an officer spoke up and started to ask questions about the new plan. It was a moment that, without really thinking about it, I shut it down. I redirected the conversation, tightened my tone, and moved on. In my mind, at the time, I was keeping order and showing command presence. But I felt a shift immediately. The room got quieter—but not in a good way. It was withdrawal. No one else asked questions. No one added anything. The rest of the briefing moved fast and completely flat.

That moment stayed with me and it reframed how I understood my leadership influence. I realized the hardest part of the transition wasn't learning

 DOI: 10.4324/9781003728849-9

policy or procedure. It was understanding that every reaction, every tone, every response was being watched and interpreted—not just what I decided, but for how I made people feel in the process. A patrol sergeant in our survey for this project shared a powerful statement: "Your officers will forgive a tough decision if they trust your intentions. What they won't forgive is feeling like they don't matter." My goal should not have been about controlling the room but instead about creating space where people stayed in it.

Leadership research consistently converges on a central truth: organizational culture is a downstream reflection of relational quality.[1] Leadership scholars emphasize that leadership is not simply a matter of position or authority, but rather a process that occurs through relationships, influence, and shared meaning among individuals within a system. Hickman reminds us that leadership is embedded in systems of meaning and influence—it is relational and contextual, not merely positional.[2]

Leader-Member Exchange (LMX) theory further illustrates the importance of relational leadership. This body of research demonstrates that the quality of relationships between supervisors and employees strongly predicts outcomes such as organizational commitment, engagement, trust, and even workplace deviance.[3,4] Trust is not a soft concept: it is an operational variable. As Covey argues, it directly impacts both the speed and cost of execution and that trust functions as a central driver of organizational effectiveness, influencing both the speed and cost of performance.[5] High-trust environments reduce friction and enable faster collaboration, while low-trust environments increase oversight, defensiveness, and delays in decision-making. When you violate relational expectations as a leader—through inconsistency, perceived injustice, dismissiveness, avoidance, or silence—employees often respond in kind, reinforcing cycles of mistrust and disengagement.[6]

Therefore, in public safety these are not abstract theories. When you as a leader, supervisor, manager, commander, or executive, are consistent, fair, and aligned with your stated values, trust accelerates performance, communication flows faster, accountability strengthens, and ethical norms hold better. When leadership behavior contradicts organizational values, trust is going to slow, friction will increase, and reciprocity shifts negatively. This is where silence grows and where culture can begin to destabilize and a slow or fast erosion begins. Trust is the bridge, or it could and should be, between values and behavior—and it is something you must continue cultivating and curating in your career advancements. Without relational integrity, ethical values lose their normative force and, with relational integrity, they gain greater speed, or at least some momentum. The leadership ripple is not metaphorical by any means: it is measurable. It shows up in communication velocity, discretionary effort, or non-effort, ethical decision-making, and organizational resilience.

RELATIONAL LEADERSHIP AND TRUST

Public safety organizations are structured hierarchically with a chain of command that is intended to ensure clarity, coordination, and accountability. Chain of command matters. Policy matters. Discipline matters. Yet, leadership research consistently demonstrates that effectiveness is shaped not merely by authority, but by the quality of leader-member relationships.[7]

Relational leadership theory (RLT) argues that leadership is a dynamic social process, one that emerges through interaction, trust-building, and mutual influences rather than positional authority alone.[8] Research shows that high-quality leader–follower relationships are associated with increased employee engagement, stronger organizational commitment, and reduced turnover.[9] In the public safety and law enforcement context, research shows that supervisory fairness and trust are strongly linked to morale, compliance with departmental values, and more procedurally just citizen encounters and internal legitimacy strengthen external legitimacy—the math is not that complicated.[10]

When we talk about pillar 7—Leadership Stewardship—it is not about personal productivity; instead, it is about cultural consequence as you are no longer simply responsible for outcomes—you are responsible for the conditions that produce those outcomes. Relational leadership is not optional at advanced levels of leadership; it is the operating system. The idea of trust is not sentimental; it is structural and the operational infrastructure. And empathy—often misunderstood in enforcement environments—is not weakness; it is operational intelligence. Emotional intelligence plays a critical role in effective leadership, as leaders who demonstrate self-awareness, empathy, and emotional regulation are better able to build trust and influence.[11] When balanced with clear standards, empathy strengthens legitimacy rather than softening authority. Those leaders who build trust have the ability to reduce resistance and those same leaders can create psychological safety which increases accountability. If you are a leader who can demonstrate empathy in a way that balances these factors, you are not lowering standards; instead, you are elevating and raising commitment. So think about relational leadership as a disciplined influence and how you apply it in all your interactions; again, those decisions and any opportunity where you can actually activate your relational leadership. LMX research tells us that high-quality exchanges evolve from transactional relationships to mature partnerships grounded in mutual trust and shared purpose.[12] When those partnerships multiply across an organization, discretionary behaviors increase—mentorship, collaboration, and initiative.[13]

So this chapter explores how leadership shifts from more of a performance to culture where it is from management to stewardship and it is from authority to legacy—your legacy.

LEGACY THINKING

Legacy thinking is the moment a leader realizes that promotion, position, and performance are not the destination—stewardship is. It is the disciplined shift from managing today's demands to shaping tomorrow's stability. Over the course of a career, it becomes clear that authority is temporary, but influence is enduring. Legacy thinking asks us to look beyond the urgency of the inbox, the metrics of the quarterly reporting, or the pressure of the moment and consider something far more consequential: who is stronger and better because of my leadership? What systems are healthier because I implemented new and innovative ideas? What values will continue to influence and guide the organization long after my title changes? True leadership is not measured by how well we occupy a role, but by how responsibly we prepare others—and the organization—to thrive well after we have served.

The mindset requires courage because leaders need to confront a deeper question: am I building dependency, or am I building durability? It is easy to become indispensable but it is far more difficult—and far more responsible—to make yourself progressively less necessary. That is the quiet discipline of mature leadership. As we advance, the metrics change. For example, in our early careers we are rewarded for individual excellence—our productivity, our decisiveness, our technical mastery. However, the higher the levels of responsibility, the measure shifts, and it becomes sometimes a moving target. Therefore, the question becomes less about what you can accomplish and more about what continues to function, grow, and improve without constant intervention. It is the transition from being the doer to becoming the developer, from problem-solver to capacity-builder, from performer to architect.

It also reframes how we approach decision-making when you adopt a legacy lens—short-term wins lose their appeal if they compromise long-term trust. Legacy thinking disciplines a leader to ask not simply: will this solve the issue? But what precedent does this set? Because every decision is not just a resolution—it is a signal, and signals accumulate into culture. It also demands intentional investment in people—mentoring someone who may one day surpass you, documenting processes others could navigate without you, sharing institutional knowledge rather than guarding it. When you understand that succession is not a threat to relevance, it is the highest validation of your impact. And this shift reframes leadership from ownership to stewardship—you do not own the organization; you are entrusted with it.

Legacy thinking cannot exist without futuring. A leader who thinks about legacy but ignores emerging shifts is preserving the past, not preparing for the future. True stewardship requires the discipline to scan the horizon, interpret signals, and prepare people before disruption arrives. This type of legacy thinking is not nostalgic; it is anticipatory. Actually, futuring is the intentional practice of examining trends, technological shifts, demographic changes, policy evolution, workforce expectation expectations, and economic volatility,[14] asking what will this mean for us five, ten, fifteen years from now? Those leaders who operate with a legacy mindset and understand that stability does not come from resisting change but that it comes from preparing for it will be most effective. This approach aligns with established foresight models such as social, technological, economic, environmental, and political (STEEP) analysis to inform strategic forecasting.[15] When you do this, it helps you to move beyond awareness and into informed preparation, positioning your organization to anticipate, adapt, and lead through uncertainty.

In every industry, public safety, non-profit leadership, corporate environments, higher education, the ground is shifting. As we see all around us, technology is accelerating decision cycles, and community expectations are evolving, and workforce generations are redefining authority, flexibility, and engagement. Let's not forget that funding models are fluctuating, and data transparency is increasing and a leader focused only on today's operational demands will always be in a reactionary mode[16]. Therefore a leader grounded in legacy thinking asks how do we build capacity now so we are not scrambling later? This is where legacy thinking becomes strategic. It might mean investing in continuous learning before it becomes mandatory, or it means strengthening emotional intelligence before conflicts escalate, or it means developing emerging leaders before vacancies appear, or it means modernizing systems before inefficiencies become crises.

Although I know most of these just mentioned are already happening in many organizations, there is still time to be able to put on your legacy thinking hat, be a future-oriented leader—and strengthen readiness cultures. Do not wait for disruption to force transformation. Create readiness on purpose.

Preparing your organization for the future requires three deliberate moves:

- First is environmental awareness. Leaders must consistently examine external signals, like industry research, workforce data, technological advancements, community expectations, and translate those signals into internal conversations. Futuring is not prediction—it is disciplined curiosity.
- Second is talent development aligned with emerging needs. If artificial intelligence, data analytics, cross-cultural communication, and adaptive leadership are becoming essential, then training cannot remain static. Legacy thinking requires aligning professional development with where the industry is going, not where it has been. You cannot afford to sit in a silo.
- Third, structural flexibility organizations that endure are not rigid; they are principled yet adaptable and policies must reflect values, although

processes must allow innovation and creative artistry. It is important that teams understand missions clearly enough to adjust tactics confidently, and this intersection of legacy thinking and futuring ultimately protects both people and purpose. It is possible it can reduce anxiety during transition before preparation replaces panic and it builds confidence because learning replaces fear, and it can foster trust because leaders demonstrate foresight rather than reaction.

If you want your influence to outlast your tenure, you must prepare your teams now, not just for the roles they hold today but for the environment they will inherit tomorrow. Legacy thinking, at its highest level, is not about being remembered; it is about ensuring your organization is ready. And when you do this as you are refining your leadership for your readiness for career advancement the implications can be significant.

CULTURAL INFLUENCE AND PSYCHOLOGICAL SAFETY

What is the risk of organizational silence from your leadership? What does that even look like? It can look like betrayal, administrative betrayal that can lead to trauma for those you lead. In 2023, Police1 conducted a survey of over 4,100 officers looking at the challenges around recruitment and retention.[17] While examining this issue, they found that the administrative silence felt like betrayal. There is a growing discussion in policing circles around what some call administrative betrayal—the experience described when your officers—or team members—feel abandoned by their own leadership during controversy, crisis, or public scrutiny.[18]

You must remember that silence is not neutral; it actually is communication and signals and shapes perception. Whether it is a high-profile incident, or more of an internal exchange, when leaders fail to respond constructively, your employees learn that speaking up carries a risk and, over time, they may withdraw their voice to protect themselves. That withdrawal is not just emotional—it is shaping culture. Your silence can run deep and undermine morale, increase cynicism, intensify stress responses, and accelerate burnout.[19]

Psychological safety research reminds us that our people evaluate safety not by the absence of discipline, but by the predictability, fairness, and consistency of leadership response.[20] Think about it. When leaders are visibly present, engaged with their teams, transparent in communication, and consistent in process, even difficult decisions can be easier to digest. But remember, fairness does not eliminate disagreement, but it does build trust in the system.

However, if leaders are absent or ambiguous, your people will fill the void with assumptions and their own narrative. That silence creates the gaps, and those gaps are rarely filled generously, so make sure you are addressing big and small issues, those rumors, policy inconsistencies, officer wellness signals, and internal and external conflicts or criticisms. Left unaddressed, subtle shifts in culture can happen quickly if you are not paying attention, and your teams may start to self-regulate without guidance, and this is where those subcultures and informal norms take shape—and I know you have seen numerous headlines on the fallout from some of those organizations that did not intervene in a timely manner, or at all. History has shown us that when organizational leaders fail to intervene early, those patterns can solidify into behaviors that ultimately damage trust, legitimacy, and public confidence. Really effective leaders recognize that culture is never static; it is constantly being shaped by what leaders reinforce, what they ignore, and how consistently they show up.

While individual leadership behavior shapes culture in powerful ways, the broader organizational environment determines whether that leadership, and the leader, can grow, advance, and sustain impact over time. Leadership development does not occur in isolation; it is reinforced, constrained, or accelerated by organizational systems, access to opportunity, and intentional investment in people.[21] In this way, career advancement is not simply a function of individual readiness: it is also a function of organizational support. Leaders may create the ripple, but organizations determine whether the ripple expands into sustained influence, increased responsibility, and long-term leadership trajectory.

To better understand how this dynamic shapes real-world advancement, we turn to lived experiences of professionals across agencies. Their insights reveal a critical reality: while leadership is earned individually, it is often enabled—or limited—systematically.

Voices from the Field Installment Six: Organizational Support

In this final traditional iteration of the *Voices From the Field* feature, we focus on leadership development and organizational support. Respondents throughout these sections have consistently highlighted the strikingly diverse skill set required at every phase of the leadership trajectory. As such, it is imperative for organizations to invest in their personnel and thus ensure successful succession planning within the organization. With these goals in the forefront, we asked our respondents: "How does your organization support your leadership development and nurture career advancement?"

Culture of Professional and Personal Betterment

As evident throughout this book and this *Voices from the Field* qualitative analysis, promotional preparation should not be viewed as a singular event, but rather as a consistent, ongoing, and intentional process. Therefore, successful organizations are going to be those that consistently, systematically, and equitably invest in their own people through education, training, mentoring, and exposure to a wide variety of organizational roles.

This sentiment was captured masterfully by a sergeant from a small municipal police department in California:

> My organization invests in training, mentorship, and creating pathways to grow. They genuinely want people to succeed, and they give us opportunities to attend courses, rotate into new assignments, and take on projects that stretch our abilities.

A lieutenant from a large municipal police department in California highlighted that their agency facilitates leadership training inside the organization and promotes additional external opportunities:

> My department hosts a Leadership Development Institute for sworn and professional staff members to take. It is a 12-month program that promotes leadership development. Additionally, my department advertises various leadership trainings within the state and higher education opportunities.

Lastly, a front line officer from a medium-sized municipal police department in Indiana reaffirmed that everyone in public safety is a leader. Moreover, they noted that both formal training and mentoring were central to their organization's culture of professional growth:

> By supporting us, sending us to schools specifically about leadership, allowing shadowing of higher positions and just being transparent. Our department wants leaders, but you don't have to be in a supervisory position to be a leader.

The Dual Benefit of "Acting" Positions

Many respondents described the strategic dual advantage of acting roles. First, acting roles can be beneficial for an individual to gain hands-on experience in a particular role and assignment. This hands-on experience can help the individual develop an introspective understanding of the skill sets they might need to enhance to perform that role in a permanent capacity. Second, acting roles can be beneficial for the organization to gain insight into an employee's strengths and weaknesses. Thereafter, an intentional organization can develop individualized training, coaching, and mentoring to set that person up to best serve the organization.

A captain from a medium-sized municipal police department in California noted the value of temporary assignments: "Our department has an acting sergeant program where we allow officers who have gone through a testing process to work as a patrol sergeant on a temporary basis dependent on staffing needs."

A federal special agent made a nearly identical point: "Support from management and encouragement to attend training, opportunities to serve in acting supervisory positions and take on challenging roles like serving in inspections."

A captain from a large municipal police department in California saw the opportunity to serve in a pseudo-acting position when their supervisor was regularly absent:

> I had a lieutenant who was absent frequently when I was a detective sergeant. I was also the senior detective sergeant at the time. I took it upon myself to fill the gap of the absent lieutenant. When doing that, I found myself reporting to the captain often, and I became accustomed to doing that while also having to report back to the absent lieutenant when he would reappear. I did not complain about it; I saw it as an opportunity to grow, and with it came some additional challenges but also a lot of freedom. I also established a reputation as someone who understood the role of a lieutenant because I frequently served in that capacity. Another powerful opportunity was volunteering to do the PIO role. The lieutenant in that official role was not comfortable doing it and had little interest, so I was allowed to do my own news releases and even press conferences as a detective sergeant.

A chief of police from a small municipal police department in California advances this theme by noting that at the executive level, acing positions may be outside the department. "My city manager supports my leadership development by providing exposure to city operations and allowing me to serve as the acting city manager in their absence."

Navigating Scant Support

Many respondents shared heartening accounts of their organizations investing in them, as part of an intentional and robust succession plan. However, in many organizations self-advocacy and a bit of savvy were required to ensure you were getting an equitable share of the available training and professional development opportunities.

An undersheriff from a large County Sheriff's Department in California candid shared their strategy for navigating the zero-sum game of organizational support:

> [My strategy] allowed me to attend many training sessions and schools. It also helped that, starting as a deputy, I developed good relations with the finance and training divisions. The people who worked in those areas were underappreciated and usually 'dumped on.' I approached them with the attitude: 'Help me learn what you need to know from me to make your job easier.' And I wrote thank-you notes whenever it was appropriate. This learning paid off as a sergeant when I wrote my own budgets, had little difficulty attending trainings, and developed the relationships necessary to be a manager.

A captain from a very large municipal police department in Colorado made a very similar point:

> Sit down and identify goals. Write them down and keep them where you can refer to them during your journey. We would use a SWOT analysis (strengths, weaknesses, opportunities, and threats) in our leadership classes. Once the aspiring leader idenitfied a goal, we had them list the S, W, O, and Ts that could help or hinder that success. Not only does this help you identify your strengths, but more importantly, it should help identify your blind spots. Work on those! Read. Listen. Ask Questions. Be Present. And participate in as many opportunities afforded you while finding ways to create opportunities for yourself. For example, I was always paying attention to upcoming classes/training. I submitted requests for many classes. I figured if others were not going to take advantage, I would. I was blessed to attend a great deal of classes over the years. Today, there are even more opportunities with online learning, podcasts, and audible books. Soak it all in! Additionally, and arguably more important, learn about people. For some, caring, taking an interest,

> and generally liking others is easy. For others, this is a challenge that must be worked on. I believe at its core, good leadership starts with just being a good person. This is predicated on having great relationships with those around you.

A captain from a large municipal police department in California candidly shared that formal professional development was essentially non-existent in their agency. This forced growth-minded personnel to seek out the few mentors available:

> My organization was neutral on that topic. Career advancement was mainly window dressing, but I did have some leaders who mentored me, gave me opportunities, and provided support along the way. There were two of them out of all the leaders in the organization.

Lastly, a lieutenant from a large municipal police department in California candidly shared that professional development opportunities

> [i]s an area that can use a little work. Anecdotally, we say we develop our future leaders, however, there are no tangible or measurable programs we can fall back on to support that claim. For managers, we are provided more opportunities for career growth than those seeking opportunities to become a sergeant or lieutenant.

This final traditional installment of *Voices From the Field* revealed that organizational opportunities for professional development exist on a continuum: many organizations seemingly provide ample support and opportunities, while in others these opportunities are essentially non-existent. Regardless of your organization's investment—or lack thereof—in its personnel, the advice and strategies shared here will hopefully provide empowering, tangible pathways to achieving your professional goals.

APPLIED LEADERSHIP AND CRITICAL THINKING QUESTIONS

- Think about a recent interaction where your tone, response, or decision may have shaped team behavior.
  - What ripple effect did it create positive or negative? What would you intentionally do differently next time to shape culture more effectively?

- In a high-pressure situation, how do you balance command presence with relational leadership?
  - What specific behaviors demonstrate both authority and psychological safety?
- Consider your current team or unit.
  - Where is trust accelerating performance, and where is it slowing it down?
  - What leadership behaviors are directly contributing to each?
- Reflect on a time when you or your organization remain silent during a critical issue.
  - What message did that silence send?
  - How might proactive communication have changed outcomes?
- Based on the concept of deliberate practice, how are you intentionally refining your leadership skills?
  - What specific behaviors are you practicing with feedback and repetition, not just performing (because remember performance alone does not equal improvement)?
- When making decisions how often do you consider long-term cultural impact versus short-term resolution?
  - What precedent are your current decisions setting for your team or organization?
- Looking ahead five to ten years, what emerging trends in technology, workforce expectations, and policy shifts will impact your organization?
  - How are you preparing your team now to meet those changes?
- If your organization lacks structured development opportunities, how are you taking ownership of your growth and of those you lead?
  - What relationships or training are you experiencing that you can proactively pursue?
  - What opportunities can you create for your teams for a climate of learning to give them experiential exposure and professional development?
- Where are you still operating as the primary problem solver instead of building others' capacity?
  - What is one area where you can intentionally shift to developing others?

KEY TAKEAWAYS

- Leadership is felt before it is measured.
  In every interaction whether it is your tone, your response, even your silence, it shapes culture. Whether you intend it or not, you are always creating a ripple.

- Trust is not a soft skill—it is operational infrastructure.
  It directly impacts speed, performance, accountability, and morale. When trust is strong, everything moves better; when it is weak, everything begins to slow down.
- Experience alone will not make you better—intentional practice will.
  Leadership growth requires deliberate effort, feedback, and refinement. Simply doing the job over and over is not the same as improving at it.
- Promotion expands influence, not just your authority.
  Leadership at higher levels is less about task and more about shaping systems—culture, norms, and how people experience the organization.
- Legacy is built in the small, daily decisions.
  Every choice sets a precedent. The question is not just did I solve the problem—it is what did this teach my team about leadership, trust, and expectations?
- SIlence is never neutral.
  When leaders do not communicate, people fill the gaps—usually with assumptions that erode trust and morale.
- Strong leaders build people not dependency.
  Their own measure of leadership is whether your team can function, grow, and succeed without constant intervention, especially by you.

KEY TERMS

Leadership Ripple—the cumulative effect of a leader's tone, decisions, silence, and behavior on trust, culture, and team climate.

Relational Leadership—a leadership approach grounded in interaction, influence, trust building, and the quality of relationships rather than position alone.

Relational Leadership Theory (RLT)—a framework that views leadership as a dynamic process shaped through relationships, shared meaning, and mutual influence.

Leader-Member Exchange (LMX)—a leadership theory focused on the quality of the relationship between leaders and employees and its impact on trust, commitment, engagement, and performance.

Legacy Stewardship—the responsibility to shape the conditions, culture, and systems that enable people and the organization to thrive beyond the leader's tenure.

Internal Legitimacy—the trust and belief personnel place in leadership fairness, consistency, and values alignment inside the organization, which strengthens external legitimacy.

Futuring—a disciplined practice of anticipating and preparing for emerging trends, disruptions, and long-term changes to position an organization for sustained success.

STEEP Analysis—a strategic foresight framework used to evaluate social, technological, economic, environmental, and political trends to inform planning and decision-making.

NOTES

1 Gill Robinson Hickman, ed., *Leading Organizations: Perspectives for a New Era*, 3rd ed. (Thousand Oaks, CA: Sage Publications, 2016).
2 Gill Robinson Hickman, ed., *Leading Organizations: Perspectives for a New Era*, 3rd ed. (Thousand Oaks, CA: Sage Publications, 2016).
3 George B. Graen and Mary Uhl-Bien, "Relationship-Based Approach to Leadership: Development of Leader–Member Exchange (LMX) Theory of Leadership over 25 Years," *Leadership Quarterly* 6, no. 2 (1995): 219–247.
4 Michal Biron, "Negative Reciprocity and the Association between Perceived Organizational Ethical Values and Organizational Deviance," *Human Relations* 63, no. 6 (2010): 875–897.
5 Covey, S. M. R. (2006). *The speed of trust: The one thing that changes everything.* Free Press.
6 Biron, M. (2010). Negative reciprocity and the relationship between leader–member exchange and employee performance. *Human Relations*, *63*(5), 661–684.
7 Aggarwal, A., Krishnan, V. R., and Bhargava, S. (2020). Leader–member exchange and organizational citizenship behavior: The moderating role of emotional intelligence. *Leadership & Organization Development Journal, 41*(1), 37–52.
8 Mary Uhl-Bien, "Relational Leadership Theory: Exploring the Social Processes of Leadership and Organizing," *The Leadership Quarterly* 17, no. 6 (2006): 654–676.
9 George B. Graen and Mary Uhl-Bien, "Relationship-Based Approach to Leadership: Development of Leader–Member Exchange (LMX) Theory of Leadership Over 25 Years," *The Leadership Quarterly* 6, no. 2 (1995): 219–247; Ankit Aggarwal, V. R. Krishnan, and Shalini Bhargava, "Leader–Member

Exchange and Organizational Citizenship Behavior: The Moderating Role of Emotional Intelligence," *Leadership & Organization Development Journal* 41, no. 1 (2020): 37–52.

10 Tom R. Tyler, *Why People Obey the Law* (Princeton, NJ: Princeton University Press, 2006); Rick Trinkner, Tom R. Tyler, and Phillip Atiba Goff, "Justice from Within: The Relations Between a Procedurally Just Organizational Climate and Police Organizational Efficiency, Endorsement of Democratic Policing, and Officer Well-Being," *Psychology, Public Policy, and Law* 22, no. 2 (2016): 158–172

11 Daniel Goleman, *Working with Emotional Intelligence* (New York, NY: Bantam Books, 1998).

12 George B. Graen and Mary Uhl-Bien, "Relationship-Based Approach to Leadership: Development of Leader–Member Exchange (LMX) Theory of Leadership Over 25 Years," *The Leadership Quarterly* 6, no. 2 (1995): 219–247.

13 George B. Graen and Mary Uhl-Bien, "Relationship-Based Approach to Leadership: Development of Leader–Member Exchange (LMX) Theory of Leadership Over 25 Years," *The Leadership Quarterly* 6, no. 2 (1995): 219–247

14 Edward Cornish, *Futuring: The Exploration of the Future* (Bethesda, MD: World Future Society, 2004).

15 Edward Cornish, *Futuring: The Exploration of the Future* (Bethesda, MD: World Future Society, 2004).

16 Edward Cornish, *Futuring: The Exploration of the Future* (Bethesda, MD: World Future Society, 2004).

17 Bob Harrison, *What Cops Want in 2023* (Police1, 2024).

18 Sgt. Sean Springer, "Administrative Betrayal: Why the Silence of Leaders Is the Greatest Trauma for Many LEOs," *Police1*, November 26, 2024, https://www.police1.com/what-cops-want/administrative-betrayal-why-the-silence-of-leaders-is-the-greatest-trauma-for-many-leos

19 Sgt. Sean Springer, "Administrative Betrayal: Why the Silence of Leaders Is the Greatest Trauma for Many LEOs," *Police1*, November 26, 2024, https://www.police1.com/what-cops-want/administrative-betrayal-why-the-silence-of-leaders-is-the-greatest-trauma-for-many-leos

20 Amy C. Edmondson and Zhike Lei, "Psychological Safety: The History, Renaissance, and Future of an Interpersonal Construct," *Annual Review of Organizational Psychology and Organizational Behavior* 1 (2014): 23–43; Alexander Newman, Ross Donohue, and Nathan Eva, "Psychological Safety: A Systematic Review of the Literature," *Human Resource Management Review* 27, no. 3 (2017): 521–535.

21 Valentine, S. R., Meglich, P., Mathis, R. L., and Jackson, J. H. (2019). *Human Resource Management* (16th ed.). Cengage Learning.

REFERENCES

Aggarwal, A., Krishnan, V. R., and Bhargava, S. (2020). Leader–member exchange and organizational citizenship behavior: The moderating role of emotional intelligence. *Leadership & Organization Development Journal, 41*(1), 37–52.

Biron, M. (2010). Negative reciprocity and the relationship between leader–member exchange and employee performance. *Human Relations, 63*(5), 661–684.

Cornish, E. (2004). *Futuring: The exploration of the future.* World Future Society.

Covey, S. M. R. (2006). *The speed of trust: The one thing that changes everything.* Free Press.

Edmondson, A. C., and Lei, Z. (2014). Psychological safety: The history, renaissance, and future of an interpersonal construct. *Annual Review of Organizational Psychology and Organizational Behavior, 1*, 23–43.

Goleman, D. (1998). *Working with emotional intelligence.* Bantam Books.

Graen, G. B., and Uhl-Bien, M. (1995). Relationship-based approach to leadership: Development of leader–member exchange (LMX) theory of leadership over 25 years. *The Leadership Quarterly, 6*(2), 219–247.

Harrison, B. (2024). What cops want in 2023. Police1.

Hickman, G. R. (Ed.). (2016). *Leading organizations: Perspectives for a new era* (3rd ed.). Sage Publications.

Newman, A., Donohue, R., and Eva, N. (2017). Psychological safety: A systematic review of the literature. *Human Resource Management Review, 27*(3), 521–535.

Springer, S. (2024, November 26). Administrative betrayal: Why the silence of leaders is the greatest trauma for many LEOs. Police1. https://www.police1.com/what-cops-want/administrative-betrayal-why-the-silence-of-leaders-is-the-greatest-trauma-for-many-leos

Trinkner, R., Tyler, T. R., and Goff, P. A. (2016). Justice from within: The relations between a procedurally just organizational climate and police organizational efficiency, endorsement of democratic policing, and officer well-being. *Psychology, Public Policy, and Law, 22*(2), 158–172.

Tyler, T. R. (2006). *Why people obey the law.* Princeton University Press.

Uhl-Bien, M. (2006). Relational leadership theory: Exploring the social processes of leadership and organizing. *The Leadership Quarterly, 17*(6), 654–676.

Valentine, S. R., Meglich, P., Mathis, R. L., and Jackson, J. H. (2019). *Human resource management* (16th ed.). Cengage Learning.

CHAPTER SEVEN

Leadership in Practice

From Promotion to Stewardship

Leadership in public safety is often discussed in terms of preparation, preparing for the next assignment, the next responsibility, or the next promotional opportunity. Yet those of us who have spent time in leadership roles understand the promotion itself is not the destination, and I know that has been said more than once. In many ways, it is simply the beginning of a different kind of responsibility. It is that moment when a leader assumes a new role, and the focus shifts from individual competence to collective influence and responsibility. Decisions are no longer measured solely by personal performance, but by how effectively leaders guide people, shape culture, and steward the mission of the organization. It sounds like it has been said before: it has. It is worth repeating, so it has been.

Leadership scholarship reinforces this transition. Research on leadership identity and development emphasizes that moving from Individual contributor to leader requires a shift in perspective, from technical expertise to relational influence and organizational stewardship.[1] In professions such as law enforcement and public safety, where trust, legitimacy, and accountability carry significant weight, the quality of leadership relationships can directly shape organizational culture and public confidence.[2,3] Throughout my career, I have seen this reality play out in ways that no textbook could fully capture because leadership is often learned not only through training or formal preparation but through experience—moments when leaders must navigate uncertainty, make difficult decisions, and remain accountable to the people they serve both inside and outside the organization. Some of the most meaningful lessons observed did not come from policy manuals or leadership models, but from watching how

DOI: 10.4324/9781003728849-10

leaders showed up for their teams, handled adversity, and carried the weight of responsibility and resilience.

For that reason, this chapter steps away from heavy theory and turns toward the lived experiences of leaders in the field. While research offers valuable insight into leadership principles, the reflections of those who practice leadership every single day provide a deeper understanding of how these principles unfold in real-world moments and organizational environments. If their testimonies are not considered as preparation for your professional development, then I do not know what is. The following section brings together reflections from practitioners, lessons learned through experience, and insights drawn from the leadership journey itself. These perspectives will highlight common challenges leaders face, the decisions that shape organizational culture, and the responsibilities that come with influence. The hope is they will also serve as reminders to all of you that leadership is not defined by position alone, but by the daily choices that you will make as leaders in service to others and the profession.

The reflections that follow offer a glimpse into those experiences—moments where leadership moves beyond theory and becomes practice.

VOICES FROM THE FIELD: A CAPSTONE

Thus far, the *Voices from the Field* have provided invaluable insights into the promotional process, organized into discrete, tangible categories focused on different elements of promotional readiness. In this final installment, the collective wisdom of over 1,500 public safety professionals will be leveraged to provide a more macro-level view of the public safety profession as a whole and the larger social context in which it exists. This section will focus disproportionately on institutional, cultural, social, and political dynamics related to the field of public safety, and those brave men and women looking to thrive within it.

The Institutional Knowledge Crisis

Many respondents spotlighted the demographic changes faced by many departments and their impact on organizational culture, knowledge, and continuity. The convergence of recruitment and retention challenges, a disproportionate number of personnel nearing retirement age, and increased mobility between agencies has left some agencies with a demographically bipolar workforce: many young officers and many nearing retirement.[4]

A sergeant from a medium department in California captured this dynamic powerfully and succinctly: "Staffing will be the most complicated challenge for every agency going forward. The exodus that is occurring is going to wipe out the number of officers and with it, institutional knowledge."

A frontline officer from a medium department in Indiana reaffirmed that recruitment is a critical challenge facing the profession: "Recruitment and retention. It's getting harder and harder to find qualified applicants to join the ranks."

A captain from a very large department in California added that the combination of political dynamics and staffing is a particularly acute challenge: "The increasing sway of outside politics [is a major challenge], along with staffing and retention."

A detective from a large department in California articulated that the very real exposure and risk that modern public safety professionals face adds to the recruitment challenge. This observation also infuses a political element, at least implicitly: "If good officers are leaving the profession due to scrutiny and lawsuits, it makes it difficult to pitch this career as a suitable choice."

A major from a very large department in Tennessee candidly shared their perspective on this demographic shift: "Getting qualified candidates, forcing the senior personnel out to me is not a good thing. Younger don't always mean better."

Dovetailing with the potential loss of institutional knowledge, several respondents reflected on the need to lead effectively across generational typologies. As a frontline officer from a medium-sized department in Indiana put it: "Some aspects of law-enforcement is [becoming less] attractive to the new generation coming out."

A sergeant from a very large department in California articulated this dynamic, arguing that generational norms and values are something leaders need to be acutely aware of: "Changes in generations, Gen X in leadership roles now with Millennials coming in next."

Other respondents were more critical. A major from a very large department in Ohio highlighted the challenge of "dealing with the younger generation that does not have the same work ethic."

A lieutenant from a large department in California added: "It was common for leaders in our profession to have 25–30 years of experience … Now, it feels there is a shift and officers only want to work 10–15 years, then move on to another vocation."

The combination of socio-political and staffing dynamics requires modern public safety professionals to be proactive in the areas of recruitment, retention, and intentionally investing in the professional development of individuals within their organization. Respondents consistently touted the value of mentoring for organizational knowledge preservation and continuity. According to a special agent in charge from a medium department in California, mentorship is the key: "Many senior leaders will be retiring and the future leadership will be much younger. Mentoring and preparing them for future success is critical ...Great leaders make future leaders."

A captain from a very large department in California noted that the scant mentors available in his organization helped overcome a lack of professional development investment by their organization:

> My organization was neutral on that topic. And that made things easier for me in some respects. Career advancement was mainly window dressing, but I did have some leaders who mentored me, gave me opportunities, and provided support along the way. There were two of them out of all the leaders in the organization.

A chief of police from a small department in California reaffirmed that the burden is on the mentee to identify and connect with potential mentors: "Seek out a network of mentors who have been successful to guide them through their career."

A frontline officer in Indiana subtly reaffirmed that the initiation burden is often on the mentee, not the mentor: "Ask supervisors what they like and don't like about different leadership styles ... have 'What am I messing up' meetings." These respondents evidence that mentoring is not only effective for individualized professional development, but it also will facilitate the preservation of institutional knowledge throughout the organization, which is in part created by demographic shifts in policing.

This evidence suggests that for an aspiring leader of any rank, these socio-political and demographic changes in the profession represent both a challenge and an opportunity. The demographically "bipolar" workforce will demand leaders who can build bridges between factions within their organization and intentionally create a collaborative, team-oriented environment across a range of experience levels among their personnel. Moreover, the institutional legacy and knowledge of more senior personnel must be institutionalized, harvested, and documented, while younger public safety professionals must be mentored, trained, and positioned to be successful, because promotional opportunities to mid-management roles are likely to be needed much more quickly than in past decades. The profession will require skilled, human-centric leaders for organizations to thrive in this complex climate.

Integrating Technology in the "Business of People"

A major theme among our respondents was the tension of integrating technology in the modern public safety environment. Policing is an inherently human endeavor and modern law enforcement is in "the business of people."[5] Simultaneously, technology is a valuable force multiplier with empirically proven impacts.[6] Contemporary law enforcement leaders must harness the advantages of technology, without losing the essential human, relational, and interpersonal elements of co-creating public safety with the community.

A chief of police from a small department in California summed up this challenge powerfully and succinctly: "Successful policing is relational and technology is steering us away from needing to engage one another."

An undersheriff from a large department in California warned that the efficacy of modern technology must not overshadow the need for community engagement and compassion: "Artificial Intelligence, recording of everything, hypercritical oversight from outside the agency ... Law enforcement leaders struggle to step out of the profession and view it from the community's perspective."

Several respondents spotlighted artificial intelligence as potentially the quintessential representation of this tension between technological advantages and a people-centric endeavor: "The responsible use of technology will be a major challenge for the next generation of leaders, especially the emergence of AI," a captain from a medium department in California stated. Similarly, a Special Agent in Charge from a medium-sized department in California agreed: "I also think technology and AI will significantly change the law enforcement field."

A lieutenant from a medium department in Florida bridged the previous discussion of institutional knowledge and leading across generations with technology. This lieutenant argued that "managing different generations of workers and the advancement in AI technology" will be a critical challenge facing the profession and its leaders.

A chief of police from a small department in California powerfully articulated the balanced approach needed to harness the advantages of technology successfully without losing the "human service" inherent in the profession: "We will be managing the integration of technology in our field, while maintaining a level of human service to our communities." This is sage advice for law enforcement professionals looking to promote and thrive in the modern socio-political climate.

The Training and Education Panacea[7]

Undeniably, a combination of professional experience, mentoring, quality training, and narrowly-tailored, professionally relevant education is key to successful professional development. This book has vigorously argued that agencies should invest heavily in the development of their people. And in the absence of that investment, individuals seeking to promote, lead, and thrive in their careers should proactively invest in themselves and seek out opportunities for training, education, and professional development.

A captain from a very large department in California highlighted the problem caused by organizations that fail to proactively train their leadership: "We need to do better [to] prepare people before they promote ... With law enforcement, you move into the position and get the training afterwards. The change would set up people for success."

A sergeant from a medium department in California cited the institutional pressure to promote as a driving force in this challenge: "Part of this issue is that most in command staff rapidly promoted and did not obtain the needed experience to handle a lot of the common issues that arise in agencies."

Several respondents cited formal education specifically as a key tool for promotion and long-term professional success.

A lieutenant from a large department in California stated: "There is a notable difference in our promotability success rates between our leaders who have sought higher education and those who have not."

A lieutenant from a large department in Washington added: "It's imperative that police leaders not only have operational expertise but also education to support their relevant experience."

A chief of police from a small tribal police department on the East Coast shared how education, along with other intentional strategies, played a critical role in their own career advancement:

> The most effective strategy I used to prepare for the promotional process throughout my career was a deliberate investment in both structured preparation and continued education. During my first career with the [redacted] Police Department, where I served 25 years and retired as Chief of Police in 2021, promotions were governed by state and local civil service requirements, meaning written examinations were essential at every rank from detective through chief. Early in my promotional journey, I invested in civil service audio and written exam guides. That decision proved to be a turning point. By committing consistent time and effort to studying, I was able to regularly score within the top three candidates, which was critical for promotional eligibility. As my career advanced, I recognized that formal education would become equally important. While serving as a lieutenant and preparing for executive leadership opportunities, I returned to complete my bachelor's degree after more than 20 years in law enforcement. I then continued my professional development by graduating from the FBI National Academy, earning graduate-level credits that I transferred to the University of San Diego to complete my LEPSL master's degree. That academic foundation played a significant role in my eventual appointment as Chief of Police.

An undersheriff from a large department in California puts the burden on the organization to create promotional processes that recognize and value diverse experience, training, and education. This serves as sage advice and a valuable antidote to the lack of preparation for leadership roles articulated throughout this section:

> The profession still relies on technical skills and expertise when selecting a candidate for promotion. Technical skills can be learned at any time and are usually learned by looking them up. Human leadership skills are far more critical to an agency's success. For example, many lieutenant tests still quiz on the laws of arrest, the Penal Code, and the Vehicle Code. The test focuses on the skill level of the assignment the candidate currently holds. But at the management level, many assignments have little to do with patrol and more with organizing and directing people to solve problems. The skills required for success at the management level can be applied to any assignment. By focusing the testing process on those skills, candidates will be required to learn them before being promoted.

Leading and Promoting with Humility

A major theme that emerged from these surveys was the importance of leading with humility and keeping humility in the forefront as you strategize for career advancement. A sound promotional process will inherently recognize and reward top performers who have earned the rank and corresponding recognition. But our respondents reaffirm, in a series of diverse arguments, that despite the accomplishments and demonstrated skill-set of meritorious leaders, the willingness to listen, learn, and be authentically humble is an essential leadership skill.

A sergeant from a medium-sized department in California put it clearly: "Ego has no place there [at the executive level]; you have to lead with humility and clarity."

An Indiana frontline officer argued that the promotional process mandates a humble approach to one's accomplishments, and the dangers of ego in the field:

> Overconfidence or entitlement. Getting ready for a promotion there's no time to be proud. Absolutely highlight successes you have had. However, be prepared to address mistakes you shouldn't have made. A lot of people have gone up for leadership positions thinking because of the successes they have had or accomplishments entitle them to this position, but that's not the case. Humility is key in a major pitfall people come across is overconfidence. When a tense scene is being done and escalation is happening over confidence can get people hurt.

A chief of police from a large suburban police department in California implies that ego can be a fatal flaw when engaging diverse stakeholders as a police executive:

> As previously stated, understanding stakeholder perspectives is critical to success as a leader and is a non-negotiable for the command/executive level roles. This understanding serves as the foundation for legitimacy. Once the stakeholder perspectives is clearly known, the next step is to find commonalities to gain influence and buy-in. This will require one to perhaps acquiesce on things they are passionate about for the greater good. This is not to be confused with selling your soul but instead, a BATNA (best alternative to a negotiated agreement). We must be willing to meet people where they are and have to abandon the "we are the cops so we know what is right" mentality. Frankly, we do not have it all figured out and there is always more to learn.

A captain from a very large agency in Colorado candidly shared a story of personal persistence, and reaffirmed the importance of avoiding the curse of ego and the value of humility in your drive to be successful:

> Want it! If your heart is not in it, you will fail. Long story, which I will spare you, I had suffered a setback and was forced to retake a promotional exam. Usually, I was fortunate that I was always prepared and was humbled to finish at the top of these exams; not bragging, just a pleasant reality. However, the time I had to retake the assessment center, I became so irritated in the middle, my performance suffered and I failed! I was devasted, but I learned a valuable lesson that I pass on to this day. If your heart is not into leading or you are distracted by outside forces, you will not be prepared and you will fail. Just as important, make sure you are doing it for the right reasons. If you want to promote for your own ego or paycheck, don't do it. You will fail to garner real followers and your reputation and success will suffer.

Purpose and Service

One of the paramount themes to emerge from our respondents, and arguably a substantively ideal point to spotlight in this final *Voices from the Field* segment, is the importance of purpose and service in the leadership journey. The passion for a selfless dedication to others, to the professional, and to social betterment as a whole is strikingly evident throughout this survey evidence. For these law enforcement leaders, promotion is ultimately not about career advancement, financial rewards, status or ego; rather, career advancement is about service to something that transcends self.

Related to this theme, a sergeant from a small police department in California advised: “Don’t chase promotion for status or recognition, chase it because you want to make things better. The badge only carries weight when your heart is in the right place. If you focus on serving others, the promotion will eventually come to you.”

Similarly, a detective from a large department in California emphasized finding your “why:”[8] “Do not seek promotion for the rank/title or money. Each promotion comes with more responsibility and expectations. When seeking to promote, you need to ask yourself why you want this role and if you are ready for the higher expectations that come with it.”

A major from a very large department in Ohio put it plainly: “If you are doing it solely for the money, then you will be very disappointed.”

Respondents continually emphasized an earnest and heartfelt investment in others, and modeling human-centric leadership approaches for the entire organization.

A sergeant from a medium-sized department in California provided some direct advice on this topic: “Avoid office politics. Do your job well. Treat people well even when you are not being treated the same way.”

A frontline officer from Indiana articulated these themes in an impactful manner:

> Development of others. Being a leader is no longer about yourself. If you wanna make your agency better, you need to make the people around you better and you should surround yourself with people that make you better. Mentoring and developing others is a key aspect of being promoted and leadership. And you don’t have to out rank somebody to develop them. You can just be a more senior officer or come a different experiences that you can teach to others. Doing so shows your knowledge, your preparation and your ability to teach … Review and assess your why. You should have a desire or a purpose for promotion. You should be able to communicate in articulate your desire or higher responsibility and accountability of others. You should prepare a need or a gap in your agency and how you believe you can assist with the promotion. You should review your departments strategic plan and how the leadership above you wants to accomplish their goals and you should prepare how you can assist in meeting those goals. However, if you’re only reason to promote is for the rank or the pay, you need to reevaluate if you are ready for the promotion or not. With a promotion and a new leadership position, it is no longer about self-serving. It’s about leading, developing, mentoring, and taking care of the people you are charged to lead.

LEADERSHIP TRUTHS I WISH SOMEONE HAD TOLD ME EARLIER

1. *Promotion does not make you a leader.* It simply gives you the opportunity to become one.
2. *Your people watch what you far more than they listen to what you say.*
3. *Trust is built in small moments.* It is rarely lost in a single dramatic event—it erodes through silence, inconsistency, or absence.
4. *Leadership will expose who you authentically are.* Rank amplifies character; it does not replace it.
5. *The hardest decisions in leadership are rarely about policy.* They are about people.

APPLIED LEADERSHIP AND CRITICAL THINKING QUESTIONS

- The chapter highlights an institutional challenge driven by retirements, staffing shortages, and workforce mobility. In your role, what concrete systems would you put in place to preserve knowledge, prepare successors, and reduce the loss of organizational wisdom?
- Several field voices emphasize that mentoring is essential for continuity and leadership development. How can a leader create a culture of mentoring that is not dependent on only a few generous individuals, but becomes part of the organization's normal way of operating?
- The chapter argues that public safety is still the business of people, even as technology and AI expand. How should leaders evaluate whether a new technology is actually improving service, and trust rather than simply creating distance from the community or over reliance on systems?
- Some respondents from Voices from the Field noted that agencies often promote people and train them afterward. What are the organizational risks of that model, and what would a more forward-looking, readiness-based leadership development pipeline look like?
- The chapter repeatedly returns to purpose and service. When someone says they want to promote, what questions should they ask themselves to determine whether they're motivation is rooted in service, ego, money, status, or a genuine desire to make the organization better?
- Public safety leaders must often lead across generational differences and expectations, communication styles, and work norms. How can leaders avoid unfair stereotypes while still addressing real tensions and building a cohesive, high performing team across generations?

- This chapter reframes advancement as stewardship and legacy. If your leadership role ended tomorrow, what evidence would show that your leadership made the organization stronger, more aligned, and better prepared for the future?

KEY TAKEAWAYS

- Promotion is not the finish line—it is the beginning of a broader leadership assignment or success is measured by influence, stewardship, and the ability to strengthen the organization beyond your own role.
- Leadership at higher levels requires a mindset shift from doing the work yourself to developing people, aligning systems, preserving institutional knowledge, and shaping cultural intentionally.
- The strongest leaders balance operational competency with human leadership. They understand the communication, humility, trust, mentoring, and credibility are not 'soft' extras—they are essential to organizational effectiveness.
- Technology, data, and AI can support modern public safety leadership, but they must never replace judgment, relational leadership, and the human service mission at the heart of the profession.
- Purpose matters. Purposeful leaders often experience greater resilience, enjoy the work more, and are better position to create long-term impact.

KEY TERMS

Leadership Stewardship—the shift from focusing on personal performance to taking responsibility for people, culture, systems, and the long-term health of the organization.

Organizational Impact—the broader effect a leader has on outcomes, alignment, accountability, trust, and future readiness across the agency.

Institutional Knowledge—the experience, history, judgment, and operational wisdom that can be lost when seasoned personnel retire or leave.

Succession Planning—intentional efforts to prepare future leaders and preserve organizational continuity before vacancies occur.

Community Trust—public confidence in the legitimacy, fairness, and effectiveness of public safety leadership and practice.

Artificial Intelligence—emerging technology that can influence decision-making, operations, and service deliver, while requiring careful ethical and relational leadership.

Legacy Thinking—leading in a way that strengthens the organization for the future and leaves behind a healthier culture, stronger people, and better systems.

PERSONAL REFLECTION

Jonni Redick

Over the course of my career—and life journey—I have come to understand that leadership is rarely defined in the moments when everything is going well. It often reveals itself in the quieter, more uncertain moments when the answers are not clear, when trust has been tested, and when people are looking to you not just for direction, but for reassurance that they matter. I did not always have the confidence or clarity that leadership required. There were times when I questioned whether I belonged in the room, whether I was prepared enough, or whether my voice carried the weight it needed to. Like many of you, I learned along the way sometimes through success, and sometimes through mistakes and failures that taught me far more than comfort ever could.

What I have learned is that advancement in this profession is about far more than passing an examination and earning the next rank, position, or title. It is about developing the judgment, humility, and courage to lead people through complexity while protecting the values of the profession we serve. Leadership, at its best, ask us to grow continually, to listen more closely, to live more intentionally, and to remain accountable to the people who place their trust in us. If there is one thing I hope this book leaves you with, it is the reminder that professional leadership readiness is not a destination. It is a daily deliberate practice. Striving for excellence should always be your priority. Every conversation, every decision, every moment of influence contributes to the culture we shape for those around us, whether that is personal or professional. The responsibility of that leadership is not simply to manage the work, or manage the people, but to care for them and to care for the profession that you are entrusted with. Remember, leadership is not defined by the authority you hold, but by the culture you leave behind. Stay ready.

Erik Fritsvold

Everything of significance that I have learned about leadership I learned by osmosis. As a career academic, my formal training in this area has been minimal. My leadership education was having the privilege of working alongside the men and women of law enforcement, public safety, and the military on a daily basis for the last dozen years of my career. Watching, albeit in an academic environment, how these leaders proactively solve problems, mentor others, think strategically, navigate turbulent organizational politics, and lead with a human-centric viewpoint is nothing short of inspiring.

From this experience, I would argue that leadership is primarily about caring for others as we all work together for a common goal. And more than motivating speeches or visionary brilliance, to me leadership is about the little things. The daily grind of being the first in the office and the last to leave. The daily grind of taking care of the minutiae and details that allow others the agility to be successful. The daily grind of always picking up the phone to co-create a solution or willingly derail your day to prioritize an unanticipated challenge. Leadership is often about showing up.

Ultimately, leadership is not a title or a theory. It is about the quiet, unglamorous, and often unrecognized persistence that is almost always required for success. It is about an unwavering dedication to the people around you and the privilege of striving to meet a goal together.

Concept Bootcamp: Cultural Growth and Organization Change in Action

As you promote in public safety throughout your career, your span of influence on the organization inherently increases. At some point you will be well-positioned to initiate, pitch, implement, and oversee complex organizational changes intended to improve your organization and the community you collectively serve. In this installment of the *Concept Bootcamp* we provide system-level examples of organizational change in action that dovetail with the design infrastructure and change management themes of this chapter.

- *The Value of Education in Law Enforcement:* Education plays a crucial role in enhancing the effectiveness and professionalism of law enforcement officers. By pursuing higher education, officers gain critical thinking skills, ethical decision-making abilities, and a deeper understanding of the communities they serve. Studies have shown that educated officers are better equipped to handle complex situations, reduce the use of force, and build stronger community relations.[9,10] Studies suggest that officers with college degrees are less likely to resort to force and more likely to use communication and de-escalation techniques effectively.[11] This not only improves public trust but also enhances the overall safety and well-being of both officers and community members.

Moreover, education fosters a culture of continuous learning and adaptability within law enforcement agencies. Officers who engage in ongoing education are more adept at staying current with evolving laws, technologies, and best practices. This adaptability is essential in addressing modern challenges such as cybercrime, terrorism, and community policing. Additionally, educational programs often emphasize the importance of mental health and wellness, equipping officers with the tools to manage stress and maintain resilience. Experts argue that investing in education for law enforcement personnel is a strategic move that yields long-term benefits, including improved job performance, reduced liability, and enhanced public perception of the profession.[12] In 2017, studies found 35.1 percent of police chiefs had a master's degree, a statistic that is likely far higher today.[13]

- *30x30 Initiative*: This movement seeks to improve gender equity in law enforcement organizations by creating a critical mass of female personnel at all levels of the organization. More specifically, the goal of 30x30 is to have women constitute 30 percent of law enforcement personnel by the year 2030. At present, approximately 14 percent of sworn law enforcement professionals nationwide are female.[14] To reach this goal, 30x30 empowers those who take the "30x30 Pledge" with tangible steps that organizations can take to engage in any organizational change necessary to facilitate this goal. The crux of the pledge is introspection about existing hiring and promotional processes related to gender equity and proactive steps to address any policies, practices, or cultural dynamics that may be obstacles to equity.[15]
- *Co-Responder Models*: In the modern era, law enforcement is tasked with managing a diverse breadth of social problems, often including homelessness, mental health crises, drug abuse, and others. While the breadth of law enforcement responsibilities is arguably expanding, the staffing challenges facing the profession remain steadfast and significant.[16] In this context, collaborative co-responder models

have proven to be effective and resource-efficient ways to respond to these "wicked problems"[17] of society.

Co-responder models generally involve interdisciplinary teams that may include law enforcement, social service providers, faith-based leaders, community leaders broadly construed, mental health practitioners, and other issue-specific subject matter experts. Proponents of co-responder models for individuals who experience mental health challenges or crisis argue that:

> [l]aw enforcement and mental health clinicians respond to these calls for service together, providing an improved and immediate response to crisis situations by conducting a more accurate needs assessment on scene for the person in distress, and connecting them and their families to community-based resources.[18]

A significant advantage of many co-responder frameworks is the sustained support they provide in the aftermath of the original call for service. Robust co-responder models for mental health issues often involve bridging resources for treatment, and follow-up care that attempt to address the root causes of the issue and avoid a revolving door of regular law enforcement responses to ongoing and repetitive crises involving the same individual.

Similarly, interdisciplinary collaborative teams have also proven effective in addressing the complex problem of homelessness. According to Lexipol: "Collaborative responses are the most successful at efficiently using resources and driving down the homeless population when properly implemented."[19]

We would argue that co-responder models also have an important symbolic component. An effective co-responder model reaffirms that positive interventions into vulnerable populations are not exclusively a police responsibility, but rather a collective community-wide priority that requires a team of professional expertise. This paradigm shift in responsibility reduces mission creep that often exhausts police resources and, more importantly, ensures that the person in crisis receives the holistic support they need.

- *Relational Policing*: Coined by then Houston Chief of Police Art Acevedo[20] and further developed by Chief Sheryl Victorian of the Waco, Texas Police Department, this is a contemporary conceptualization of longstanding community-policing principles. The fundamental argument is that creating meaningful and sustainable long-term relationships with community members is pivotal to public safety and helping to create healthy communities and societies. Chief Victorian[21] and others describe the core tenets of relational policing using the acronym TREEAT:

- Transparency
- Respect
- Engagement
- Emotional Capital
- Accountability
- Trust .

This perspective on police-community relations emphasizes mutual-respect, and collaborative approaches to mitigating many social problems, including crime.

Proponents of relational policing argue that its principles are valuable and appropriately applied in the community, as well as within police organizations. These same principles centered on trust, transparency, procedural justice and mutual respect should be applied to management, personnel challenges, discipline, coaching, resource allocation, decision-making, and the other various functions of modern public safety agencies. When leaders employ relational policing, they are modeling its importance for personnel at all levels of the organization, and thus reinforcing it as a core principle of the agency that should be applied in a wide variety of contexts.

FINAL CLOSING MESSAGE

Ultimately, career advancement in law enforcement and public safety is not simply achieving the next rank or title—it is about becoming the kind of leader others trust to steward people, decisions, and culture responsibility. The journey you have taken through these chapters is an invitation to lead with intention, humility, grit, grace, and courage. Remember, promotions may place you in positions of authority, but it is your character, consistency, and commitment to those you serve that will define your legacy. As you continue forward, keep this in the forefront of your mind: leadership is not a destination but a practice—one built daily through relationships, accountability, and the quiet choices that shape culture around you. The future of our profession will not be defined by policy alone, but by the leaders who choose to rise, serve, and lead with purpose. Therefore, the question is not whether you will hold a leadership position, but whether you will become the kind of leader whose presence makes the nobility of the profession stronger and brighter for those who will follow.

NOTES

1 Mary Uhl-Bien, "Relational Leadership Theory: Exploring the Social Processes of Leadership and Organizing," *The Leadership Quarterly* 17, no. 6 (2006): 654–676.
2 Rick Trinkner, Tom R. Tyler, and Phillip A. Goff, "Justice from Within: The Relations Between a Procedurally Just Organizational Climate and Police Organizational Efficiency, Endorsement of Democratic Policing, and Officer Well-Being," *Psychology, Public Policy, and Law* 22, no. 2 (2016): 158–172.
3 Tom R. Tyler, *Why People Obey the Law*, 2nd ed. (Princeton, NJ: Princeton University Press, 2006).
4 Police Executive Research Forum. (2023). Responding to the staffing crisis: Innovations in recruitment and retention. https://www.policeforum.org/assets/RecruitmentRetention.pdf
5 B. Goldberg, personal communication, March 21, 2026
6 As evident in the many technology-centric Concept Boot Camp entries in this book
7 Fritsvold, E. (2018, May). The education panacea. Police Chief, 85(5), 40–45.
8 Sinek, S. (2009). Start with why: How great leaders inspire everyone to take action. Portfolio.
9 Bond, M. (2014, July 30). How education impacts police performance. *In Public Safety.* http://inpublicsafety.com/2014/07/how-education-impacts-police-performance
10 Sereni-Massinger, C., and Wood, N. (2016). Linking educational institutions with police officer training programs. *Journal of Education and Learning, 10*(2), 139–146.
11 Bond, M. (2014, July 30). How education impacts police performance. *In Public Safety.* http://inpublicsafety.com/2014/07/how-education-impacts-police-performance
12 Fritsvold, E. (2016). The education panacea: Addressing wide-ranging challenges with advanced education. *Police Chief Magazine.* https://www.policechiefmagazine.org/the-education-panacea-addressing-wide-ranging-challenges-with-advanced-education/

13 Gardiner, C (2017). Policing Around the Nation: Education, Philosophy, and Practice. National Policing Institute. https://www.policinginstitute.org/publication/policing-around-the-nation-education-philosophy-and-practice/
14 30x30 Initiative. (n.d.). About 30x30. Retrieved January 6, 2026, from https://30x30initiative.org/about-30x30/
15 30x30 Initiative. (n.d.). The 30x30 pledge. Retrieved January 6, 2026, from https://30x30initiative.org/the-30x30-pledge/
16 Police Executive Research Forum. (2023). Responding to the staffing crisis: Innovations in recruitment and retention. https://www.policeforum.org/assets/RecruitmentRetention.pdf
17 Rittel, H. W., and Webber, M. M. (1973). Dilemmas in a general theory of planning. Policy Sciences, 4(2), 155–169. https://doi.org/10.1007/BF01405730
18 Esserman, D. M. (2021, September 13). Co-responder models in policing: Better serving communities. Police1. https://www.police1.com/community-policing/articles/co-responder-models-in-policing-better-serving-communities-hKy6a1mHLq3Hlrcw/
19 Lexipol Staff. (2020, July 1). Coordinated homeless outreach: Where does law enforcement fit in? Police1. https://www.police1.com/patrol-issues/articles/coordinated-homeless-outreach-where-does-law-enforcement-fit-in-XXqsW88sdBcRHUDB/
20 California State University, San Bernardino (n.d.) Art Acevedo Bio. Institute for Public Management & Governance. https://www.csusb.edu/institute-public-management-governance/agency-transformation-symposium/art-acevedo
21 Blue Leadership Episode 19 (2023). Chief Sheryl Victorian. University of San Diego, Law Enforcement & Public Safety Leadership MS Program. https://www.youtube.com/watch?v=EL11oKxFScl&list=PLaVHrclV0Clf1aedpAjCgOZEB8WJcdRJF&index=31&t=5s

REFERENCES

30x30Initiative. (n.d.). About the 30x30 pledge. https://30x30initiative.org/about-30x30/
Blue Leadership. (2023). Chief Sheryl Victorian (Episode 19) [Video]. University of San Diego, Law Enforcement & Public Safety Leadership MS Program. https://www.youtube.com/watch?v=EL11oKxFScl
Bond, M. (2014, July 30). How education impacts police performance. In Public Safety. http://inpublicsafety.com/2014/07/how-education-impacts-police-performance
California State University, San Bernardino. (n.d.). Art Acevedo bio. Institute for Public Management & Governance. https://www.csusb.edu/institute-public-management-governance/agency-transformation-symposium/art-acevedo

Esserman, D. M. (2021, September 13). Co-responder models in policing: Better serving communities. Police1. https://www.police1.com/community-policing/articles/co-responder-models-in-policing-better-serving-communities-hKy6a1mHLq3Hlrcw/

Fritsvold, E. (2016). The education panacea: Addressing wide-ranging challenges with advanced education. *Police Chief Magazine*. https://www.policechiefmagazine.org/the-education-panacea-addressing-wide-ranging-challenges-with-advanced-education/

Fritsvold, E. (2018, May). The education panacea. *Police Chief, 85*(5), 40–45.

Gardiner, C. (2017). Policing around the nation: Education, philosophy, and practice. National Policing Institute. https://www.policinginstitute.org/publication/policing-around-the-nation-education-philosophy-and-practice/

Lexipol Staff. (2020, July 1). Coordinated homeless outreach: Where does law enforcement fit in? Police1. https://www.police1.com/patrol-issues/articles/coordinated-homeless-outreach-where-does-law-enforcement-fit-in-XXqsW88sdBcRHUDB/

Police Executive Research Forum. (2023). *Responding to the staffing crisis: Innovations in recruitment and retention*. https://www.policeforum.org/assets/RecruitmentRetention.pdf

Rittel, H. W., and Webber, M. M. (1973). Dilemmas in a general theory of planning. *Policy Sciences, 4*(2), 155–169. https://doi.org/10.1007/BF01405730

Sereni-Massinger, C., and Wood, N. (2016). Linking educational institutions with police officer training programs. *Journal of Education and Learning*, *10*(2), 139–146.

Sinek, S. (2009). *Start with why: How great leaders inspire everyone to take action*. Portfolio.

Trinkner, R., Tyler, T. R., and Goff, P. A. (2016). Justice from within: The relations between a procedurally just organizational climate and police organizational efficiency, endorsement of democratic policing, and officer well-being. *Psychology, Public Policy, and Law, 22*(2), 158–172.

Tyler, T. R. (2006). *Why people obey the law* (2nd ed.). Princeton University Press.

Uhl-Bien, M. (2006). Relational leadership theory: Exploring the social processes of leadership and organizing. *The Leadership Quarterly, 17*(6), 654–676.

Index

Note: **Bold** page numbers indicate tables, *italic* numbers indicate figures.

For Product Safety Concerns and Information please contact our EU representative GPSR@taylorandfrancis.com
Taylor & Francis Verlag GmbH, Kaufingerstraße 24, 80331 München, Germany

www.ingramcontent.com/pod-product-compliance
Ingram Content Group UK Ltd.
Pitfield, Milton Keynes, MK11 3LW, UK
UKHW022035091026
476426UK00010B/601
9781041217497